Hebrew Talk

101 Hebrew Roots and the Stories They Tell

Hebrew Talk

101 HEBREW ROOTS
AND THE STORIES THEY TELL

Joseph Lowin

EKS PUBLISHING CO.
Oakland, California

For information, contact the publisher:
EKS Publishing Co.
Berkeley, CA 94709-0750
E-mail: orders@ekspublishing.com
Phone: (510) 251-9100
Fax: (510) 251-9102

ISBN 0-939144-47-6

First Printing, June 2004

Library of Congress Cataloging-in-Publication Data:

Lowin, Joseph.
Hebrew talk : 101 Hebrew roots and the
stories they tell / Joseph Lowin.
p.   cm.
Includes bibliographical references.
ISBN 0-939144-47-6 — ISBN 0-939144-48-4 (pbk.)
1. Hebrew language—Word formation.
2. Hebrew language—Roots. 3. Hebrew language—Etymology.
4. Hebrew language—Usage. I. Title.
PJ4603.L69 2004
492.4'2—dc22
2004050628

For the Lowins of Stari-Sambor
May Their Memory Be for a Blessing

יְהִי זִכְרָם בָּרוּךְ

And For Shari, David, and Benjamin Lowin
May Their Blessing Be to Remember

תְּהִי בִּרְכָתָם לִזְכּוֹר

בִּנְעָרֵינוּ בִזְקֵנֵינוּ וּבִלְשׁוֹנֵנוּ נֵלֵךְ

INTRODUCTION

There we were, the five of us—my wife Judy and I, our son Benji, and David and Rachel Wolfe, the "summer landlords" of our apartment in Raanana—sitting around a table in *Pundak Sha'ul*, a quintessentially Israeli restaurant nestled in the colorful *Kerem Ha-Teimanim* section of Tel Aviv.

We had come to Raanana that summer primarily because there are no hotels there and, probably for that reason, few tourists. Although it's a city with a rich history—a city that even has a captivating Zionist story to tell—there is in truth nothing of a monumental nature to see in Raanana. It is, however, a good place just to "look around"—at the signs on the storefronts, at the placards on the landscaping, and at the posters on the walls—and to listen, by discreet (and sometimes indiscreet) eavesdropping, to the conversations of its good citizens.

We were charmed by the fact that the window of the local barbershop carried the legend מִסְתַּפְּרִים אֵצֶל בָּרוּךְ (*mistaprim etsel barukh*), People-Get-Their-Hair-Cut-at-Barukh's-Place (Benji loves stores that are named for what they sell or do), and that the neighborhood takeout food store was called הָאִמָּא שֶׁל דוּדוּ (*ha-imma shel dudu*), Dudu's Mom. (Was it really Dudu Fisher's mom, or Dudu Topaz's mom, as we were variously told? Or was she just the mother of a plain Dudu, a kid from around the block?)

Although Raanana has plenty of אַנְגְלוֹ-סַקְסִים (*anglo-saksim*)—the way Israelis bundle together all Americans, British, Australians, and South Africans—it is a good city to practice one's Hebrew, the goal of our stay. Plenty of native-born Israelis live there too, including the editor of שַׁעַר לַמַּתְחִיל (*sha'ar la-mathil*), the Israeli newspaper in easy Hebrew, designed for non-natives who are studying and learning the language.

Admittedly, some of the Hebrew in Raanana has a decidedly

אַנְגְלוֹ-סַקְסִי (anglo-saksi) flavor. The sidewalk café where we took our daily קָפֶה הָפוּךְ (kafeh hafukh), Israeli *cappuccino*, and flaky croissants is called, in "Hebrew," Lady Di, and the Hebrew conversations we eavesdropped on there were sprinkled repeatedly with the "Hebrew" word קַנְטְרִי (kantri), for the new Country Club in town. But there were also signs on the median that divided Ahuza, the main boulevard. These told us, in pure Hebrew, that this was a city that took care of its פְּנֵי הָעִיר (penei ha-ir), literally, face of the city, i.e., its flowerbeds, and streets, and sidewalks. The public Hebrew that gave us greatest insight into the culture of Raanana in particular and of Israel in general were the two words carved into the sidewalks at every street corner, indented so that baby carriages could make the crossing with the least effort: לָאֵם וְלַיֶּלֶד (la-em ve-la-yeled), for mother and child. And sometimes the Hebrew was scary too. Benji and I would go fairly regularly to play tennis at the Israel Tennis Center down the road from Raanana. But one day we found some courts (for free) in the adjacent town of Kfar Saba. There, on a wall at the tennis court, we noticed some graffiti that brought home to us that sometimes the only way to confront the daily threat of terrorism in Israel—in this case by poisonous mustard gas—is to take it with a bit of morbid humor. What did the handwriting on the wall say? תִּקְנוּ נַקְנִיקִיּוֹת—הַחַרְדָּל בַּדֶּרֶךְ (tiknu naknikiyyot—ha-hardal ba-derekh), Buy hot dogs—the mustard is on the way.

But let's get back to *Pundak Sha'ul* and to the festive dinner to which we had invited David and Rachel at the end of our stay. We wanted to share with them the stories of our stay in David's mother's apartment and to regale them with stories of our Hebrew experiences.

After an evening of pleasant banter about Hebrew, there was one more Hebrew experience to which they were going to be eyewitnesses themselves. At the end of the meal, the waiter—as officious as any waiter at Sardi's in New York (or, to keep it kosher,

Prime Grill)—brought me the check. I looked it over and, perceiving a charge that I took to be for שֵׁרוּת (*sherut*), service, I asked the waiter what I would later learn was a שְׁאֵלַת קִיטְבַּג (*she'elat kitbag*) —from the Israel army joke about the sad sack who always asks the sergeant when ordered to move if he should bring along his weighted down "kitbag" and is always told בְּוַדַּאי (*be-vaddai*), of course. Innocently, I thought, I asked the waiter if the שֵׁרוּת (*sherut*) was כָּלוּל (*kalul*), included. The waiter didn't say בְּוַדַּאי (*be-vaddai*), nor did he say בְּוַדַּאי שֶׁלֹּא (*be-vaddai she-lo*), of course not. Rather he looked down at me with the most supercilious glare I had ever seen and said in his baritone voice, like a Hebrew-speaking Rex Harrison, עֲשֵׂה כְּאַוַּת נַפְשֶׁךָ (*aseh ke-avvat nafshekha*), Act according to your heart's desires. As I plunked down an extra twenty-dollar tip, David had a hearty laugh at this American פְרָיֶר (*frayer*), sucker. "Don't you know that he's playing you like a violin? Of course the service is included." Frankly, the situation was worthy of a domestic comedy at Tel Aviv's Cameri Theater; the waiter had put on a show that was revelatory of the culture in which he was a major player and I was his stooge. But to me it was more than worth it to hear a phrase—אַוַּת נַפְשֶׁךָ (*avvat nafshekha*), heart's desire—that I knew from its several repetitions in the Tanakh, plucked from Scripture to roll so mellifluously and naturally off a waiter's lips.

This story portrays vividly what I try so hard to capture in this book. In the 101 "talks" about Hebrew that make up *HebrewTalk*, I strive to demonstrate how the language "talks" to us today. What I am interested in learning—and teaching—is how Hebrew makes its way, through the three-letter roots that are at the origin of the language, to the creation of the various worlds that make up Jewish civilization through the ages. A good deal of time-travel is involved, to be sure, from Biblical times to the rabbinic period, from the middle ages to modern times, and on, and on to the streets and restaurants of Raanana and Tel Aviv (and Jerusalem, too, of course). Almost every word spoken in these places—or written on the walls—resonates with echoes of Jewish history.

Readers of *HebrewTalk* are invited to listen too, in the hope that they will hear these echoes and that these echoes will resonate with them just as clearly as the words produced by our waiter's voice.

A WORD ABOUT TRANSLITERATION
AND TRANSLATION OF HEBREW

Generally, *HebrewTalk* follows the transliteration rules of the *Encyclopedia Judaica* (Jerusalem: Keter, 1972), Vol. I, p. 90. In addition, because even transliteration is not immune to trends, fashions, and elaborations, we have also looked for guidance to an updated treatment of transliteration in the "Guide to Transliteration Style" of *The Torah U-Madda Journal*, edited by Dr. David Shatz, 9(2000):280-81, also found online at www.ivrit.org/html/study/TranslitGuide-02.pdf.

These authorities not withstanding, we have arrogated to ourselves the right to deviate from the rules when it has appeared prudent to do so for the sake of our readers' comfort. For example, unlike both of our sources, we reserve the transliteration [z] for the letter ז (*zayin*) and transliterate the Hebrew letter צ (*tsadi*) with a [ts]—e.g., מַצָּה (*matsah*) and מִצְוָה (*mitsvah*). Nevertheless, the reader will find these words spelled, as in everyday English, matzah and mitzvah when used in the body of the text.

On another note, not all of our translations are literal or exact. In many cases we have tried to find equivalents of Israeli slang in American idioms. Thus the reader will find that the Hebrew expression תִּשְׁכַּח מִזֶּה (*tishkah mi-zeh*) is translated as "Fuhgeh-dahboudit." In addition, many of our illustrations of biblical usage come from the chapter in the book of Proverbs dealing with the person we term the "proverbial Woman of Valor." While we are aware that there is a tendency in modern scholarship to translate the expression אֵשֶׁת חַיִל (*eshet hayil*) as "the wife of a man of substance," we have decided to use the more popular translation, so as not to sow confusion where none is needed.

Finally, we beg the reader to understand that while consistency is almost an absolute good, we believe that it is even better to exercise one's judgment from time to time and as a matter of principle to deviate a bit from the rules.

ACKNOWLEDGEMENTS

In Hebrew it's called *hakarat ha-tov*, literally, recognizing the good. Figuratively, the expression is used for the public acknowledgement of service rendered above and beyond the call of duty. It's something I take pleasure in doing here.

First of all I would like to thank my wife, Judy, who, for the past twenty years, has been the first reader of every Hebrew column I have written for *Hadassah Magazine*, the basis for the vast majority of the chapters of this book. Her sharp eye is responsible for detecting and eliminating needlessly flowery, hyperbolic, or overly technical language in the column.

Only after Judy had her go at a column would I send it off for publication. There it was gone over by a scrupulously exacting editorial staff. I would like to thank in particular Leah Finkelshteyn and Zelda Shluker, of *Hadassah Magazine*, who were mainly responsible for seeing that the finished product was polished to a fine sheen. Some of the columns were written for the *Jewish Heritage Online Magazine* (www.jhom.com), whose editor, Simcha Shtull, played a similarly exacting role.

When it came time to turn these columns into a second book (the first, *Hebrewspeak*, had been published nearly a decade earlier), my son Benji, during the summer between his graduation from college and his first year of law school, spent many hours putting a first version of the book manuscript in order, highlighting repetitions, underlining inconsistencies, and pointing out ways the various articles could be made to read like chapters of a unified book. Without Benji's help I might never have had the courage to undertake the daunting task of getting this material between covers.

One impetus for the publication of the book was the promotion of the goals and values of the National Center for the Hebrew Language (NCHL), which I have directed for many years. In many ways, this volume aims to serve as an NCHL book of Hebrew roots. My more-than-assistant at the NCHL, Osnat Eitan, oversaw the next step in the preparation of the manuscript. During Ossi's tenure at the NCHL, it happened more than once that I could be heard saying to myself, in admiration of her work ethic and in awe of her varied talents, "Is there anything Ossi cannot do?" Her most outstanding contribution to the book—among many—consisted of going over the manuscript to suggest ways the entries in each chapter would reflect the latest Hebrew usage. To the extent that the book truly traces the development of a Hebrew root from its use in Scripture to its use on the streets of Israel today, it is due to Ossi's *yozmah*, initiative.

The editing of a book such as this requires a great amount of knowledge and many technical skills, including a keen eye for proper English, knowledge of Hebrew grammar, and expertise in what is called Information Technology. I was fortunate to find this combination in Richard White, who expertly edited this book. I am also fortunate to call him a friend.

Finally, I would like to thank my publisher, Claudia Valas, whose enthusiasm for this project, both when it was presented to her and throughout the publication process—with her excellent publishing team of Irene Imfeld and Scott Perry—equaled mine. Her passion for Hebrew is reflected in every book she publishes and is mirrored in the chapters of this book.

CONTENTS

Hebrew Talk

101 Hebrew Roots
and the Stories They Tell

LOST AND FOUND

Your daughter brings her college roommate home for the Passover Seder and explains what is about to take place: "Judaism is a religion where, before they feed you, they give you a history lesson." It just so happens that the Passover Haggadah echoes Deuteronomy's instructions for another meal, the Feast of the First Fruits. There, too, you must first recite a formulaic History of the Jews, beginning with אֲרַמִּי אוֹבֵד אָבִי (arammi oved avi), "A wandering Aramean was my father." When the Seder reaches those words, your daughter amends her explanation: "They also give you a Hebrew lesson."

It all has to do with the Hebrew root אָ-ב-ד (alef, bet, dalet), among whose many meanings are to wander, to be destitute, and to be forlorn. Certainly, our father Jacob, who is the subject of the phrase above, was a wanderer both before and after his twenty-year stint with "Laban the Aramean." In the beginning, Jacob was destitute and, in his transactions with Laban, forlorn. And so, the Haggadah tells us that the verb אוֹבֵד (oved) in our verse should be rendered midrashically as "An Aramean [Laban] tried לְאַבֵּד (le-abbed), to destroy, my father [Jacob]." That he did not succeed is a reason for the feast.

The root's sense of destruction is found more than a dozen times in relation to Purim. The majestic words of Queen Esther, וְכַאֲשֶׁר אָבַדְתִּי אָבָדְתִּי (ve-kha-asher avadeti avadeti), "If I perish [in trying to save my people], I perish," have become emblematic of Jewish heroism. In modern Israel, Esther's words are used as the Hebrew equivalent of Che sarà sarà, "Whatever will be, will be."

According to the Rabbis, אֲבַדּוֹן (*avadon*), destruction, is one of the seven names of Hell. When someone dear passes away, there is an Aramaic expression to be said חֲבָל עַל דְּאָבְדִין (*haval al deavdin*), "Woe is our loss." Another use of our root also has to do with loss. On the battlefield, one hopes that there will not be אֲבֵדוֹת קָשׁוֹת (*avedot kashot*), heavy casualties. A tragic way of losing oneself is to commit suicide, לְהִתְאַבֵּד (*le-hitabbed*). Of one "at a loss" about what's going on, we say אָבְדוּ עֶשְׁתּוֹנוֹתָיו (*avdu eshtonotav*), literally, his thoughts have been lost. One of our biggest little mitzvot is הֲשָׁבַת אֲבֵדָה (*hashavat avedah*), going out of one's way to return lost property. Perhaps because we celebrate Passover the way we do, as a history and vocabulary lesson first, we have earned the merit to sing the Israeli national anthem at the end of the Seder, especially the line עוֹד לֹא אָבְדָה תִּקְוָתֵנוּ (*od lo avdah tikvatenu*), "We have not yet lost our [bi-millennial] hope," to be a free nation in our own land.

And since the haroset on our Seder plate is אָבֵד (*aved*), perishable, perhaps it is time, finally, to eat.

ROCKS WITHOUT ROLLS

Jewish folk wisdom observes that, whether a rock falls on a pot or a pot falls on a rock it is always the pot that gets dented by the אֶבֶן (even), rock.

The Hebrew word אֶבֶן (even) is found in dozens of expressions —a veritable גַל אֲבָנִים (gal avanim), pile of stones, of expressions —that encapsulate the Jewish worldview. God himself is termed אֶבֶן יִשְׂרָאֵל (even yisrael). According to tradition, the אֶבֶן שְׁתִיָּה (even shetiyah), the concrete, primordial foundation stone of the world, is located in Jeruaslem. Today it is found in the Mosque of Omar on the Temple Mount. The Ten Commandments were inscribed on שְׁנֵי לוּחוֹת אֲבָנִים (shenei luhot avanim), two tablets of stone. And let us not forget the beautiful stone that distinguishes Jerusalem from every other city in the world, אֶבֶן יְרוּשַׁלְמִית (even yerushalmit), Jerusalem stone. Our word is found in combination with other words, as in the expression for criterion, אֶבֶן בּוֹחַן (even bohan), touchstone. The Rabbis looked at a scholar and saw an אֶבֶן פִּנָּה (even pinnah), a cornerstone on which to build a civilization.

A game resembling Jacks uses five "stones"—known as kugelach in Yiddish and חָמֵשׁ אֲבָנִים (hamesh avanim) in Hebrew—and is played in some circles by children in Israel today. It also teaches us that the gender of אֶבֶן (even) is feminine.

The Torah uses the word אֶבֶן (even) twice in one aphorism to teach us an important lesson in business ethics. A merchant who sells his product by weight may not carry in his pouch אֶבֶן וָאֶבֶן (even va-even), that is, one stone for regular transactions and another for cheating. Today the expression אֶבֶן וָאֶבֶן (even va-even) is used for "double standard." The book of Psalms employs our word to teach a psychological lesson about usefulness. There we are told that אֶבֶן מָאֲסוּ הַבּוֹנִים (*even ma'asu ha-bonim*), a stone that was disdained by some builders, can be used by others as a cornerstone.

In ancient times, the word was used in situations that range from the sublime to the artisanal and from the legal to the superstitious. Did you know, for example, that one of the earliest instances of a Lost-and-Found, a place called the אֶבֶן הַטּוֹעִים (*even ha-to'im*), was situated in Jerusalem (perhaps on a rock) during the period of the Second Temple? Because a potter's wheel is made from a pair of stones, it was called אָבְנַיִם (*ovnayim*), using the יִם_ (*-ayim*) ending for things that come in pairs. The third volume of Rabbi Joseph Caro's Shulhan Arukh, dealing with laws pertaining to women, is entitled אֶבֶן הָעֵזֶר (*even ha-ezer*), using a word for woman found in the Creation story. And the Talmud tells us that among the amulets prevalent at the time was the אֶבֶן תְּקוּמָה (*even tekumah*), figuratively, survival stone, worn to prevent miscarriages.

The word אָבְנַיִם (*ovnayim*), mentioned above, has a secondary meaning, birthing stool. It has led to some interesting give-and-take among the founders of Hebrew etymology. Both Rabbi Jonah Ibn Jannah and Rabbi David Kimhi, the Radak, agree that this word does not derive from אֶבֶן (*even*), stone, but from בֵּן (*ben*), child. For Rabbi Jonah, it is the place where the baby lands upon emerging; for the Radak, it is the place from which the baby emerges, i.e., the womb. The Radak concludes by quoting his father, who held that the word אָבְנַיִם (*ovnayim*) comes neither from אֶבֶן (*even*) nor from בֵּן (*ben*) but from בִּנְיָן (*binyan*), building. Ironically, if not etymologically, this takes us back to the vocabulary of cornerstones and to the idea that as long as they sustain and promote life, both the pot and the rock are desirable utensils.

GOING POSTAL

There are some people who can find poetry anywhere, even in the database on their computer. Then there are those who find poetry in a Hebrew expression for database, מַאֲגַר מֵידָע (ma'agar meida).

The word מַאֲגַר (ma'agar), comes from the root ר-ג-א (alef, gimmel, resh), to gather, collect. It is found in a locution for something as low-tech as a reservoir, מַאֲגַר מַיִם (ma'agar mayim). Additionally, a מַאֲגוֹר (ma'agor) is a very large storage receptacle, especially for grain, and אֲגִירָה (agirah) is the act of storing it. An אָגוּר (agur) was a laborer who was hired, at a salary called an אֲגוֹרָה (agorah), to gather the grain. The grain itself, when it was of superior quality and therefore fit for storage, was called אִיגְרוּ (igru). You can learn a useful ethical lesson from the Aramaic proverb לְפוּם צַעֲרָא אַגְרָא (le-fum tsa'ara agra), "According to the pains taken is the reward." Or as they say today, "No pain, no gain."

If you are yourself an אַגְרָן בּוּלִים (agran bulim), stamp collector, you are aware of the superior quality of Israeli stamps. If you are a collector of Hebrew words, you should have a look at a recently-published lexicon of Hebrew synonyms by Aryeh Komay called, using our root, אֱגְרוֹן לְמִלִּים נִרְדָפוֹת (egron le-millim nirdafot).

If, however, you are a modern-day lexicographer, you will have difficulty assigning the word אִגֶּרֶת (iggeret), letter (i.e., message or note), to our root. And that's where the poetry comes in, in an argument across the centuries. While most modern linguists believe that אִגֶּרֶת (iggeret) does not come from our root but is a foreign loan-word, medieval Hebrew lexicographers David Kimhi, the Radak, and Jonah Ibn Jannah had no trouble seeing an epistle as a storehouse for thoughts. They found the expression אִגֶּרֶת הַפּוּרִים (*iggeret ha-purim*), the Purim "collection," in Esther's megillah itself.

Moreover, both Maimonides and Nachmanides were masters of the art of correspondence. They bequeathed to us two of the most quoted letters in the Jewish textual tradition. The Rambam's אִגֶּרֶת תֵּימָן (*iggeret teiman*) was a letter written both in support of Yemen's Jews, who were being forced to convert to Islam, and against a false messiah. The אִגֶּרֶת הָרַמְבַּ״ן לִבְנוֹ (*iggeret ha-ramban li-vno*), Ramban's Letter to His Son, is an ethical will in which he warns against anger as man's downfall.

In the old days—say, ten years ago—if your child was on a program in Israel, you could count on receiving an אִגֶּרֶת אֲוִיר (*iggeret avir*), aerogramme, every once in a while. Today with the advent of e-mail, you just log on to your computer to retrieve correspondence. Press "Save" to create your own מַאֲגָר (*ma'agar*), collection, of letters. That's also a form of poetry.

LIGHTENING UP

In December, in cosmopolitan shopping districts, one sees signs in a multitude of languages offering season's greetings. Lately, in a breakthrough for Hebrew, one also sees a greeting for Hanukkah, חַג אוּרִים שָׂמֵחַ (*hag urim same'ah*), Happy Festival of Lights.

The Hebrew root אָ-ו-ר (*alef, vav, resh*), used as a verb, means to give light. We welcome the Shabbat by singing קוּמִי אוֹרִי (*kumi ori*), "Rise and shine."

Verbs or nouns, it's all very positive. The first commandment in the Creation narrative is יְהִי אוֹר (*yehi or*), "Let there be light." The oracular breastplate of the High Priest bears the words אוּרִים וְתֻמִּים (*urim ve-tumim*), loosely but perhaps accurately translated as "Clarity and Truth." The victory of the Jews at Purim is marked by אוֹרָה וְשִׂמְחָה (*orah ve-simhah*), where the words for "light" and "joy" are virtually synonymous.

The Bible uses the word מָאוֹר (*ma'or*), derived from our root, to designate both the sun and the moon. The Rabbis use it to characterize Rabbenu Gershom, whom they called the מְאוֹר הַגּוֹלָה (*me'or ha-golah*), the Light of the Exile. When they mention a colleague in writing, they follow his name by the letters נ"י (*nun, yud*), meaning נֵרוֹ יָאִיר (*nero ya'ir*), "May his flame illuminate."

In the Dead Sea Scrolls, the Israelites are referred to as the בְּנֵי אוֹר (*benei or*), sons of light. Poet Chaim Nachman Bialik beseeches the Sabbath Queen בְּזִיוֵךְ נָא אוֹרִי (*be-zivekh na ori*), "May your splendor cast its light upon us." The many Hebrew names derived from the root testify to Jewish culture's esteem for light. The female names one hears include מְאִירָה (*me'irah*), אוֹרָה (*orah*), and אוֹרְנָה

(*ornah*). Among the males are: מֵאִיר (*me'ir*), יָאִיר (*ya'ir*), אוּרִי (*uri*, from which we get the name of Israel's first comic-book superhero, Uri-On [Power-Light]), אוּרִיָּה (*uriah*), and אוּרִיאֵל (*uriel*).

The uses of the root in Modern Hebrew are subtle, varied, and plentiful. For example, the word לִכְאוֹרָה (*li-kh-ora*), seemingly, is used in contexts where the speaker wishes to assert that the way something appears "as it first comes to light" is false. The light of day is a very special place for authors in Israel where a publisher is called a מוֹצִיא לָאוֹר (*motsi la-or*), one who brings to light. A good teacher will provide useful הֶאָרוֹת (*he'arot*), clarifications or notes, to a difficult book. Did you know that there are nine and a half billion kilometers in a שְׁנַת אוֹר (*shenat or*), lightyear? If you give someone an אוֹר יָרוֹק (*or yarok*), green light, you are giving him the "go-ahead." Often, אוֹר is so successfully absorbed into other words that its *alef* disappears. You cross the street at a רַמְזוֹר (*ramzor*, from *remez-or*, a light signal), traffic light; onstage, the זַרְקוֹר (*zarkor*, from *zarak-or*, to cast light), the spotlight, shines on the star. If you are נָאוֹר (*na'or*), enlightened, you are probably studying Hebrew using an אוֹרְקוֹלִי (*orkoli*), audio-visual, method.

At the end of the day a parent might call out that it's time for כִּבּוּי אוֹרוֹת (*kibbui orot*), lights out. At the end of the day, it's also important to remember that the Jews, like light, are created for a purpose. A good one to strive for is to be an אוֹר לַגּוֹיִים (*or la-goyim*), a light unto the nations. Perhaps then, in these dark days of our winter, we'll be able to see the אוֹר בִּקְצֵה הַמִּנְהָרָה (*or bi-ktseh ha-minharah*), the light at the end of the tunnel.

ALL TOGETHER NOW

When we speak of "Pluralism in Jewish Life," we are necessarily confronted by a thorny question: How are we to achieve collective harmony in an ambience of plural agendas? Interestingly, אַחְדוּת (*ahdut*), the Hebrew word for unity, also addresses this problem.

Many people will recognize the Hebrew word for the number one, אֶחָד (*ehad*), in אַחְדוּת (*ahdut*). But even אֶחָד (*ehad*) has a whole rainbow of meanings. In the Shema, אֶחָד (*ehad*), referring to God, means "unique." In the mouth of Haman, the arch-enemy of the Jews in the book of Esther, the expression עַם אֶחָד (*am ehad*) is a rather pejorative term for a stubbornly unassimilable nation. After a hotly-contested election in Israel, especially in times of crisis, the two leading parties might decide to form a מֶמְשֶׁלֶת אַחְדוּת (*memshelet ahdut*), unity government.

A newspaper in Israel might carry an article on the observance of אֶחָד בְּמַאי (*ehad be-mai*), the Hebrew way of saying May Day. And a ketubah, a Jewish marriage contract, might begin with the words בְּאֶחָד בְּשַׁבָּת (*be-ehad be-shabbat*), the Jewish way of saying that the wedding takes place on a Saturday night or a Sunday.

And then, there is the poetry. Probably the greatest love story ever told is that of forefather Jacob for foremother Rachel. Jacob's lyricism is expressed in his comment on the first seven years he spent working to earn Rachel's hand in marriage. These years were to him כְּיָמִים אֲחָדִים (*ke-yamim ahadim*), "like a mere few days." In the writings of the twentieth century's Jewish national poet, Chaim Nachman Bialik, we find the expression שְׁכֶם אֶחָד (*shekhem ehad*),

9

"a single shoulder." Bialik uses this expression metaphorically to praise the Jewish people's innate ability to work together—bearing a burden on their collective shoulder—to accomplish a common goal.

The Jewish community in America is particularly famous for this שְׁכֶם אֶחָד (*shekhem ehad*) attitude. It must honestly be said, however, that every once in a while you will meet someone for whom the Hebrew expression אֶחָד בַּפֶּה וְאֶחָד בַּלֵּב (*ehad ba-peh ve-ehad ba-lev*), "one thing in the mouth and another in the heart," is an apt description. Sometimes, we call these people diplomats.

For a variety of historical reasons, the letter alef is sometimes missing from the word אֶחָד (*ehad*). This happens in modern Israel in the expression for a one-way street, רְחוֹב חַד-סִטְרִי (*rehov had-sitri*). It occurs as well in the Aramaic goat-ditty חַד-גַּדְיָא (*had-gadya*)—for which you may have some use at your next Passover Seder.

And it may also have happened in the pre-history of the Hebrew language, where, according to some theories, two-letter roots were a part of the norm. This phenomenon may give us a useful insight into the concept of Jewish unity. Just think about this: Words as disparate in meaning as חַד (*had*), sharp, חֶדְוָה (*hedvah*), joy, and חִידָה (*hidah*), puzzle—to say nothing of יָחִיד (*yahid*), individual, and אַחְדוּת (*ahdut*), unity—are all united by a common ancestor.

Just like the Jewish people.

AFTER ALL

When a speaker of French permits another to pass in front with a polite *après vous,* he or she is performing, according to French Jewish thinker Emmanuel Lévinas, the ultimate ethical act—putting the "other" before oneself. When a speaker of Hebrew says אַחֲרֶיךָ (*aharekha*) in similar circumstances, he or she makes an ethical statement about Jewish culture itself. For the word אַחֲרֶיךָ (*aharekha*), after you, not only contains the word אַחֵר (*aher*), other, but alludes as well to the word אַחֲרָיוּת (*aharayut*), responsibility, conveying the sense that one not only places the other before oneself but that one also "stands behind" the other.

Sensitivity to others is not at all trivial. In fact, it is more "natural" to view others inimically, even in Judaism. When the Rabbis wanted to stigmatize apostate Elisha ben Abuya, they did not call him the רָשָׁע (*rasha*), evil one, but rather אַחֵר (*aher*), the quintessential "other." The root turns up in more benign religious circumstances. Anonymous talmudic opinions are ascribed to אֲחֵרִים (*aherim*), as in "Others say." A sarcastic way of saying "Speak only good of the dead" is to allude to the names of two biblical chapters often read together, אַחֲרֵי מוֹת-קְדוֹשִׁים (*aharei mot kedoshim*), "After death, everyone is holy."

The root א-ח-ר (*alef, het, resh*) originally had a temporal sense, obvious in the noun אִחוּר (*ihur*), lateness, the adjective מְאוּחָר (*me'uhar*), late, and the preposition אַחַר (*ahar*), after. In the popular Adon Olam prayer we chant, at the end of the Shabbat service, that God will continue to reign even אַחֲרֵי כִּכְלוֹת הַכֹּל (*aharei ki-khlot ha-kol*), "after everything will have come to an end."

What do Isaiah, Jeremiah, and Ezekiel have in common? They are among the נְבִיאִים אַחֲרוֹנִים (*nevi'im aharonim*), Latter Prophets.

Messianically speaking, the world will end at the אַחֲרִית הַיָּמִים (*aharit ha-yamim*), the End of Days. The Kabbalists were wary of the סִטְרָא אַחֲרָא (*sitra ahara*, Aramaic), Other Side, where Satan dwells. In the book of Esther, Mordechai encourages his ward to spring to action; אַחֶרֶת (*aheret*), otherwise, salvation will come, he says, מִמָּקוֹם אַחֵר (*mi-makom aher*), "from another place," that is, God. It is curious that אַחֲרוֹן (*aharon*), the commonly-used expression for "last," originally meant "the one coming after." Perhaps this etymology explains the popular Hebrew equivalent for "last but not least," אַחֲרוֹן אַחֲרוֹן חָבִיב (*aharon aharon haviv*), the literal sense of which would be "The one after the last one is beloved."

Most Israeli parents asking their children to straighten out their room, have undoubtedly encountered the response אַחַר כָּךְ (*ahar kakh*), later. Wiseacre children who answer מָחָר כָּךְ (*mahar kakh*), slang for "never," are etymologically correct if not behaviorally so. Many scholars believe that מָחָר (*mahar*), tomorrow, derives from our root, some speculating that מָחָר (*mahar*) is a contraction of יוֹם אַחֵר (*yom aher*), another day.

What can we say, except that the Jewish value system, expressed in Hebrew, takes responsibility both for those who say *après vous* and for those who say *mañana*.

FOOD FOR THOUGHT

Like many of the commonplaces of Judaism, food raises difficult questions. Is food central to Jewish culture because we make such a tzimmes about it, with our prohibitions, admonitions, and conditions? Or perhaps Jewish food is central because, with its kugels, kishkes and khremzlakh, it just tastes good.

A close look at the uses of the Hebrew root א-כ-ל (*alef, kaf, lamed*)—source of the verb "to eat" and of three nouns for food אֹכֶל, אָכְלָה, מַאֲכָל (*okhel, akhlah, ma'akhal*)—raises more questions about Jewish life and thought. For example, what are we to make of the exhortation by the prophet Isaiah, אָכוֹל וְשָׁתוֹ כִּי מָחָר נָמוּת (*akhol ve-shato ki mahar namut*), "Let us eat and drink for tomorrow we die"? Are we to be disciples of Epicurus? Why did Isaiah leave out the "Be merry"? Perhaps he foresaw that toward the end of the twentieth century some wise-guy would translate Horace's *carpe diem* as "Gefilte fish every day."

In the narrative of the Garden of Eden, Adam is told מִכֹּל עֵץ הַגָּן אָכוֹל תֹּאכֵל (*mi-kol ets ha-gan akhol tokhel*), "You shall surely eat from every tree in the garden." When Adam ignores God's subsequent restrictive clause about eating certain fruits, he is banished with the curse בְּזֵעַת אַפֶּיךָ תֹּאכַל לֶחֶם (*be-ze'at apekha tokhal lehem*), "By the sweat of your brow shall you eat bread," i.e., you'll earn a living only by dint of hard work.

The beginning of the Exodus story displays yet another meaning of our root. Moses comes upon a bush that אֵינֶנּוּ אֻכָּל (*einennu ukkal*), "is not consumed." Using that meaning, Eliezer ben Yehudah coined the modern word for tuberculosis, אַכֶּלֶת (*akkelet*), known also as consumption. In the biblical narrative of the Akedah, why is the knife that Abraham uses on his substitute sacrifice called a מַאֲכֶלֶת (*ma'akhelet*)—a word clearly derived from our root? Does a knife consume? Or is consumption, as the disease hints, merely another word for destruction?

Modern-day Israelis love to play with their food, er, words. When they say, in a register quite different from that of the Ten Spies, that Israel is an אֶרֶץ אוֹכֶלֶת יוֹשְׁבֶיהָ (*erets okhelet yoshveha*), "a land which consumes its inhabitants," they are playfully bragging about the toughness needed to flourish in their socio-politico-economic environment. A restaurant in Israel recently posted a sign that plays on the biblical source for the Grace after Meals וְאָכַלְתָּ וְשָׂבַעְתָּ וּבֵרַכְתָּ (*ve-akhalta ve-savata u-verakhta*), "Eat, be satisfied, and bless." The sign reads וְאָכַלְתָּ וְשִׁלַמְתָּ וּבָרַחְתָּ (*ve-akhalta ve-shilamta u-varahta*), "Eat, pay up, and leave quickly." A woman who works in an office with a nasty boss tells a friend who is complaining about a single unpleasant incident with this person אֲנִי אוֹכֶלֶת אֶת זֶה כָּל יוֹם (*ani okhelet et zeh kol yom*), "I have to take it every day."

But let's not dwell on these negatives, however colorful. Remember the positive Passover prescription, שִׁבְעַת יָמִים תֹּאכַל מַצֹּת (*shiv'at yamim tokhal matsot*), "You shall eat matzot for seven days." You don't like matzah? Take our word for it, עִם הָאֲכִילָה יִגְדַּל הַתֵּאָבוֹן (*im ha-akhila yigdal ha-te'avon*), "The appetite will grow in the very eating."

Please pass the *khremzlakh*.

THE MILLENNIUM AND THE JEWISH ELEPHANT PROBLEM

The advent of the millennium, aside from its religious and hi-tech significance, provides us with an entrée into the fascinating facets of the Hebrew root פ-ל-א (*alef, lamed, peh*). Today, the word, which is also the first letter of the alphabet, means to grow very big and, once big, to be tamed, to learn, as in an אֻלְפָּן (*ulpan*), a school for learning Hebrew.

Hebrew has a knack for expressing size by multiplying the root. Thus, if אֶלֶף (*elef*) is a thousand, then אַלְפֵי אֲלָפִים (*alfei alafim*) is a million and אֶלֶף אַלְפֵי אֲלָפִים (*elef alfei alafim*) is a billion. Figuratively, אֶחָד מִנִּי אָלֶף (*ehad mini alef*) one in a thousand, means very few.

The word אֶלֶף (*elef*) is applied to many big things. The expression in Psalms הַרְרֵי אָלֶף (*harerei alef*) means high mountains, and may be where we get the name for the Alps. It also means any big number, but not necessarily the biggest. When the book of Samuel tells us that King Saul הִכָּה בַּאֲלָפָיו (*hikkah ba-alafav*), "smote his thousands," it is only to compare him unfavorably to King David, who smote tens of thousands. Officers in a biblical army were called שָׂרֵי אֲלָפִים (*sarei alafim*), leaders of thousands. This locution gave rise to expressions like אַלּוּף (*aluf*), army officer, and, by extension, champion. A question on the lips of Israeli soccer fans is: Did you hear what team is going to be in the playoffs for the אֲלִיפוּת אֵירוֹפָּה (*alifut eiropah*), European Championship? The book of Judges uses אַלְפִּי (*alpi*) to signify "my family." And אַלְפֵי

15

מְנַשֶּׁה (*alfei menashe*) meant originally a large part of the tribe of Manasseh.

During a recent bank scandal, an Israeli comedian versed in Scripture asked: "Do you know the bank teller's motto?" He answered with a verse from Psalms that begins with the words, יִפֹּל מִצִּדְּךָ אֶלֶף (*yipol mi-tsidkha elef*), "A thousand shall fall to your [left] side." He continued with the rest of verse 91:7: "And ten thousand [shall fall] to your right. It will not reach you. Just look at it with your eyes and you shall see the payments of the scoundrels."

The verb לְאַלֵּף (*le-allef*), to tame—as in אִלּוּף הַסּוֹרֶרֶת (*illuf ha-soreret*), Shakespeare's *Taming of the Shrew*—is very מְאַלֵּף (*me'allef*), instructive. That's possibly where the word "elephant" comes in. The letter אָלֶף (*alef*) in ancient Hebrew script is said to resemble the head of an ox, giving rise to a word meaning big tamed animal. The Oxford English Dictionary sees a possible connection between that Hebrew word for ox, אֶלֶף (*elef*), and the English word elephant.

And if you can't train an ox or an elephant, you can surely train an American to learn Hebrew, and that's why during the coming millennium we will all become אַלְפָאבֵּתִים (*alfabetim*), literate, in Hebrew, by studying at an אֻלְפָּן (*ulpan*), Hebrew-language school, and getting the grade of אָלֶף-אָלֶף (*alef-alef*), excellent.

THE RED HORSE OF COURAGE

What is the connection between an aliyah to the Torah and an Israeli Boy Scout? What does courage have to do with constipation? And how is an adopted child related to a reddish-brown horse? Believe it or not, all these relationships—and more—come to us from the Hebrew root צ-מ-א (*alef, mem, tsadi*), to be valiant.

The root is found in the familiar exhortation חֲזַק וֶאֱמַץ (*hazak ve-emats*), "Be strong and intrepid," the greeting of choice among Israeli צוֹפִים (*tsofim*), scouts. Sefardi Jews, having been congratulated for receiving a synagogue honor with a hearty חֲזַק וּבָרוּךְ (*hazak u-varukh*), "May you be strong and blessed," respond with an even more vigorous חֲזַק וֶאֱמַץ (*hazak ve-emats*).

In the Tanakh, our root is found in the names of אֲמַצְיָה (*amatsyah*), king of Judah, and אָמוֹץ (*amots*), father of the prophet Isaiah. It is also found in connection with two valiant biblical heroines. Of the proverbial Woman of Valor it is said, וַתְּאַמֵּץ זְרוֹעוֹתֶיהָ (*va-te'ammets zero'oteha*), "She invigorates her arms." In the book of Ruth, Naomi relents when she sees that her daughter-in-law Ruth מִתְאַמֶּצֶת (*mitammetset*), persists, in her determination to accompany her mother-in-law. In rabbinic literature, a tuneful prayer of the High Holy Day liturgy requests of God, הַיּוֹם תְּאַמְּצֵנוּ (*ha-yom te'amtsenu*) "Strengthen us today." Maimonides, a physician, writes, rather clinically, that certain foodstuffs מְאַמְּצִין (*me'amtsin*), harden, the intestines, and cause constipation.

Did you ever see someone make such a strong מַאֲמָץ (*ma'amats*), effort, that, לְאַמֵּץ כּוֹחוֹתָיו (*le-ammets kohotav*), to gather his strength,

17

he practically squeezes his eyes closed in concentration? Hebrew has an expression for that, לְאַמֵּץ עֵינַיִם (le-ammets einayim), to strive with one's eyes closed. This expression is also used for for closing the eyes of a corpse.

Gathering strength must be like gathering an orphan into one's family, because one meaning of the verb לְאַמֵּץ (le-ammets) is "to adopt." A new oleh to Israel will often want לְאַמֵּץ שֵׁם עִבְרִי (le-ammets shem ivri), to adopt a Hebrew name. And anyone might want לְאַמֵּץ תַּחְבִּיב (le-ammets tahbiv), to take up a hobby.

And what of the red horse? Several grammarians point out that one of the colors on the Hebrew palette is the reddish-brown אָמוֹץ (amots), of a bay horse, a word that emphasizes the color's intensity. Nobody, it seems, makes a connection between the red horse and the cut of red beef called the אוּמְצָה (umtsah), steak, which apparently comes from a different language family. But what good is a book about Hebrew if you can't sometimes find a little אַמִּיצוּת (ammitsut), boldness, in its conjectures?

GATHER IN MEETINGS WHILE YE MAY

O ne of the more serious issues all societies have to deal with is the relationship of the individual to the collective. In Jewish life, of one thing we may be certain: Jews know that it's more important to gather in meetings than to gather rosebuds. According to Rabbi Samson Raphael Hirsch, Moses, blessing his kinsmen, assures them that, when the heads of the Jewish people gather together in unity, בְּהִתְאַסֵּף רָאשֵׁי עָם (be-hitassef rashei am), then we have an ideal Israel, one whose sovereign is the Torah itself.

The most prominent of the several synonyms for "meeting" is the word אֲסֵפָה (asefah), whose root, א-ס-פ (alef, samekh, peh), means to gather and to collect, as well as to heal and to die.

It is not unlikely that the root had originally to do with agriculture. Every day, in the recitation of the Shema, we repeat God's promise that, as a reward for our good behavior, וְאָסַפְתָּ דְגָנֶךָ (ve-asafta deganekha), "You shall gather in your grain." The harvest festival of Sukkot is called חַג הָאָסִיף (hag ha-asif).

The root is also associated with names. One of the most important musicians in King David's court was אָסָף (asaf), to whom were dedicated no fewer than eleven of the Psalms. Foremother Rachel was probably the first to play etymologically with our root. Naming her first-born son, she uttered thanks that אָסַף אֱלוֹקִים אֶת חֶרְפָּתִי (asaf elokim et herpati), "God has taken away my disgrace," and then she named her son יוֹסֵף (yosef).

From God's perspective, it appears that a person can also be harvested. The poetic expression נֶאֱסַף אֶל עַמָּיו (ne'esaf el ammav), "He was gathered unto his people," is used with slight variations to describe the deaths of both Abraham and Moses.

Some gatherings have low status. Witness the epithet applied to the camp followers who gathered themselves to the Israelites during the Exodus, הָאֲסַפְסֻף (ha-asafsuf), the "rabble."

One of the most important Jewish publications of the eighteenth century was the periodical הַמְאַסֵּף (ha me'assef), which "collected" together articles promoting the use of Hebrew among the Jewish Maskilim, as the Enlighteners were called.

To show how far we've come since then, when you take a bus in Israel today, as you roam around or between cities, you will find the same word, מְאַסֵּף (me'assef), on the front of some of these buses. This word indicates that the bus makes all local stops, picking up passengers along the way. That sounds like as good a metaphor as there is for all types of meetings in Israel, including the great אֲסֵפָה (asefah) known as the ingathering of the Jewish people.

BLESS YOU

Ask a Jerusalemite what the appropriately brief response to a sneeze is, and you're likely to get the following long answer: "In Tel-Aviv, they say אָסוּתָא (*asuta*), Aramaic for 'Health!' (like gezuntheit!). Since Assuta is also the name of a hospital in Tel-Aviv, here in Jerusalem we naturally counter with הֲדַסָּה (*hadassah*), the name of our trophy hospital."

This true story leads one to muse about health words. The word אָסוּתָא (*asuta*), for example, contains within it the verb אַסִּי (*assi*), to cure, originally, to know the "waters," that is, the medicines. It also leads to the noun אָסְיָא (*asya*), physician, and to an Aramaic expression, אָסְיָא אַסִּי חִגַּרְתָּךְ (*asya, assi higartakh*), well-known in English as "Physician, heal thyself."

Hadassah, the Women's Zionist Organization of America, also has healing inscribed within it, not in its name, perhaps, but in its motto אֲרוּכַת בַּת עַמִּי (*arukhat bat ammi*), literally, "the healing of the daughter of my people." In the book of Jeremiah אֲרוּכַת בַּת עַמִּי (*arukhat bat ami*) is a metaphor for "the restoration of my people's land." (According to Bible scholar Umberto Cassuto, בַּת (*bat*) is an idiom meaning "land.") The figurative "restoration" comes from the ancient Hebrew sense of אֲרוּכָה (*arukhah*), the new skin that grows over a wound, further extending the symbolic appropriateness of the motto for a Zionist medical organization.

According to many Hebrew philologists (e.g., David Kimhi, Jonah Ibn Jannah, and, with a question mark, Abraham Even-Shoshan), the word אֲרוּכָה (*arukhah*) is related to the Hebrew root כ-ר-א (*alef, resh, kaf*), to lengthen, and implies that somewhere in the misty past people looked on a scab as a lengthening of the skin.

In Scripture (Exodus 34:6), the root is used to describe one of the Thirteen Attributes of God, אֶרֶךְ אַפַּיִם (*erekh apayim*), forebearance, because He "takes long" to get angry. The Fifth Commandment, to honor one's parents, adds a coda and a reward, לְמַעַן יַאֲרִיכוּן יָמֶיךָ (*le-ma'an ya'arikhun yamekha*), "so that your days may be lengthened" (Exodus 20:12). One of the cantillation marks used in chanting the Torah is called a מֵרְכָא (*merkha*), which, missing one of the letters of our root, is ironically a contraction of מַאֲרְכָא (*ma'arkha*), "that which lengthens."

For the Rabbis, the adjective אָרוּךְ (*arukh*), perhaps related to the idea of dressing a wound—or just as likely because it is a homonym of עָרוּךְ (*arukh*), prepared—also meant arranged. For them, a completely well-arranged world, עוֹלָם שֶׁכֻּלּוֹ אָרוּךְ (*olam she-kullo arukh*), could be found only in the hereafter, the hereafter being eternally אָרוֹךְ (*arokh*), long. Perhaps that's why we, in our entangled world of nets and webs, continue to need an enduring and healthy organization working toward both meanings of אֲרוּכַת בַּת עַמִּי (*arukhat bat ammi*), the restoration of the body's health and of the people's land.

HOSPITALITY SUITE

When you go outside on Sukkot—if you've done your "home" work—you'll see a makeshift roof on a hut in front of you. According to the mystical tradition, when you go inside the hut, you'll find a group of honored guests waiting to be greeted by you.

Known collectively as the אֻשְׁפִּיזִין (ushpizin), the guests, seven men—and, since the gender revolution, seven women—from Jewish antiquity are traditionally (and not so traditionally) invited into our sukkah to help us celebrate the holiday.

The word אֻשְׁפִּיזִין (ushpizin) is obviously not originally a Hebrew word, but came into the Hebrew from the Aramaic. Its root has entered the Hebrew language, however, and even displays three fascinating characteristics worthy of note (and of a chapter).

Did you know, for example, that some Hebrew words mean not only themselves but also their opposite? Thus, the word חֶסֶד (hesed) means not only "goodness" but also "abomination." as in the "Holiness Code" of the book of Leviticus (20:17), which teaches that if a man marries his sister, חֶסֶד הוּא (hesed hu), "it is an abomination." To get back to our subject, the word אֻשְׁפִּיז (ushpiz) originally meant both "guest" and "host." It is more than a curiosity that the Latin word hospes, from which we get "hospital" and "hospitality," meant both "host" and "guest" as well. If you listen closely, you'll recognize that hospes and אֻשְׁפִּיז (ushpiz) are indeed the same word.

The wonderful ambiguity of the word אֻשְׁפִּיז (ushpiz) is highlighted in a briskly narrated legal ethics story in the Talmud.

Tractate Sanhedrin (7b-8a) relates how the אֻשְׁפִּיזְכָן (*ushpizkhan*), host, of Rav—a leading Babylonian *amora* of the third century—asks him to be a judge in a case he is bringing to court. The punctilious jurist finds it necessary to recuse himself.

As we learned but a moment ago, the word hospital comes from the Latin hospes. Intriguingly, the Modern Hebrew verb לְאַשְׁפֵּז (*le-ashpez*) means "to hospitalize." The verb derived from our noun has not a three- but rather a four-letter root א-שׁ-פּ-ז (*alef, shin, peh, zayyin*). This structure is rare enough in Hebrew and is usually found in vocabulary items artificially derived from foreign words, such as לְאַקְלֵם (*le-aklem*), to acclimate, or from words artfully constructed from whole cloth, like לְאַבְגֵּד (*le-avged*), to alphabetize, from the first four letters of the Hebrew alphabet, *alef, bet, gimmel* and *dalet.*

The modern verb לְאַשְׁפֵּז (*le-ashpez*) has led to a great language controversy in Israel. Is the noun for hospitalization אִשְׁפּוּז (*ishpuz*) or אַשְׁפָּזָה (*ashpazah*)? Both have fervent adherents and the outcome is still being fought on the linguistic battlefield.

Who would have thought that when we entered our sukkah to greet our אֻשְׁפִּיזִין (*ushpizin*) we would be drawn into such a contentious language debate? Maybe it's time to warm up our brains by going back into the house. Hag same'ah, nevertheless.

WITH NOTHING ON THE SIDE

One of the consequences of having a monotheistic religion is that you're likely to have a lonely God—and a lonely people as well.

The latter case is described in the story of Balaam, hired by Balak to curse the nation of Israel. The best Balaam can come up with is הֶן עָם לְבָדָד יִשְׁכֹּן (*hen am le-vadad yishkon*), "This is a people that dwells apart," using the Hebrew root ב-ד-ד (*bet, dalet, dalet*), to be alone, separated, isolated. The root is applied to God as well in the biblical pronouncement אֵין עוֹד מִלְבַדּוֹ (*ein od mi-le-vado*), "There is none beside him." Then there is, of course, the case God himself makes for marriage, לֹא טוֹב הֱיוֹת הָאָדָם לְבַדּוֹ (*lo tov heyot ha-adam le-vado*), "It is not good for man to be alone."

The root can be played in both a major and a minor key. At Hanukkah, we use our root to chant that we are permitted לִרְאוֹתָם בִּלְבַד (*li-rotam bi-le-vad*), "only to look at" the candles (and enjoy their glow). On Tisha be-Av, with the same root, we mourn the destruction of the Temple with the lament אֵיכָה יָשְׁבָה בָדָד (*eikhah yashvah vadad*), "Alas, lonely sits the City [once great with people]."

Hasidic lore is replete with narratives in which the Rebbe—perhaps as a way of imitating God—goes into הִתְבּוֹדְדוּת (*hitbodedut*), mystical seclusion. The same word, הִתְבּוֹדְדוּת (*hitbodedut*), is used in the Talmud to describe a punishment—exile.

The doubling of the dalet in the root hints that it may come from a primordial two-letter root, ב-ד (*bet, dalet*), and that roots that begin with these letters may be related to each other, as in the root ל-ד-ב (*bet, dalet, lamed*), to be detached or differentiated, which gives us havdalah, the ceremony that separates the Sabbath from weekdays. In any case, the two-letter word בַּד (*bad*), portion or part, does come from our root, and gives us בְּבַד בַּד (*bad be-vad*), alongside.

The word בּוֹדֵד (*boded*) has many interesting uses, as a noun, adjective, and verb. A word that appears only once in Scripture is called in Hebrew a בּוֹדֵד בַּמִּקְרָא (*boded ba-mikra*), *hapax legomenon*, in scholarly circles. A new oleh serving in the Israeli army is called a חַיָּל בּוֹדֵד (*hayyal boded*), because he doesn't have a local family to give him moral support. A doctor may decide לְבוֹדֵד (*le-voded*), to put in isolation, an infectious patient. From isolation to keeping out the cold is but a small step, as the word בִּדּוּד (*biddud*), insulation, attests.

When you wish to make sure that a check is not cashed by the wrong person, you write לַמּוּטָב בִּלְבַד (*la-mutav bi-le-vad*), for recipient only. And לֹא זוֹ בִּלְבַד (*lo zo bi-le-vad*), not only that, there is the tree made lonely by the בָּדִיד (*badid*), moat, placed around it to water it more efficiently. Often a pair of lovers will seek לְהִתְבּוֹדֵד (*le-hitboded*), to be alone together, in a מָקוֹם מְבוּדָד (*makom mevudad*), a deserted place. Sometimes, like God and the Jewish people, you need a little בְּדִידוּת (*bedidut*), loneliness, to thrive.

FEAR OF CRYING

The Jewish people have no fear of crying. The Hebrew root ב-כ-ה (*bet, kaf, heh*) is found in many a biblical narrative and is associated with several biblical figures. First, there are the "other" sons of the patriarchs, Ishmael and Esau. Curiously, there is a neat linguistic parallelism in both episodes. In the Ishmael story (Genesis 21:16), though God hears the son's voice, it is his mother Hagar who cries: וַתִּשָּׂא אֶת קֹלָהּ וַתֵּבְךְ (*va-tissa et kolah va-tevk*), "She lifted her voice and wept." In the Esau episode, in Genesis 27:38, וַיִּשָּׂא עֵשָׂו קֹלוֹ וַיֵּבְךְ (*va-yissa esav kolo va-yevk*), "Esau lifted his voice and wept."

Jews weep nationally for their condition of exile. As the Psalmist says in Psalm 137:1, "By the waters of Babylon" שָׁם יָשַׁבְנוּ גַּם בָּכִינוּ (*sham yashavnu gam bakhinu*), "there we sat and wept." Mainly, however, Jews follow King Solomon's dictum in Koheleth 3:4—עֵת לִבְכּוֹת וְעֵת לִשְׂחוֹק (*et li-vkot ve-et li-sehok*)—"There is a time for tears and a time for laughter."

But because Jewish culture frowns on the tragic outlook on life, crying will often lead to laughter. The book of Psalms tells us repeatedly and metaphorically that crying is merely a first step toward redemption. Thus we have, in Psalm 30:6, בָּעֶרֶב יָלִין בֶּכִי וְלַבּוֹקֶר רִנָּה (*ba-erev yalin bekhi ve-la-boker rinnah*), "In the evening, one may lie down weeping; but at dawn there are shouts of joy."

The vision of a crying Mother Rachel in Jeremiah 31:15—רָחֵל מְבַכָּה עַל בָּנֶיהָ (*rahel mevakkah al baneha*)—uses our words in a prophetic consolation.

In some instances crying has the same function as prayer, as a

27

tool to ask God for more life. When, in I Samuel 1:8, Hannah cries because she is childless, her husband Elkanah reminds her that his love for her transcends her fertility and that she therefore has no need to cry, חַנָּה לָמֶה תִבְכִּי (hannah lameh tivki), "Hannah, why should you cry?" David stops crying when the infant he fathered with Bathsheba dies. As David explains to his advisors, בְּעוֹד הַיֶּלֶד חַי צַמְתִּי וָאֶבְכֶּה (be-od ha-yeled hai tsamti va-evkeh), "I fasted and cried as long as the child was alive," now that he is dead we must go on with living (II Samuel 12:22).

And then there is the story of Joseph for whom kissing and crying out of happiness go together. Even though he is viceroy to the Pharaoh, Joseph cannot restrain his sentimental side when his brothers come to Egypt for food. He finally breaks down, in Genesis 45, and, after weeping with Benjamin וַיְנַשֵּׁק לְכָל אֶחָיו וַיֵּבְךְּ עֲלֵיהֶם (va-yenashek le-khol ehav va-yevk aleihem), "He kissed all his brothers and wept upon them."

The expression בָּכָה עַל (bakhah al) has a different connotation in modern Israeli Hebrew. It is used in cases where things just do not "go well." Thus, a woman discussing her friend's ill-fitting item of clothing might say הַשִּׂמְלָה בָּכְתָה עָלֶיהָ (ha-simlah bakhtah aleiha), "The dress did not suit her at all."

Nobody likes a whiner and that includes speakers of Modern Hebrew, who will not hesitate to take on a constant complainer with אַל תִּהְיֶה בַּכְיָן כָּזֶה (al tihyeh bakhyan ka-zeh), "Don't be such a whiner." If you're ever gotten soap in your eyes you surely cried. Miriam Yalan Shtekelis, a major Israeli poet, bids us to think of the soap itself in the poem הַסַּבּוֹן בָּכָה מְאוֹד (ha-sabon bakhah me'od), "The Soap Cried a Lot."

From weeping matriarchs to weeping dresses to weeping bars of soap, it shows how far we've come.

WHAT'S IN A NAME? LIGHTNING

The 1999 elections in Israel sent some Torah-savvy Zionists scurrying for scriptural confirmation of the results. They didn't have far to look. Before the election, they noted, there was only one Barak ensconced in a seat of power, the Chief Justice of the Israel Supreme Court, Aharon Barak. Then came the elections. They confirmed the verse in Exodus 19:12, וַיְהִי קֹלֹת וּבְרָקִים (va-yehi kolot u-verakim), translatable not only as "There was thunder and lightning," but, alternatively, as "There were votes (קֹלֹות means both thunder and votes) and there were בְּרָקִים (berakim), plural Baraks," to include the new Prime Minister, Ehud Barak.

Does it matter that Ehud Barak changed his family name by finding a Hebrew word that would refer back phonically to his original Diaspora moniker, Brug? (His brother, by the way, has kept the original name.) Does it help that there is also a first name בָּרָק (barak), given to both the scriptural general in service to the prophetess Deborah in the book of Judges and to the father of the hero in Leon Uris's novel *Exodus*?

The Hebrew root ק-ר-ב (bet, resh, kof) originally meant a gleam or a flash, especially a flash of lightning. That is the sense found in the poem "*Halikhah le-Kesariah*" by Zionist heroine Hannah Senesh. Also set to music, it sings of בְּרַק הַשָּׁמַיִם (berak ha-shamayim), the heavenly lightning, that is like a human prayer. The Torah speaks of a gleaming stone called a בָּרֶקֶת (bareket), the lustrous emerald found in the High Priest's breastplate. And when you meet a long-lost friend, don't your eyes light up? In Hebrew, you have בָּרָק בָּעֵינַיִם (*barak ba-einayim*), literally, a glimmer in the eyes.

How do we know that a new day is dawning? Just look up at the sky, says the Tractate Yoma of the Talmud, and you will see the בַּרְקַאי (*barkai*), morning star, that announces the new month.

Today, if we wish to send a message to the Prime Minister's office, we can send a fax or an e-mail. In the old days, as many as ten years ago, one could send a מִבְרָק (*mivrak*), telegram, that would get there with the speed of lightning. Today, no one working in the PM's office can even tell you the מַעַן לַמִּבְרָקִים (*ma'an la-mivrakim*), cable address.

In the army, where Ehud Barak made his first career, soldiers were required to shine their shoes to a gleaming finish, לְהַבְרִיק אֶת הַנַּעֲלַיִם (*le-havrik et ha-na'alayim*). Some people also have gleaming eyes, to be sure, but one does have to watch out for the eye ailment called בַּרְקִית (*barkit*), glaucoma. Nowadays, with laser technology, some eye diseases can be treated in a בֶּרֶק עַיִן (*berak ayin*), a flash. Everyone will agree that that is a רַעֲיוֹן מַבְרִיק (*ra'ayon mavrik*), bright idea.

You say you want to increase your Hebrew vocabulary? A good study aid would be a set of כַּרְטִיסֵי הַבְרָקָה (*kartisei havrakah*), flash cards. Or, you can take a Hebrew root—or a former Prime Minister's name—and play with it until you uncover all the vocabulary items hidden within.

LIGHT AND CLARITY

Probably the most storied couple in all of talmudic literature is that of Rabbi Meir and his scholarly wife Beruriah. So many legends have been woven about their life that the Rabbis were inclined to treat even their names allegorically. He was called מֵאִיר (me'ir), from אוֹר (or), light, because he enlightened the eyes of the wise. She was בְּרוּרְיָה (beruryah), from the root ב-ר-ר (bet, resh, resh), pure, clear, because she clarified the words of God.

Both the marriage and the root of Beruriah's name were obviously made in language heaven. The prophet Zephaniah, foreseeing a day when all people will call upon the name of the Lord, tells us that they will do so in a שָׂפָה בְרוּרָה (safah verurah), "pure language."

The root is found not only in aggadic (story-telling) portions of the Talmud but also in its halakhic (legal) sections. One of the thirty-nine categories of work prohibited on the Sabbath is called בּוֹרֵר (borer), sifting. A בּוֹרֵר (borer) is also an "arbitrator" or a "referee," someone who chooses between right and wrong.

That the root contains a nuance of cleanliness can be gleaned from a word for soap that derives from it, בּוֹרִית (borit). If you listen carefully, you will hear an echo of "borax" in the latter word.

It will surprise no one to learn that our root is found in the Siddur, which insists that all those who unify God's name are כֻּלָּם בְּרוּרִים (kulam berurim), flawless. To be בַּר לֵבָב (bar levav), is to be "pure in heart."

In Israel today, the tendency is לְדַבֵּר בְּרוּרוֹת (le-dabber berurot), to speak plainly, for example, by reminding people that הַקַּבְּצָן

הַקַּבְּצָן אֵינוּ יָכוֹל לִהְיוֹת בַּרְרָן (*ha-kabtsan eino yakhol li-hyot bareran*), Beggars can't be choosers. The reason some Israelis give for their success in war is to call it a מִלְחֶמֶת אֵין בְּרֵירָה (*milhemet ein bereirah*), "a war of no other choice." And if בְּרָרָה (*berarah*) is the traditional word for "fruit of inferior quality" (because the best fruit has been chosen out), it is also a slangy and somewhat snooty idiom for soldiers who don't make it into an elite army unit.

At play here is what Charles Darwin, had he spoken Hebrew, might have called הַבְּרֵרָה הַטִּבְעִית (*ha-bereirah ha-tiv'it*), Natural Selection. Darwin might have been astonished that an Israeli music group from the 1970s had adopted his theory as its name. But Rabbi Meir, Beruriah, and their colleagues knew that names have a resonance beyond their simple meanings.

THE COOKING LESSON

Whenever Jewish holidays draw near, the importance of food percolates into the collective consciousness. A look at the Hebrew root for the preparation of food, by both nature and man—ב-שׁ-ל (*bet, shin, lamed*)—makes us realize how fundamental making food ready for consumption is.

One of the meanings of our root is "to ripen." One would not pick a fruit that is not בָּשֵׁל (*bashel*), ripe. Rather, one waits patiently for the fruit's בָּשִׁיל (*bashil*), the season when it gets ripe. (The *bashil* of an orange, for example, is in the winter.) Ripeness is also applied to human beings, especially when speaking of the בְּשֵׁלוּת (*beshelut*), maturity, of a young person.

In Hebrew, however, ripeness is only half the story, nature's half. The other half of the meaning of our root refers to the human activity of cooking. The verse in the Torah from which the laws of kashrut derive is לֹא תְבַשֵּׁל גְּדִי בַּחֲלֵב אִמּוֹ (*lo tevashel gedi ba-halev immo*), "Thou shalt not seethe a kid in its mother's milk." If you've ever wondered whether this prohibited dish ever existed in reality, just look at the food column in the New York Times Magazine (July 11, 1999), which speaks of *abbacchio*, "the Italian baby lamb simmered in its mother's milk."

The culinary term יַיִן מְבֻשָּׁל (*yayin mevushal*), boiled wine, has the virtue of being immune to ritual contamination. An עֵרוּב תַּבְשִׁילִין (*eruv tavshilin*), the ritual mixing of cooked foods, permits one to cook for Shabbat on a Friday holiday.

The most common word for the person who does the cooking is טַבָּח (*tabbah*), cook, from which we get the word for kitchen,

מִטְבָּח (*mitbah*). But our root contributes three other synonyms: מְבַשֵׁל (*mevashel*), בַּשְׁלָן (*bashlan*), and, in modern slang, בַּשֵׁל (*bashal*) or, when talking about one's mother, בַּשְׁלָנִית (*bashlanit*).

If you've wondered at the meaning of the English expression "hoist by his own petard," you need look no further than the idiom's Hebrew equivalent for clarification. One might say of Haman, for example, who gets hung on his own gallows, that בַּקְּדֵרָה שֶׁבִּשֵׁל בָּהּ נִתְבַּשֵׁל (*ba-kederah she-bishel bah nitbashel*), literally, "in the pot that he boiled he was cooked," or, more idiomatically, הוּא אוֹכֵל אֶת מַה שֶׁהוּא בִּשֵׁל (*hu okhel et mah she-hu bishel*), "He eats what he himself cooked." In Hebrew, of someone who washes his dirty linen in public, one says, הִקְדִיחַ תַּבְשִׁילוֹ בָּרַבִּים (*hikdi'ah tavshilo ba-rabbim*), metaphorically, "he caused his pot to boil over in public." Some people cook cereal, while others stir up trouble. Of both, one says, בִּשֵׁל דַּיְסָה (*bishel daissah*). Of such a troublemaker we might also say, "Let him stew in his own juices," שֶׁיִּתְבַּשֵׁל בַּמִּיץ שֶׁל עַצְמוֹ (*she-yitbashel ba-mits shel atsmo*).

Sooner or later, in every social interaction, one realizes that מַשֶׁהוּ מִתְבַּשֵׁל כָּאן (*ma-she-hu mitbashel kan*), "Something strange is going on here." The proof of this cooking lesson is in the reading. Or, as they say in Hebrew, מִי שֶׁאָכַל אֶת הַתַּבְשִׁיל יוֹדֵעַ אֶת טַעֲמוֹ (*mi she-akhal et ha-tavshil yode'a et ta'amo*), "He who has eaten this food once before knows how it's supposed to taste."

Bon appétit! Or, better yet, בְּתֵאָבוֹן (*be-te'avon*).

LOOKING FOR MR. BIG

Quiz: What do the third day of the Jewish year, an Islamic chant, Mary Magdalene, and a tassel have in common? If you answered that they are all connected to the same Hebrew root, ג-ד-ל (*gimmel, dalet, lamed*), to grow, to become great, אַתָּה גָּדוֹל (*attah gadol*), "You the man."

The root is found throughout Scripture. Pharaoh, appointing Joseph viceroy, assures him, רַק הַכִּסֵּא אֶגְדַּל מִמֶּךָ (*rak ha-kisse egdal mi-meka*), "only the Throne will I elevate over you." Exodus relates that Moses was גָּדוֹל מְאֹד (*gadol me'od*), pre-eminent. His brother Aaron was כֹּהֵן גָּדוֹל (*kohen gadol*), High Priest. The book of Esther reports that Mordechai, after foiling Haman's plot, הוֹלֵךְ וְגָדוֹל (*holekh ve-gadol*), becomes increasingly influential, in Persia. A fast on the third day of Tishrei commemorates the assassination of the governor of Judaea, גְּדַלְיָה (*gedaliah*), whose name means, like the Islamic chant Allahu Akbar, "God is Great."

During Second Temple times the 120 אַנְשֵׁי כְּנֶסֶת הַגְּדוֹלָה (*anshei kenesset ha-gedolah*), members of the supreme council, were both judges and preservers of tradition. The importance of Passover is brought home clearly in the name given to the Sabbath preceding the holiday, שַׁבַּת הַגָּדוֹל (*shabbat ha-gadol*), the Great Sabbath.

Rabbinic literature reveals a possible link among a גְּדִיל (*gedil*), tassel, a גַּדָּל (*gadal*), hairdresser, and our root. Twisting a cord to make a tassel or plaiting the hair to make a braid makes them strong; and a strong person is plausibly great.

Our root is found most prominently beginning the Mourner's Kaddish, יִתְגַּדַּל (*yitgadal*), "[May His name] be glorified," and in the expression גְּדוֹל הַדּוֹר (*gedol ha-dor*), the outstanding Rabbi of his generation. Do not confuse the talmudic euphemism גְּדוֹלִים (*gedolim*), bowel movement, with the modern Yiddish-inflected הַגְּדוֹילִים (*ha-gedoilim*), big shots.

A rabbinic dictum, גָּדוֹל מְצֻוֶּה וְעוֹשֶׂה (*gadol metsuvveh ve-oseh*), teaching that it is more meritorious to do what you are commanded than to volunteer for something you are not commanded, requires some commentary, perhaps from your local Rabbi.

Every parent can understand the expression צַעַר גִּדּוּל בָּנִים (*tsa'ar giddul banim*), the pain of child rearing. The use of our root in the word אֲגוּדָל (*agudal*), thumb, big toe, is transparent as well. Less transparent is the relationship of Mary Magdalene to our root. It appears she was from the Galilean town of Magdala, either *gadol*, an important town, or, a town with a מִגְדָּל (*migdal*), tower.

Some may choose to retreat from life in a מִגְדַּלּוֹר (*migdalor*), lighthouse, and others in a מִגְדָּל שֵׁן (*migdal shen*), ivory tower. Neither of these options is attractive to a certain type of modern Israeli whom we would call a רֹאשׁ גָּדוֹל (*rosh gadol*), one who always thinks big and can always be counted on. To that that type of person, we attribute גֹּדֶל (*godel*), significance; גְּדוּלָה (*gedullah*), honor; and גַּדְלוּת (*gadlut*), greatness. Or is that just a Zionist's way of looking through a זְכוּכִית מַגְדֶּלֶת (*zekhukhit magdelet*), magnifying glass?

CUTTING TO SIZE

"**M**easure twice; cut once." That's easy enough if you're a carpenter or a tailor. In Hebrew, with over fifty synonyms for "to cut," you'll be exhausted before you've found the right verb for the semantic path you wish to travel.

A good illustration of "semantic path" is provided by the root ג-ז-ר (*gimmel, zayin, resh*), which leads away from cutting into Jewish life and Hebrew letters.

In Hebrew Scripture, the verb גָּזַר (*gazar*) often means to cut in two. The Psalmist sings the praises of the One Who, גּוֹזֵר יַם סוּף לִגְזָרִים (*gozer yam suf li-gzarim*), divides the Red Sea in two. When King Solomon is confronted by two mothers who lay claim to the same infant, he uses our root wisely to render his judgment: גִּזְרוּ אֶת הַיֶּלֶד הַחַי לִשְׁנַיִם (*gizru et ha-yeled ha-hai li-shnayim*), "Cut the living child in half," thus inducing the real mother to relinquish her claim and save her baby's life.

Solomon's use of our root to render his verdict leads to its use as a word for rendering a גְּזַר דִּין (*gezar din*), verdict. The Rabbis of the Talmud operate on the principle that אֵין גּוֹזְרִין גְּזֵרָה (*ein gozrin gezerah*), "One does not issue a decree" that the majority of the populace is unable to fulfill. One of the thirteen principles of textual analysis proposed by Rabbi Ishmael is the גְּזֵרָה שָׁוָה (*gezerah shavah*), an analogy based on the repetition of a word in two texts.

Among the most pernicious decrees ever handed down were what historians call the גְּזֵרוֹת תַּ"ח וְתַ"ט (*gezerot tah ve-tat*), the edicts of 1648-49, which permitted anti-Semite Chmelnitzki and his marauding Cossacks to attack the Jews of Poland.

A more benign use of our root is found in Hebrew grammar and etymology. When you talk about גִּזְרַת הַשְּׁלֵמִים (*gizrat ha-shelemim*), for example, you are describing a verb that uses all three letters of the root in its conjugations. Even-Shoshan's dictionary contains a useful section called הַשָּׁרָשִׁים וְנִגְזְרֵיהֶם (*ha-shorashim ve-nigzereihem*), roots and their derivations. While you will still hear the word *etimologia*, the Hebraically correct word for etymology is גִּזְרוֹן (*gizron*).

Today, writers who wish to save time will use their computer's גְּזוֹר וְהַדְבֵּק (*gezor ve-hadbek*), "cut and paste" function as they edit their text. Also, political pundits talk about a מִגְזָר (*migzar*), sector, of the populace. Fashionistas will describe how a dress highlights a woman's גִּזְרָה (*gizrah*), waist. And a מַגְזֵרָה (*magzerah*) is both a saw and a paper-cutting machine.

There are two groups of Hebrew lovers and they both ask the same question: אֵיךְ גּוֹזְרִים גֶּזֶר? (*eikh gozrim gezer?*). The first group wants to know, "How do you cut a carrot? Into long strips or round coins?" The second group is asking, "How do people גּוֹזְרִים (*gozrim*), derive, the Hebrew word גֶּזֶר (*gezer*), carrot, from our root?" The answer to the first question is shrouded in mystery. The answer to the second question is answered by the first. A carrot is called גֶּזֶר (*gezer*) because it looks like a log, something נִגְזָר (*nigzar*), cut, from a tree. And a carrot may be cut in one of two ways because it resembles a log of wood, which may be cut either into long planks or round tabletops.

To buy a pair of wire-cutters, go into the hardware store and ask for מִגְזָרַיִם (*migzarayim*). If the merchant doesn't know what you're talking about, be patient. Sometimes we have to measure our words twice before we can cut with them.

THE EXILE MENTALITY REVEALED

One of the most crucial Jewish-identity questions today is not "Who am I?" but "Where am I?" Should those of us who live outside the Jewish State consider ourselves to be in גָּלוּת (*galut*), exile, or not? For once, the Hebrew root does not solve the problem. In this case, ג-ל-ה (*gimmel, lamed, heh*), only serves to compound the confusion.

The root itself has two seemingly unconnected meanings, "to reveal" and "to depart." It has been suggested, splitting a few hairs, that one who moves away from his homeland removes the "protective covering" that a homeland provides.

The first meaning, to uncover, gives us the expression, גָּלוּי שְׁכִינָה (*gillui shekhinah*), divine revelation. But it also gives us גָּלוּי עֲרָיוֹת (*gilui arayot*), illicit sexual relations. Fifty years ago, when Crick and Watson made the תַּגְלִית מַדָּעִית (*taglit mada'it*), scientific discovery, of the Double Helix, any journalist reporting its significance would have been credited with a גָּלוּי מַרְעִישׁ (*gillui mar'ish*), scoop. On the same tack, a student on a Birthright Israel trip, called in Hebrew תַּגְלִית (*taglit*), discovery, will be sure to send home at least a postcard, called in Hebrew a גְּלוּיָה (*geluyah*), because its message is גָּלוּי (*galui*), revealed to all.

The Ethics of the Fathers uses the other meaning of our root to suggest that we should move away to a Torah center, הֱוֵי גּוֹלֶה לִמְקוֹם תּוֹרָה (*hevei goleh li-mekom torah*). But, בֹּא נְדַבֵּר גְּלוּיוֹת (*bo nedabber geluyot*), let's speak frankly, the word גָּלוּת (*galut*), unlike its near-synonym גּוֹלָה (*golah*), has a strong negative connotation of banishment and expulsion, even captivity. And yet, both can also be synonymous with תְּפוּצָה (*tefutsa*), the less emotion-laden word meaning Diaspora.

While an Israeli abroad is merely חוּץ לָאָרֶץ (*huts la-arets*), outside the Land, one can be in *galut* in Israel as well, and you don't even have to be a Jew to be there. On the "street" in Israel you will hear Israelis berate their fellow citizens for having a גָּלוּתִי (*galuti*), ghetto-like, mentality. According to Dan Ben-Amotz and Netiva Ben Yehudah, in their dictionary of spoken Hebrew, an Israeli soccer team, forced to play its home games in another city, is said to be in *galut*. And not so long ago Israeli journalists used to remind us that Iran's Ayatollah Khomeini was once a גּוֹלֶה פּוֹלִיטִי (*goleh politi*), political exile, in Paris.

Jewish pilgrimage holidays have a day tacked on for Diaspora residents, called יוֹם טוֹב שֵׁנִי שֶׁל גָלוּיוֹת (*yom tov sheni shel galuyyot*). Is that a blessing or a curse? Just ask the person doing the cooking and serving. And pray for קְבּוּץ גָלוּיוֹת (*kibbuts galuyyot*), the Ingathering of the Exiles.

OVERFLOWING ABUNDANCE

In Hebrew, one word always leads to another. Often, the road a word takes to its new series of meanings seems both convoluted and discomfiting.

Take the example of the Hebrew root ג-ל-שׁ (*gimmel, lamed, shin*), to glide down. This is a word that appears only once in Scripture, in the Song of Songs, as the Lover compares his Beloved's hair to a flock of goats שֶׁגָּלְשׁוּ (*she-galshu*), "streaming down," from Mount Gilead.

How did this poetic description of a woman's abundant head of hair, in Modern Hebrew שֵׂעָר גּוֹלֵשׁ (*se'ar golesh*), lead to the rabbinic use of our root for both baldness and publishing? It has to do with a boiled-over pot of liquid. Here's how it goes. It seems that when a boiling pot of milk, for example, overflows, the milk, like the cascading goats above, גּוֹלֵשׁ מִן הַסִּיר (*golesh min ha-sir*), flows down its sides. A liquid that's scorching can easily scald the hair off someone's head, causing, in rabbinic Hebrew, גָּלֵשׁ (*gelesh*), baldness. Since a bald head is shiny and reflects light, then, in rabbinic terms, one can use the verb לְהַגְלִישׁ (*le-haglish*) for to publish, i.e., to bring to light.

The modern use of our root is easier to follow, but it also has its adventurous twists and turns. Be careful, you can get a skin disease, גַּלֶּשֶׁת (*galleshet*), eczema, from our root, as the skin "boils over" to form lesions. Every little park in Israel has a מַגְלֵשָׁה (*magleshah*), sliding pond, for the kiddies. At the amusement park in summer, one of the most popular rides is the מַגְלֵצָ׳ת מַיִם (*magletchat mayim*), water slide. Notice the pronunciation, adapted from a

Yiddish word, *glitshn*, to slide, that—amazingly—fits its Hebrew near-homonym, *magleshah*.

A trendy winter vacation spot in Israel is Mount Hermon, where you'll find גַּלָּשִׁים (*gallashim*), skiers, coming down the mountain on their מִגְלָשַׁיִם (*miglashayim*), skis; the less adventurous, perhaps worried about a גְּלִישָׁה (*gelishah*), avalanche, will glide down a safer slope on their מִגְלָשָׁה (*miglashah*), sled.

At the beach, if you look up, you'll see an adventurous type on a גִּלְשׁוֹן (*gilshon*), hang glider. Look out on the water, and listen carefully, and you're likely to encounter a young muscular type on a גַּלְשָׁן גַּלִּים (*galshan gallim*), surfboard, singing to himself the up-to-the-minute שִׁיר הַגַּלְשָׁן (*shir ha-galshan*) surfer's song.

Of course, the most popular sport using our root is played by גּוֹלְשִׁים בָּאִינְטֶרְנֶט (*golshim ba-internet*), the non-athletic types who surf the net, sometimes looking for a good Hebrew site and sometimes looking for a new love with flowing hair.

gimmel shin mem מ-שׁ-ג   22

RAINMAKERS AND WINDBREAKERS

And you thought Hamlet had a problem. In Israel, at one time, youths preparing to join a kibbutz ultimately had to ask themselves: ?לְהַגְשִׁים אוֹ לֹא לְהַגְשִׁים (le-hagshim o lo le-hagshim?), literally, to concretize or not to concretize? In other words, "Shall I indeed put the ideology I imbibed in the youth movement into practice and make a commitment to become a kibbutz member?"

These youngsters are using the meaning of the Hebrew root ג-שׁ-מ (gimmel, shin, mem) that has to do with substance, matter, the concrete. The Hebrew term גַשְׁמִיּוּת (gashmiyyut), materialism, may be the polar opposite of רוּחָנִיּוּת (ruhaniyyut), spirituality, but, in some circumstances, it represents a higher value. Just ask the members of Young Judea, the American Zionist youth movement, whose senior group, destined for aliyah to Eretz Yisrael, is called הַמַּגְשִׁימִים (ha-magshimim), the implementers.

There is another meaning to the root ג-שׁ-מ (gimmel, shin, mem)—or is it another root entirely?—that gives us the word גֶּשֶׁם (geshem), rain. While some scholars are dubious about a linguistic connection between the two meanings of גֶּשֶׁם (geshem), others believe that a convincing case might nevertheless be made.

First of all, in the תְּפִלַּת הַגֶּשֶׁם (tefillat ha-geshem), Prayer for Rain, which we recite every year during the holiday of Shemini Atzeret, we say מַשִּׁיב הָרוּחַ וּמוֹרִיד הַגֶּשֶׁם (mashiv ha-ru'ah u-morid ha-gashem), "Who causes the wind to blow and the rain to fall." Is it possible that wind is the opposite of rain the way spirituality is the opposite of physicality?

43

It is a matter of no small consequence, perhaps, that when גֶּשֶׁם (geshem) appears in Scripture, it is usually associated with a heavy rain. The word גֶּשֶׁם (geshem) materializes twice in the story of Noah's flood. In addition, we have גֶּשֶׁם נְדָבוֹת (geshem nedavot), "bounteous rain" in Psalms; גֶּשֶׁם גָּדוֹל (geshem gadol), "a big rain," and הֲמוֹן הַגֶּשֶׁם (hamon ha-geshem), "abundant rain," in the book of Kings; and גֶּשֶׁם שׁוֹטֵף (geshem shotef), "torrential rain," three times in the book of Ezekiel.

The word is also tied to literary heroes, both classical and modern. The Talmud tells a charming tale of Honi the Circlemaker, whose prayer for rain is, on a deeper level, a demand that God do justice for his people. In more modern times, when the education department of the World Zionist Organization inaugurated its Gesher series of books in "Easy Hebrew," the very first title it chose to publish was Aharon Megged's short story, גֶּשֶׁם נְדָבוֹת (geshem nedavot), "Bounteous Rain."

Perhaps the most convincing argument for a linguistic affiliation between rain and concreteness comes from an Arabic word for "solid substance," jism. Curiously, in several dictionaries of American slang, the word "jism" is reported as a synonym for sperm, that is, a thick liquid. Are we not to conjecture that rain is called גֶּשֶׁם (geshem), a Hebrew cognate of Arabic jism, when it, too, appears to be thick, substantial?

There are some who will contend that this piece has not hewn to a Hamlet-like train of thought but, to stay with Shakespeare, has been Much Ado About Nothing. They will nevertheless have to contend with the expression in the book of Proverbs for "much ado about nothing," נְשִׂיאִים וְרוּחַ וְגֶשֶׁם אָיִן (nesi'im ve-ruah ve-geshem ayin), "clouds and wind but no rain." This idiom argues that only when we have rain do we have something of substance.

MODEL BEHAVIOR

You can learn a great deal about a civilization not only from its laws but also from the words used in its laws. Take, לְדֻגְמָא (le-dugma), for example, the word דֻגְמָא (dugma), example, which during the rabbinic period made its entrance into Hebrew from the Greek language.

What insights can we gain from the legal opinion in the Talmud prohibiting dyers from wearing on Shabbat הַדֻּגְמָאוֹת שֶׁבְּצַוָּארָן (ha-dugma'ot she-be-tsavaran), their color-sample necklace? We can infer, first of all, that Jews have been involved in all aspects of the *shmatte* trade for a long time. We can deduce further that they knew how to market their services. (Does this story not show us that they invented four-color advertising?) It also teaches us that it is proper to shed one's business persona on Shabbat. And, finally, it shows us that the Rabbis did not shy away from adopting a Greek word when a biblical Hebrew word was not available to them.

The Hebrew word דֻגְמָא (dugma), example, is borrowed directly from the Greek word *deigma*, sample or pattern. In modern Israel, you will marvel at the exquisite דֻגְמָאוֹת (dugma'ot), design patterns, on knitted kippot. A comfortable and natty-looking shirt, with epaulets on the shoulders and button-down flap pockets on the front, was once all the rage in Israel. All haberdashers once carried the חוּלְצָה דֶגֶם אֶל-עַל (hultsa degem el-al), a shirt in the El-Al style.

At the Holyland Hotel in Jerusalem you will marvel as you walk around the דֶגֶם בַּיִת שֵׁנִי (degem bayit sheni), scale model of the Second Temple. The word is also found in the name of an elementary school in Jerusalem, דּוּגְמָא לְבָנִים (*dugma le-vanim*), literally, "a model for boys." Their role model will be a מוֹרֶה לְדוּגְמָא (*moreh le-dugma*), a model teacher.

The Greek word has undergone several changes to make it fit the various Hebrew language patterns—conjugations and declensions and all that. To illustrate, לְהַדְגִּים (*le-hadgim*), this phenomenon, we can provide several דּוּגְמָאוֹת (*dugma'ot*), instances. Thus, when an architect wishes to exhibit a scale model of a building to a city planner, she will present a דֶּגֶם (*degem*), model, for consideration. A tailor will use a דּוּגְמָן (*dugman*), tailor's dummy, on which to pin his creation. And an Israeli fashion designer will hire a דּוּגְמָנִית (*dugmanit*) or a דּוּגְמָן (*dugman*), fashion model, to parade his or her wares on the runway or for a photo spread. If a scientist, for a further example, wishes to learn the overall character of a commodity, he may conduct a דְּגִימָה (*degimah*), sampling, of some of its constituent parts. At the urologist's office, the nurse will hand you a cup and ask you provide a דְּגִימַת שֶׁתֶן (*degimat sheten*), urine specimen. At election time you will hear a lot about a מִדְגָּם (*midgam*), sample poll. A fancy term for these language patterns is פָּרָדִיגְמוֹת (*paradigmot*), paradigms, a word that comes from the same Greek word as our root but has entered Hebrew only very recently, borrowed most likely not from ancient Greek but from modern English.

This chapter has been דּוּגְמָתִי (*dugmati*), exemplary, in its הַדְגָּמָה (*hadgamah*), demonstration, of the ability of Hebrew to naturalize and neutralize outside influences. Readers familiar with the modern American business buzzword "paradigm shift" will be able to perceive from this discussion how Hebrew might provide an acceptable model for a paradigm shift to a new openness in Jewish life.

GONE FISHIN'

Some people fish for food, others fish for relaxation. Still others fish for compliments or are said to be going on a fishing expedition. Then there is the spelling "ghoti" which, as astute readers will surmise, is pronounced "fish" ("gh", as in rough; "o", as in women; and "ti", as in nation).

Although at first glance it looks straightforward, the Hebrew word for fish, דָּג (*dag*), is no less kaleidoscopic. Turn it around and around and you'll discover all sorts of fascinating patterns. First of all there is the proximity of the sound of ד-י-ג (*dalet, yod, gimmel*), to fish, to that of ד-ג-ה (*dalet, gimmel, heh*), to multiply. Forefather Jacob squashed the two verbs together in his blessing of the sons of Joseph, saying וְיִדְגּוּ לָרֹב (*ve-yidgu la-rov*), "like fish may they grow to a multitude."

Another quirky route followed by our root goes through the name of the Philistine god, דָּגוֹן (*dagon*), half-man and half-fish. When he became the Philistine god of grain, he didn't even have to change his name. The Hebrew word for grain, not related to דָּג (*dag*), fish, is דָּגָן (*dagan*).

Fish is central to Jewish lore. The whale in whose belly the prophet Jonah lands is not precisely a whale; rather the text mentions a דָּג גָּדוֹל (*dag gadol*), a "big fish." When the Israelites in the desert complain to Moses about the menu, they do so by remembering the fish they had in Egypt, זָכַרְנוּ אֶת הַדָּגָה (*zakharnu et ha-dagah*). Is that perhaps why Israelis today call the fried filet of flounder they eat on Thursday evenings דָּג מֹשֶׁה רַבֵּנוּ (*dag moshe rabbenu*), literally, the fish of Moses our Teacher? Those Israelis who call salmon דָּג שְׁלֹמֹה (*dag shelomo*) do so for another reason entirely—the proximity of the sounds "salmon" and "Solomon." Along the Dan River in today's Israel is a fish restaurant where the tables are placed alongside the flowing water filled with trout. Naturally, the restaurant is called דָּג עַל הַדָּן (*dag al ha-dan*).

Some fish you eat, some you wear, and some you merely observe. Bite into a דָּג מָלוּחַ (*dag malu'ah*) and you'll savor the salty taste of a herring. Tie a דָּג מָלוּחַ (*dag malu'ah*) underneath your shirt collar and you'll be wearing a bow tie. There, the connection is purely visual. When you talk about דְּגֵי רְקָק (*degei rekak*), you are referring to small fish, that is, the common folk.

The zodiac sign for the month of Adar—a lucky month for the Jews—is מַזַּל דָּגִים (*mazal dagim*), Pisces. In Eastern Europe, if you wanted your son to grow up lucky, you gave him the Yiddish name Fishl. Did you know, by the way, that there is one character in the Torah named "Fish?" Give up? It's Nun, the father of Joshua as in יְהוֹשֻׁעַ בִּן-נוּן (*yehoshua bin nun*). Nun means fish in Aramaic.

There is a theology of fish and a philosophy of fish. The Talmud tells us that, in the world to come, the righteous will dine on a gigantic fish called לִוְיָתָן (*livyatan*), from which we get the English word Leviathan. To get a foretaste of the heavenly world to come on Shabbat, many Ashkenazi Jews eat דָּגִים מְמֻלָּאִים (*dagim memulla'im*), stuffed, or gefilte, fish. Curiously, not respecting the meaning of the words, the gefilte fish most Jews eat today is not "stuffed fish" but merely the stuffing that used to be put into the fish.

Getting back to philosophy, our ethicists ask, is it better to have a דָּג קָטָן בַּקְּדֵרָה (*dag katan ba-kederah*), "a small fish on the plate," or a דָּג גָּדוֹל בַּבְּרֵכָה (*dag gadol ba-berekhah*), "a big fish in the pond?" We haven't yet found the correct answer to that one, but we're still fishing.

RES IPSA LOQUITUR

There are many types of Zionists in this world, from those for whom מְדִינַת יִשְׂרָאֵל (*medinat yisrael*) is the Jewish State to those for whom it is the State of the Jews. And then there are the lawyers and the language mavens, for whom it all comes down to a matter of jurisdiction.

The word מְדִינָה (*medinah*) derives from the root ד-י-נ (*dalet, yod, nun*), judgment. The verb form demonstrates that judgment and power are intertwined, since an early meaning of דָּן (*dan*) is to rule.

In ancient times a מְדִינָה (*medinah*) was a province or a city. In the book of Esther, Ahashverosh's Persia has 127 מְדִינָה (*medinah*), provinces. In Islam, there is Mecca and there is Medina, the latter an abbreviation for "City of the Prophet."

Not surprisingly, Aramaic expressions using our root have a decidedly diasporic ring to them. The widespread expression דִּינָא דְּמַלְכוּתָא דִּינָא (*dina de-malkhuta dina*), "the law of the land is the Law," reflects the subordinate position of the Jews in the lands of their dispersion. In contrast, Israel conducts its own מְדִינָאוּת (*medina'ut*), diplomacy, and sets its own מְדִינִיּוּת (*medini'ut*), policy.

The root is also found in religious contexts. Submission to God's will especially on learning of someone's death, is traditionally expressed with a resigned בָּרוּךְ דַּיָּן אֱמֶת (*barukh dayyan emet*), "Blessed be the Judge of Truth." When the Jews feel abandoned by their God, they are likely to remonstrate that לֵית דִּין וְלֵית דַּיָּן (*let din ve-let dayyan*), there is neither justice nor judge. In the Talmud there are two categories of laws: laws of property, on the one hand, and, on the other, דִּינֵי נְפָשׁוֹת (*dinei nefashot*), capital cases.

Our root is found in many Hebrew names, from Abraham's son (by his second wife Ketura), מִדְיָן (*midian*), to Jacob's son and daughter דָּן (*dan*) and דִּינָה (*dinah*). Even the name of the Greek god Adonis is likely to come from our root, by way of the Hebrew word אָדוֹן (*adon*), lord.

Before you pounce on the writer for this last conjecture, don't forget the injunction in Pirkei Avot to דָּן לְכַף זְכוּת (*dan le-khaf zekhut*), lean toward a favorable judgment. The נִדּוֹן (*niddon*) here —the item under discussion—is a set of Jewish values that ask us to judge לִפְנִים מִשּׁוּרַת הַדִּין (*lifnim mi-shurat ha-din*), leniently.

This דִּיּוּן (*diyyun*), discussion, constitutes a דו"ח (*du-akh*), a report—from דִּין וְחֶשְׁבּוֹן (*din ve-heshbon*)—on a Hebrew concept of Zionism. If you have any objections, you can always contact my עוֹרֶכֶת דִּין (*orekhet din*), lawyer. She'll tell you who has jurisdiction in cases where law and language intermingle.

50

IMAGINE THIS

Perhaps no Jewish narrative has done more to awaken the creative imagination—in Hebrew הַכֹּחַ הַמְדַמֶּה (*ha-koah ha-medammeh*), imaginative power—than the story of Purim. Just think of the costume balls, the Purimshpiels, the annual journalistic spoofs, and even Racine's classical French drama, *Esther.*

Moreover, perhaps no Hebrew word has inspired more metaphorical musings than the Hebrew root ד-מ-ה (*dalet, mem, heh*), originally, to smooth, make even, and from there to compare, visualize in one's mind, imagine.

The root is found prominently in Scripture in a dramatic conversation between the דְּמוּיוֹת מֶרְכָּזִיּוֹת (*demuyyot merkaziyyot*), central characters, of the Purim megillah, Mordechai and Esther. There, Mordechai warns his niece, אַל תְּדַמִּי בְנַפְשֵׁךְ (*al tedammi be-nafshekh*), don't imagine, as queen, you might escape Haman's evil plot.

In the Genesis story of man's creation, God muses, "Let us make man כִּדְמוּתֵנוּ (*ki-dmutenu*), in our image." In the fantastic vision of the prophet Ezekiel, the word דְּמוּת (*demut*), image, is found some sixteen times. In the Song of Songs, the beloved, saying דּוֹמֶה דוֹדִי לִצְבִי (*domeh dodi li-tsevi*), compares her lover to a deer. The prophet Isaiah reminds us that, had not God left us a small remnant on which to rebuild our people, לַעֲמֹרָה דָּמִינוּ (*la-amorah daminu*), we would have vanished as a people like Gomorrah's residents.

The Talmud uses our root to introduce a parable, asking formulaically, לְמָה הַדָּבָר דּוֹמֶה? (*le-mah ha-davar domeh?*), "To what can this story be compared?" The composers of the Siddur remind us, in the Yigdal prayer, that אֵין לוֹ דְמוּת הַגּוּף (*ein lo demut ha-guf*), "God does not have a bodily image"; in the Nishmat prayer they ask God, מִי יִדְמֶה לָךְ (*mi yidmeh lakh*), "Who can be likened unto thee?" They also teach us to speak up for what is right when they assert in Aramaic, שְׁתִיקָה כְּהוֹדָאָה דָּמְיָא (*shetikah ke-hoda'a damya*), silence is equivalent to acquiescence.

Of identical twins one might say דּוֹמִים כְּמוֹ שְׁתֵי טִפּוֹת מַיִם (*domim kemo shetei tipot mayim*), they resemble each other like two drops of water. Have you seen the Hebrew Language Academy's סֶרֶט תַּדְמִית (*seret tadmit*), promotional film? In arithmetic class you surely came into contact with a שֶׁבֶר מְדוּמֶּה (*shever medummeh*), improper fraction, in which the denominator is less than the numerator. Remember?

A devout capitalist will exercise his דִּמְיוֹן (*dimyon*), imagination, to visualize how the word דָּמִים (*damim*), money, is related to our root. It seems to me, כִּמְדֻמַּנִי (*ki-medummani*), that money, equal in value to the thing it purchases, can be said לִדְמוֹת (*li-demot*), to resemble it. You might answer נִדְמֶה לְךָ! (*nidmeh lekha*), "That's what you think!" Of a contemporary use of our root one might say אֵין לוֹ דָּמִים (*ein lo damim*), it is priceless. This meaning is found in the expression דְּמֵי לֹא יֶחֱרַץ (*demei lo yeherats*), hush money, an allusion to the night of the Exodus when, Scripture says, *lo yeherats kelev*, not even a dog barked to give the departing Israelites away.

It's always good to have a little דְּמֵי כִּיס (*demei kis*), pocket money, so that we can give our children דְּמֵי פּוּרִים (*demei purim*), Purim *gelt*. That way, no matter what תַּדְמִית (*tadmit*), model, they choose for their costume, even one that is מְדֻמֶּה (*medummeh*), imaginary, they can have a good דְּמוּי עַצְמִי (*dimmui atsmi*), self-image.

Just imagine.

PRAISE BE

"Hallelujah!" It's on everyone's lips, especially at holiday time. Like amen, which can be found in a thousand languages, the Hebrew word hallelujah has traveled from Hebrew to many cultures worldwide. It has gone, for example, from King David's Psalms to Handel's "Hallelujah Chorus," in his *Messiah*.

The word hallelujah, literally, two words meaning "Praise the Lord," appears exclusively in Psalms and nowhere else in Scripture. It derives from the Hebrew root ל-ל-ה (*heh, lamed, lamed*), to praise. Originally, this root meant to shout liturgically—sometimes for joy and sometimes in terror.

The religious aspect of a wedding feast is evident from the Aramaic name for it, הִלּוּלָא (*hillula*), a shout for joy. Today, in Israel, the word הִלּוּלָה (*hillulah*) is used, for example, for the pilgramage to the grave of Rabbi Shimon Bar Yohai on Lag ba-Omer. Psalm 150 tells us seven times to praise God with musical instruments, especially by blowing the shofar, הַלְלוּהוּ בְּתֵקַע שׁוֹפָר (*haleluhu be-teka shofar*).

The most common nouns formed from the root are the Hebrew word for psalms, תְּהִלִּים (*tehillim*), and the word הַלֵּל (*hallel*), used to denote six chapters (113 through 118) of the book of Psalms recited on Jewish holidays that celebrate the Land of Israel.

The root is also found in many famous personal names, including that of the beloved talmudic sage הִלֵּל (*hillel*) and of the heroine of S.Y. Agnon's powerful novella, תְּהִלָּה (*tehillah*), from which we get the English name Tillie. The prophet Jeremiah uses the expression עִיר תְּהִלָּה (*ir tehillah*), "city of renown," to characterize, not Jerusalem, but, surprisingly, Damascus.

The Wissotsky Tea Company in Israel takes a biblical expression in Leviticus, פְּרִי הִלּוּלִים (*pri hillulim*), "fruit worthy of praise," and turns it around to describe one of the flavors of its teas, הִלּוּלֵי פֵּירוֹת (*hillulei peirot*), "fruit galore."

One of the key words of the Mourner's Kaddish, וְיִתְהַלָּל (*ve-yithallal*), "May He be praised," helps us to understand that the Kaddish is not a prayer for the dead but rather an expression of praise for God. Most of the various forms found in Scripture of the verb לְהַלֵּל (*le-hallel*), "to praise," have God as their direct object. There is one striking exception, however. When the book of Proverbs uses the verb, it often refers to the Woman of Valor.

In Modern Hebrew הִתְהוֹלְלוּת (*hit'holelut*) is not necessarily a praiseworthy thing, often meaning either boasting or drunken reveling. Jewish wit uses our root playfully to bring bombast down to earth. Modern Hebrew takes a verse from Scripture, אַל יִתְהַלֵּל חוֹגֵר כִּמְפַתֵּחַ (*al yit'hallel hoger ki-mefate'ah*), "The one who is first putting on his armor before he has even gone into battle should not boast like the one who is removing his after a successful skirmish." This tells boasters to wait until they've finished a project successfully before they open their mouth.

The book of Proverbs admonishes, יְהַלֶּלְךָ זָר וְלֹא פִיךָ (*ye-hallelkha zar ve-lo pikha*), "Let a stranger praise you, and not your own mouth." Putting the comma after the word וְלֹא changes the meaning of the proverb drastically: "Let a stranger praise you; if he doesn't, then blow your own horn."

But Psalm 150, the last Psalm, also has the last word, which is, of course, "Hallelujah!"

AU CONTRAIRE

The story of Purim, as told in both the book of Esther and Tractate Megillah of the Talmud, contains tales of palace intrigue, a beauty contest, examples of loyalty and heroism, reminders of the importance of both minor characters and historical archives, and dramatic reversals of fortune.

This last aspect, represented in the text by the Hebrew root ה-פ-כ (*heh, peh, kaf*), to change, adds a magical quality to the story. A time of grief and mourning, we are told, was נֶהְפַּךְ (*nehepakh*), magically transformed, into one of festive joy. Furthermore, instead of Haman's forces having the upper hand, נַהֲפוֹךְ הוּא (*nahafokh hu*), the opposite happened.

The Torah demonstrates that not only events but also language itself can be changed by God's intervention. When Balaam curses the Jewish people, we are told וַיַּהֲפֹךְ אֶת הַקְּלָלָה לִבְרָכָה (*va-yahafokh ha-kelalah li-verakhah*). "God changed the curse to a blessing," as if in mid-air.

The way the Rabbis expressed their belief that the Torah is a virtual encyclopedia of universal knowledge was to proclaim הֲפוֹךְ בָּהּ וְהַפֵּךְ בָּהּ דְכוֹלָּא בָּהּ (*hafokh bah ve-hapekh bah de-khola bah*), "Turn it over and over again, for everything is in it."

The Talmud calls the Persian King Ahashverosh, הֲפַכְפְּכָן (*hafakhpekhan*), capricious, a person who changes his mind on a whim.

Before "Operation Iraqi Freedom," many Western leaders hoped for a הֲפִיכָה (*hafikhah*), a coup d'état, in troublesome Iraq. There were also some who would not have been satisfied with anything

55

less than a complete מַהְפֵּכָה (*mah'pekhah*), revolution. Today, many are willing לַהֲפוֹךְ עוֹלָמוֹת (*la-hafokh olamot*), to move heaven and earth, to find a peaceful solution to the problems of the Middle East.

Speaking of magic, there is something akin to magic in what is popularly called (if anything in grammar may be deemed popular) the וָו הַהִפּוּךְ (*vav ha-hippukh*), the "conversive vav." This is a letter that turns the past into the future and the future into the past. For example, when the Torah wishes to say "Moses spoke," it takes the future form, e.g., the phrase יְדַבֵּר מֹשֶׁה (*yedabber moshe*), "Moses shall speak," adds the וָו הַהִפּוּךְ (*vav ha-hippukh*), and "Presto Changeo," we have וַיְדַבֵּר מֹשֶׁה (*va-yedabber moshe*), "Moses spoke."

Another prophet who spoke, but who spoke perhaps too soon, was Jonah, who walked into the sinful city of Nineveh and proclaimed, using another meaning of our root, that in forty days Nineveh נֶהְפָּכֶת (*nehpakhet*), shall be utterly destroyed. That is not exactly what happened. Au contraire, or, as they say in Hebrew, לְהֶפֶךְ (*le-hefekh*), the inhabitants of Nineveh repented and the city was spared.

Another linguistic phenomenon represented by our root is the elegantly named דָּבָר וְהִפּוּכוֹ (*davar ve-hippukho*), inelegantly translated as "the thing and its opposite." One of the most striking examples of this curiosity is the Hebrew word הֶקְדֵּשׁ (*hekdesh*), which means, depending on the circumstances, both a holy and an unholy place.

In modern Israel during Purim, you might want to unwind from a topsy-turvy day of blessing Haman and cursing Mordechai. Walk into your local café and ask for a קָפֶה הָפוּךְ (*kafe hafukh*). As if by magic, it turns a cup of espresso into the best-tasting *caffè latte* you've ever had.

TIME IN

O *tempora! O mores!* (The times! The customs!) When the
Latin orator Cicero was thunderously lamenting Roman
times and Roman behavior, might he have also been foreshadowing
modern Jewish life? Time, perhaps, will tell.

The Hebrew language so celebrates time that it has at least six
synonyms for the concept. One of the richest of these is the word זְמַן
(*zeman*). Even the Hebrew Bible's Ecclesiastes, normally associated
with pessimism, teaches us that לַכֹּל זְמָן (*la-kol zeman*), there is
a time for everything, for joy as well as for sorrow. The Torah,
enjoining us to celebrate the three holidays—of our freedom, of
the giving of the Torah, and of our joy—calls each of these, זְמַן
(*zeman*), time, holiday. The Rabbis, in the *sheheheyanu* blessing,
proposed that we thank God for allowing us to live לִזְמַן הַזֶּה (*la-
zeman ha-zeh*), to this season.

When we recite the Kiddush for the holidays, we assert that
God מְקַדֵּשׁ יִשְׂרָאֵל וְהַזְּמַנִּים (*me-kaddesh yisra'el ve-ha-zemanim*),
sanctifies the people of Israel and the appointed times. Yeshivah
students take vacation בֵּין הַזְּמַנִּים (*bein ha-zemannim*), between
semesters. In Hebrew grammar the word זְמַנִּים (*zemannim*) has yet
another connotation, tenses.

In Modern Hebrew, to describe something passé, one might
borrow an expression from Jewish ritual vocabulary, עָבַר זְמַנּוֹ בָּטֵל
קָרְבָּנוֹ (*avar zemanno batel korbano*), literally, if the sacrifice is not
offered at its appointed time it is invalid.

Idioms using our root ז‎-מ‎-ב‎ (*zayin, mem, nun*) abound. A
favorite expression, חֲבָל עַל הַזְּמַן (*haval al ha-zeman*), is used

to mean "don't waste time." Hebrew folk wisdom teaches that patience helps us avoid bad consequences: מַה שֶּׁיַּעֲשֶׂה הַזְּמַן לֹא יַעֲשֶׂה הַשֵּׂכֶל (*ma she-ya'aseh ha-zeman, lo ya'aseh ha-sekhel*), what time accomplishes, reason will not, that is, solve our problems. On the sports fields of modern Israel a player may call for a פֶּסֶק זְמַן (*pesek zeman*), time out.

Sometimes, when you call a friend on his cell phone you will hear the message that it is not זָמִין (*zamin*), currently available, and that you should try later.

A morning blessing says כָּל זְמַן שֶׁהַנְּשָׁמָה בְקִרְבִּי (*kol zeman she-ha-neshamah ve-kirbi*), as long as my soul is within me, I shall thank You. A Passover Seder pre-blessing announces: הִנְנִי מוּכָן וּמְזוּמָּן (*hineni mukhan u-mezumman*), behold I am ready to perform a mitzvah. Modern speakers of Hebrew recognize that הַזְּמַן חוֹלֵף (*ha-zeman holef*), time is running away, and that one can therefore מַחְמִיץ הִזְדַמְנוּת (*mahmits hizdamnut*), miss an opportunity. At times it's not even necessary לְזַמֵּן פְּגִישָׁה (*le-zamen pegishah*), to arrange a meeting; all you need is לְהִזְדַמֵּן לַמָּקוֹם (*le-hizdammen la-makom*), to happen on a place, to meet an important opportunity or person. One of the most flexible of the words using our *shoresh* is הַזְמָנָה (*hazmanah*), which, depending on the context, can refer to receiving an invitation, reserving a ticket at the theater, or placing an order at the store.

Of course, בּוֹ בַּזְּמַן (*bo ba-zeman*) or, as they say in *Tsahal*-speak, (in the language of the IDF) בּוֹ-זְמַנִּית (*bo-zemanit*), at the same time, it is also important to be aware of the רוּחַ הַזְּמַן (*ru'ah ha-zeman*), spirit of the times, where לְאַף אֶחָד אֵין זְמַן (*le-af ehad ein zeman*), no one has time, and to remember, nostalgically perhaps, that in the past, as the popular Israeli song goes, הָיוּ זְמַנִּים (*hayu zemannim*), there were better times than these, and also, as Cicero failed to remark, better mores.

THE BONDS THAT TIE

It's hard to be a Jew, they say; but it's even harder to be a Jew alone. That's why the tying of social bonds is at the root of all Jewish communal activity. And that's why the root for tying social bonds, ר-ב-ח (*het, bet, resh*), is so prevalent in the Hebrew language.

The expression חָבֵר ,שָׁלוֹם (*shalom, haver*), used by former U.S. President Bill Clinton to bid a fond adieu to assassinated Israeli Prime Minister Yitzhak Rabin, retains a strong sense of the mysteriousness that is at the source of the word חָבֵר (*haver*), friend.

Curiously, the closely related word חֶבֶר (*hever*, accent on the first syllable) means magic. Apparently, early acts of wizardry were performed by the tying of magic knots. (If you doubt the connection between casting a spell and tying a knot, think of the English word *spellbound*.)

The tying of social bonds is at the root of words like חֶבְרָה (*hevrah*), society, and the Israeli slang word חֶבְרֶה (*hevreh*, accent on the first syllable), usually translated as the gang or the guys. If you join a kibbutz one day you can hope to become a חָבֵר (*haver*), member. The Israeli band Tipex sings יֵשׁ לִי חֲבֵרָה (*yesh li haverah*), "I have a girlfriend." A ten-year-old might write a note to the prettiest girl in class, אֶפְשָׁר לְהַצִּיעַ לָךְ חֲבֵרוּת? (*efshar le-hatsia lakh haverut?*), "Will you be my girlfriend?" On a more elevated plane, the expression כָּל יִשְׂרָאֵל חֲבֵרִים (*kol yisrael haverim*), All Jews are bound together, is also the Hebrew name for the French-based Alliance Israélite Universelle. On perhaps an even higher plane, Rashi comments on the injunction in the Sayings of the

Fathers עֲשֵׂה לְךָ חָבֵר (*aseh lekha haver*), "Acquire for yourself a friend," that the word חָבֵר (*haver*) in that expression means a book.

Many of today's Jewish communal leaders were initiated into Jewish society by what was at the time promoted as the counter-cultural חֲבוּרָה (*havurah*) movement. Because of the centrality of our root in Jewish culture, we can say that Havurot (which no one found necessary to translate into English) are as mainstream as a traditional Talmud study group, known as a חַבְרוּתָא (*havruta*).

One thing that ties together virtually all American Jews who have gone to Hebrew school is the ubiquitous מַחְבֶּרֶת (*mahberet*), notebook, we all used. Nostalgia buffs will remember fondly the special lines to accommodate the placement of Hebrew vowels.

Words closely related to מַחְבֶּרֶת (*mahberet*), like חִבּוּר (*hibbur*), composition (in math, addition), מְחַבֵּר (*mehabber*), writer, תַּחְבּוּרָה (*tahburah*), communications or transport, and תַּחְבִּיר (*tahbir*), syntax, should awaken us to the realization that it is by combining Hebrew letters into words and Hebrew words into Jewish thoughts that we create חֲבֵרוּת (*haverut*), the social bond that is at the center of our peoplehood.

Or, as Honi the Circlemaker of Jewish legend said, אוֹ חַבְרוּתָא אוֹ מִיתוּתָא (*o havruta, o mituta*), "Give me social life or give me death."

POWER TO THE PEOPLE

In an age when winning is everything, we sometimes need to be reminded to take courage from partial victories. The message of בִּרְכַּת עָם (*birkat am*), "The People's Blessing," a poem by Chaim Nachman Bialik, is that the person who builds the foundation is not also required to build the scaffolding. The first word of the poem is תֶּחֱזַקְנָה (*tehezaknah*), [May your hands] be strengthened.

The root ק-ז-ח (*het, zayin, kof*), to be strong, leads to many terms expressive of power. Scripture often attributes to God an anthropomorphic חֹזֶק יָד (*hozek yad*), hand-strength. Maimonides's *Mishneh Torah*, his treatise on Jewish law, is also called יָד הַחֲזָקָה (*yad ha-hazakah*), not only because י״ד (*yod + dalet*) equals fourteen (the number of the treatise's chapters) but also because in this book Maimonides lays down the law "strongly."

Everybody can always use a little חִזּוּק (*hizzuk*), moral support. In the army it's called חִזּוּק חִיּוּבִי (*hizzuk hiyuvi*), reinforcement. In Jewish law a חֲזָקָה (*hazakah*) is the presumption of ownership by a person who has "held" a piece of property for three years, possession granting power over the property. An Israeli student of algebra will tell you that another way of saying "eight" in Hebrew is שְׁתַּיִם בַּחֲזָקָה הַשְּׁלִישִׁית (*shetayim ba-hezkah ha-shelishit*), 2^3, two to the third power, power being the operative word in both languages. In Israeli law, as in American law, an accused is בְּחֶזְקַת חַף מִפֶּשַׁע (*be-hazkat haf mi-pesha*), presumed innocent, innocent until proven guilty.

Don't confuse חֶזְקַת כַּשְׁרוּת (*hezkat kashrut*), the presumption that an establishment is kosher, with חֶזְקַת כֹּשֶׁר (*hezkat kosher*),

61

a system by which one is judged on merit or ability alone. Of someone who owns both a regular and vacation home, one says that he מַחֲזִיק שְׁנֵי בָּתִּים (*mahazik shenei batim*). In both places you should tell a young child walking down the stairs, using our root twice, תַּחֲזִיק חָזָק (*tahazik hazak*), hold on tight.

The rallying cry of the Israeli Scouting Movement, taken from the book of Joshua, is חֲזַק וֶאֱמַץ (*hazak ve-emats*), "Be strong and take courage." In Sefardi communities, when a congregant steps down from his aliyah to the Torah, he is greeted with a hearty חָזָק וּבָרוּךְ (*hazak u-varukh*), "More power and blessing to you."

At the conclusion of the reading in the synagogue of each of the five books of Moses, the congregation rises as one to proclaim חֲזַק חֲזַק וְנִתְחַזֵּק (*hazak hazak ve-nithazzek*), "Be strong, be strong, and may all of us grow strong." It is perhaps more than a literary curiosity that twentieth-century America's most important man of letters, Edmund Wilson, had adopted this expression as his motto. He הֶחֱזִיק בַּדֵּעָה (*hihzik ba-de'ah*), held very strongly, that Hebrew is so important that he even had the motto חֲזַק חֲזַק וְנִתְחַזֵּק (*hazak hazak ve-nithazzek*) inscribed in Hebrew on a plaque over his desk and engraved on his tombstone in the Berkshires.

Hebrew lovers take strength from the Jewish nation's language in two ways, with a resounding חֲזַק חֲזַק וְנִתְחַזֵּק (*hazak hazak ve-nithazzek*) and with a prayerful תֶּחֱזַקְנָה (*tehezaknah*). And let us build on partial victories.

ONE GOOD RETURN DESERVES ANOTHER

A commitment to returning—and to returnees—is a hallmark of many religions. So central is return to Jewish culture, however, that there are even two words for it in Hebrew. Tellingly, both חָזַר (*hazar*) and שָׁב (*shav*) are found in the Hebrew expression for religious penitent, חוֹזֵר בִּתְשׁוּבָה (*hozer bi-teshuvah*), a "returner in returning."

A curious aspect of the root ח-ז-ר (*het, zayin, resh*), to return, is that it is nowhere to be found in all of Tanakh. Of course—like the medieval authority on Hebrew roots David Kimhi or like modern Bible Concordance author Solomon Mandelkern—you might want to allow the biblical word חֲזִיר (*hazir*), pig, to crawl into our root in, so to speak, a roundabout way. But let's not emphasize this possibility too much, since it may be wrong. And, as they say in Modern Hebrew when urging the correction of an error, טָעוּת לְעוֹלָם חוֹזֶרֶת (*ta'ut le-olam hozeret*), "a mistake will always come back," presumably to haunt us.

The Rabbis, who believed strongly in the principle of return, were particularly enamored of our root. One of the most poignant scenes in talmudic lore involves our root, when Rabbi Meir entreats apostate Elisha ben Avuyah חֲזוֹר בָּךְ (*hazor bekha*), "Retrace your steps," with the double meaning "go back" and "return to Judaism." The root is found most prominently in the prayer recited upon awakening, when one thanks God שֶׁהֶחֱזַרְתָּ בִּי נִשְׁמָתִי (*she-hehezarta bi nishmati*), "for having given me back my soul." When, in the synagogue, the cantor repeats the Amidah prayer, we are involved in חֲזָרַת הַשַּׁ"ץ (hazarat ha-shats), the repetition of the congregation's emissary. It is uncanny how this root finds itself in both religious and secular settings. In the language of the Yeshivah, to make a חֲזָרָה (hazarah) is diligently to go over a portion of Talmud recently learned; in the theater, a חֲזָרָה (hazarah) is a play rehearsal.

The root is also found in the word, coined in the middle ages, for the holiday prayer book, the מַחְזוֹר (mahzor), used to convey the cyclical nature of the Jewish liturgy. In Modern Hebrew the word מַחְזוֹר (mahzor) can mean one's graduating class or, in a Hebrew camp setting, the hour at which your group takes lunch. In the diagnostic lab, technicians will measure the מַחְזוֹר הַדָּם (mahzor ha-dam), the circulation of the blood. A fact of nature is the מַחְזוֹר חָדְשִׁי (mahzor hodshi), women's menstrual cycle.

Life has its ups and downs, or as they say גַּלְגַּל חוֹזֵר בָּעוֹלָם (galgal hozer ba-olam), because the wheel always turns and returns. Sometimes it is necessary לְשַׁחְזֵר (le-shahzer), to reconstruct a scene from memory, and then לָקַחַת בַּחֲזָרָה (lakahat be-hazarah), to take back, what you've said.

A letter that "circulates" among many people is called a חוֹזֵר (hozer), a circular. A repetitive article חוֹזֵר עַל עַצְמוֹ (hozer al atsmo), literally, returns to itself. And when you want to indicate that what you're talking about comes up again and again, you need only add to your statement the expression וְחוֹזֵר חֲלִילָה (ve-hozer halilah), and so on, as if repeated into eternity.

Let us recall the universal piece of wisdom that teaches that "Home is where, when you return there, they have to accept you." In Judaism, this applies to both the Jewish family and the Jewish State.

And let us all sing אֲנִי חוֹזֵר הַבַּיְתָה (ani hozer ha-baytah), "I'm coming home."

DREAM ON

Ever since the publication in 1900 of Sigmund Freud's *The Interpretation of Dreams*, we and our contemporaries have wrestled with the concept that dreams have meanings beyond themselves. Interestingly, the same can be said for the Hebrew word for dream, חֲלוֹם (*halom*).

Some scholars believe that the verb חָלַם (*halam*), to dream, and the verb חָלַם (*halam*), to be in good health, are related. Moreover, they hold, both of these words are connected to חֶלְמוֹן (*helmon*), the yolk of an egg, and to חוֹלָם (*holam*), the vowel וֹ (*o*).

A skeptic may well ask, "How so?" It goes something like this: The root ח-ל-מ (*het, lamed, mem*) originally meant to be soft, moist, viscous. One might say that one is healthy because one has good humors and that the verb חָלַם (*halam*) means to gather humors, that is, to sleep well, therefore to dream. And, maintaining the liquid imagery associated with the term, a highly authoritative biblical dictionary says that the Hebrew word for dreaming can also mean to experience an emission of seminal fluid.

And what does this have to do with the yellow of an egg or a vowel? According to a medieval book of Hebrew roots, the yolk is called חֶלְמוֹן (*helmon*) because, cholesterol notwithstanding, it is the healthful (i.e., nutritious) part of the egg. The word הַחְלָמָה (*hahlamah*), recuperation from an illness, is a not-so-distant relative. And the חוֹלָם (*holam*)? When you write a חוֹלָם (*holam*), you are creating what the grammarians call a plene (i.e., a full) reading. Says grammarian Abraham Ibn Ezra: Make the sound O and then look at your lips; they make a strong, full circle.

It appears from this discussion that dreaming is a good thing, no? Not necessarily. As used in the Tanakh, the word חֲלוֹם (halom), when it means dream, may be good, bad, or indifferent. Just ask Joseph's brothers, who derisively referred to their sibling as, בַּעַל הַחֲלוֹמוֹת הַלָּזֶה (ba'al ha-holomot ha-lazeh), that damned dream-master. Or ask Pharaoh's baker who lost his head to a dream.

The Rabbis were similarly divided about the beneficence of dreams. The Talmud relates that a חֲלוֹם שֶׁל שַׁחֲרִית (halom shel shaharit), morning-dream, is likely to be true. If the dream portends evil tidings, there is a way to nullify it: One can take on oneself—even on Shabbat, when it is normally forbidden to fast—a תַּעֲנִית חֲלוֹם (ta'anit halom), dream-fast. If you are not sure whether a dream is bad or good, you may recite the Ribbono Shel Olam meditation of the Priestly Blessing, in which you aver אֲנִי שֶׁלָּךְ וְחֲלוֹמוֹתַי שֶׁלָּךְ (ani shelakh ve-halomotai shelakh), "I am yours and my dreams are yours." The Shir ha-Ma'alot Psalm we sing before the Grace After Meals reminds us that הָיִינוּ כְּחוֹלְמִים (hayyinu ke-holmim), "We were like dreamers."

In modern Israel, somebody who crosses the street without looking might be said to be having חֲלוֹמוֹת בְּהָקִיץ (halomot be-hakits), daydreams. And when you tuck the children into bed at night, you always wish them חֲלוֹמוֹת פָּז (halomot paz), literally, dreams of gold.

We conclude our discussion by mentioning another ground-breaking book written during the twentieth century, whose title echoes that of Freud's: Eliezer Ben Yehudah's הַחֲלוֹם וְשִׁבְרוֹ (ha-halom ve-shivro), The Dream and Its Interpretation. When you hear little children speaking Hebrew on the streets of Israel, you realize that Ben Yehudah's dream of a Hebrew-speaking nation has not been buried in the collective subconscious. It is right out there on the surface for all to see and hear.

SLIDING AND DIVIDING

W hat does a herring have to do with a skating rink? A housedress with the world to come? And a weather report with flattery? In Hebrew, all of the above are somehow associated with the letters ק-ל-ח (*het, lamed, kof*), one of the most slippery, difficult-to-take-hold-of, Hebrew roots.

One might say that it all started in Genesis with forefather Jacob and his brother Esau. Talking primogeniture strategy with his mother Rebecca, Jacob reminds her that it might not be easy for him, an אִישׁ חָלָק (*ish halak*), a smooth-skinned man, to impersonate his hairy brother, an אִישׁ שָׂעִיר (*ish sa'ir*). In an uncanny verbal echo of the Jacob and Esau narrative, Joshua, in the narrative of the conquest of Canaan, travels from הָהָר הֶחָלָק (*ha-har he-halak*), the bald mountain, to הַר שֵׂעִיר (*har se'ir*), the hairy mountain—so called perhaps because the latter was studded with trees and the former was treeless. And what about the place where David and Saul part from each other, סֶלַע הַמַּחְלְקוֹת (*sela ha-makhlekot*), Rock of Separation? With all these metaphors flying about, is it any wonder that the book of Daniel warns against חֲלַקּוֹת (*halakkot*), smooth talking, flattery?

In Modern Hebrew, one uses our root to describe blunt speaking. An exasperated home renovator in Israel, wearing her plain and simple חָלוּק בַּיִת (*haluk bayit*), housedress, might tell her neighbor, I told the contractor חַד וְחָלָק (*had ve-halak*), plain and simple, either he finishes tomorrow or he doesn't get paid.

Of course our root is not so simple. There is a חִלּוּקֵי דֵעוֹת (*hillukei de'ot*), difference of opinion, among Hebrew etymologists whether חָלַק (*halak*), to glide, to slip, and חָלַק (*halak*), to divide, share, distribute, assign, are from the same root. What are we to make of the חֵלֶק (*helek*), a smooth stone that is used for dividing up parcels of land by lots? Today walking in the river, one should be careful not to step on the חַלּוּקֵי נַחַל (*halukei nahal*), smooth stones found underfoot. The noun חֵלֶק (*helek*), is found in the famous mishnaic saying that all Israel has a חֵלֶק לָעוֹלָם הַבָּא (*helek la-olam ha-ba*), a share in the world to come, and that one should be שָׂמֵחַ בְּחֶלְקוֹ (*same'ach be-helko*), happy with his lot.

The noun חֵלֶק (*helek*), meaning part, share, and, by extension, destiny, has a host of derivatives. Many Jews wanted to have a חֶלְקַת אֲדָמָה (*helkat adamah*), parcel of land, in Israel. An important activity in pre-state history was the חֲלוּקָה (*halukkah*), the distribution of charity to the learned and needy of the yishuv. In 1948, תָּכְנִית הַחֲלוּקָה (*tokhnit ha-halukkah*), the proposal to divide Palestine, was hotly debated. Another Zionist activity, because of the way it's done, with no Shabbat delivery, is חֲלוּקַת הַדּוֹאַר (*halukkat ha-do'ar*), mail distribution. This shows that Zionism did not start with a לוּחַ חָלָק (*lu'ah halak*), tabula rasa.

In a sovereign state you're just as likely to find a מַחֲלֹקֶת (*mahloket*), dispute, as a מַחְלָקָה (*mahlakah*), department. To describe someone devoid of common sense, an Israeli might joke that he was out of town כְּשֶׁחִלְּקוּ אֶת הַשֵּׂכֶל (*ke-she-hilku et ha-sekhel*), when they distributed brains. And does not the news reader on Israel Radio announce a rather sunny day with the words מְעֻנָּן חֶלְקִית (*me-unnan helkit*), partly cloudy?

And what about the herring? O.K., I lied about the herring. The herring's purported mishnaic Hebrew name חִלַּק (*hilak*), has nothing to do with our root, but comes not too directly from the Latin. We warned you that this was going to be a slippery chapter.

DELIGHT IN DESIRE

Two assignments: Next time you're in synagogue look up from your Siddur and glance at the Ten Commandments above the Ark. Scrolling down to the bottom-left, take note of the Tenth Commandment, לֹא תַחְמֹד (*lo tahmod*), "Thou Shalt Not Covet." Then, next time you're in Israel, for a family gathering at Doda Sarah's apartment, listen as she dotingly addresses her nephew: "Come חֲמוּדִי (*hamudi*), my precious one, give your auntie a kiss."

How the Hebrew language meanders around the root ח-מ-ד (*het, mem, dalet*) to include the guilt-inducing injunction of *lo tahmod* and the effusive term of endearment *hamudi* is, as they say in Modern Hebrew, a חֶמֶד שֶׁל סִפּוּר (*homed shel sippur*), a lovely story.

In Arabic the root means to praise, and that's where we get the name of Islam's prophet מוּחַמָּד (*muhammad*), the blessed one. An Arabic expression equivalent to the Hebrew *barukh ha-shem*, has entered modern colloquial Hebrew as חַמְדוּלְלָה (*hamdulelah*), Praise God.

In Hebrew Scripture, the root means to desire and to delight in, sometimes both at the same time. The Garden of Eden, we are told, has every tree that is נֶחְמָד לְמַרְאֶה (*nehmad le-mar'eh*), "delightful to look at," and we know from the subsequent story how seductive that can be. The lover of the Song of Songs is described in a sensuous passage as כֻּלּוֹ מַחֲמַדִּים (*kullo mahamaddim*), "totally delightful [and desirable]."

The sexual connotation of the root is found copiously in rabbinic literature, where a חַמְדָן (*hamdan*) is a lustful person, חָמוּד

(*himmud*) is, bluntly, sexual appetite and the verb חָמַד (*hamad*) means both to be excited and to be hot. According to the medieval Hebrew grammarian David Kimhi (Radak), it is no coincidence that the word חַם (*ham*), hot, makes up two-thirds of our root. He reminds us that לֶחֶם חֲמוּדֹת (*lehem hamudot*) is taken by some to mean fresh, hot, tasty bread.

The root is also found in all sorts of upbeat settings, including the fact that the Land of Israel is called אֶרֶץ חֶמְדָּה (*erets hemdah*), a delightful land. Look back into your Siddur and you'll see that God has proclaimed Shabbat חֶמְדַּת יָמִים (*hemdat yamim*), the most delightful of all days. A popular girl's name is חֶמְדָּה (*hemdah*). The Israeli moshav שְׂדֵי חֶמֶד (*sedei hemed*), delightful fields, was named after a scholarly book.

In modern times, the root lends itself to innocent rhyming games. A good little boy is often addressed אוּדִי חֲמוּדִי (*udi hamudi*) and one way to describe a charming-looking couple is צֶמֶד חֶמֶד (*tsemed hemed*), a delightful pair.

Finally, one can use the biblical expression וַיֵּלֶךְ בְּלֹא חֶמְדָּה (*va-yelekh belo hemdah*) when someone takes leave without anyone regretting his departure. Your next assignment, then, is to vote on whether it is a good idea to end a Hebrew chapter with this expression.

A FACE FOR FIFTY

In English, it's called "The Big Five-O." It is the age at which, according to Israeli novelist David Grossman's mother, "you get the face you deserve." Since the Hebrew language is one of the prominent features of the face of Israel in her fifties, the Jewish people must be very deserving indeed. Just think of the Hebrew expression for this occasion, יוֹבֵל הַחֲמִישִׁים (*yovel ha-hamishim*). Not only do we get to celebrate a יוֹבֵל (*yovel*), jubilee, which has given to the languages and cultures of the world the notion of jubilation; we also get to dilate on the word for fifty, חֲמִישִׁים (*hamishim*) and to talk about its contributions to the culture of the Jewish people.

Did you know, for example, that in Jewish lore bargaining traditionally begins at fifty? That's what we learn from Abraham's negotiation with God concerning the latter's plan to destroy the wicked city of Sodom. In his opening gambit, Abraham asks God, What if there are חֲמִישִׁים צַדִּיקִים (*hamishim tsaddikim*), fifty righteous people, in Sodom? There weren't, and that's how we got *hondling*. The Jewish holiday of Shavuot is called Pentecost from the biblical injunction to count חֲמִישִׁים יוֹם (*hamishim yom*), fifty days, after the first day of Passover.

One of the more interesting uses of the root ח-מ-שׁ (*het, mem, shin*), five, from which the word fifty obviously derives, occurs in the Exodus story, relating that the Israelites were חֲמוּשִׁים (*hamushim*), as they left Egypt. How is this word, usually translated simply as "armed," connected to our root? There are several theories. One of them relates the word to the fifth rib (and to the word חֹמֶשׁ

[*homesh*], belly), a vulnerable area right near the heart and a good place for armor. Another theorizes that armies were traditionally arrayed in five divisions and that when the Israelites left Egypt, they too were arrayed for battle. In either case, the modern word תַּחְמֹשֶׁת (*tahmoshet*), ammunition, comes from this sense of our root.

The relationship of Hebrew to Arabic is found in the word for the heat wave that hits the Middle East for about fifty days a year, in Hebrew, חַמְסִין (*hamsin*), and in the five-fingered amulet against the evil eye nearly ubiquitous in Israel, the חַמְסָה (*hamsah*).

Now that we've opened the door to "five," we can let it in without worrying about the evil eye. The word is found in Modern Israel in a whole slew of familiar expressions, ranging from חֲמֵשֶׁת הַחוּשִׁים (*hameshet ha-hushim*), the five senses, to תָּכְנִית חֹמֶשׁ (*tokhnit homesh*), five-year plan. A plant biologist in Israel will study the חַמְשָׁן (*hamshan*), the five-leaved cinquefoil, under her microscope while the mathematician will describe the properties of the מְחֻמָּשׁ (*mehummash*), pentagon. At the sports arena, the announcer, often חָמוּשׁ בְּמִשְׁקָפַיִם (*hamush be-mishkafayim*), equipped with eyeglasses, will tell us which basketball players make up the חֲמִשִׁיָּה הַפּוֹתַחַת (*hamishiyyah ha-potahat*), starting five, of Maccabi Tel-Aviv. If your team wins you can turn to your little nephew and exult, תֵּן חֲמִישִׁיָּה (*ten hamishiyyah*), "Slap me five." When that nephew turns חֲמֵשׁ עֶשְׂרֵה (*hamesh esreh*), fifteen, some unkind pundits will call him, however lovingly, a טִפֵּשׁ עֶשְׂרֵה (*tipesh esreh*), dumb teenager.

But of course the best way to celebrate the role of Hebrew in creating Israel's expressive face in her fifties is to invite all the budding poets out there to compose a חַמְשִׁיר (*hamshir*), a five-line limerick, from חָמֵשׁ (*hamesh*), five, and שִׁיר (*shir*), poem or song. Do you think fifty people will do it? What about ten? Even for five, it's worth it.

HANUKKAH SWEET TALK

There are two types of Jews at Hanukkah time. There are those who believe that Israelis eat jelly donuts on Hanukkah because the oil in which the donuts are fried is connected to the miracle commemorated on Hanukkah. Others hold that Israelis eat jelly donuts because somehow the sweetness of the jelly inside is related to the festival. Etymologically, if not historically, "Others" have a good case.

Some readers may remember having learned that חֲנוּכָּה (*hanukkah*) is so called because חָנוּ כ"ה (*hanu khaf heh*), "They [the Maccabees] rested on the 25th [of Kislev]." Quaint idea; wrong *shoresh*. Scripture records many types of חֲנוּכָּה (*hanukkah*) before the clash of Antiochus Epiphanes and Judah Maccabee. None of them speaks of "resting," from the root ‫ח-נ-ה‬ (*het, nun, heh*); all of them are related to inauguration, from ‫ח-נ-כ‬ (*het, nun, kaf*). Deuteronomy teaches, for example, that a man who has built a new house וְלֹא חֲנָכוֹ (*ve-lo hanakho*), "and has not 'dedicated' it," is exempt from military service. Today there is חֲנוּכַּת הַבַּיִת (*hanukkat ha-bayit*), a party one gives when moving into a new home.

A second verbal form derived from our root has to do with initiating the young into the Jewish community via education. The book of Proverbs tells us חֲנֹךְ לַנַּעַר עַל פִּי דַרְכּוֹ (*hanokh la-na'ar al pi darko*), "educate the youth in a way appropriate for him" and he will continue to behave properly into old age. According to a scriptual midrash, חֲנוֹךְ (*hanokh*), Enoch, was taken to Heaven without dying. It may fairly be said of Eliezer Ben Yehudah, the Hebrew מְחַנֵּךְ (*mehannekh*), educator, par excellence, that he almost

73

single-handedly חָנַךְ תְּקוּפָה חֲדָשָׁה (*hanakh tekufah hadashah*), inaugurated a new era, for the Jewish people.

And what does all this have to do with jelly donuts? If we remember that the letter נוּן (*nun*) has a habit of slipping in and out of words, we come to the two-letter root-word חֵךְ (*hekh*), palate. This word is found in a whole range of idiomatic expressions, from the phrase in the Jewish pledge of allegiance to Jerusalem, תִּדְבַּק לְשׁוֹנִי לְחִכִּי (*tidbak leshoni le-hikki*), "may my tongue cleave to the roof of my mouth," to the expression for "a really fine orator," חִכּוֹ מַמְתַּקִּים (*hikko mamtakim*), literally, "his palate is [like] sweets."

More to our point, and sweeter yet, is an ancient initiatory ceremony in which the חֵךְ (*hekh*), palate, of a young pupil was rubbed with dates, assuring that the learning be sweet in the pupil's mouth. (There is a similar ceremony using honey.) In Arabic, this palate-rubbing ceremony of initiation is called *hannaka*. The connection to חִנּוּךְ (*hinnukh*), education, on the one hand, and to the ceremony known in Hebrew as חֲנוּכָּה (*hanukkah*), on the other, is clear.

Nowadays, when you light the lamp of learning by publishing a book dedicated to teaching the Jewish heritage through Hebrew, you also have a חֲנוּכָּה (*hanukkah*) of sorts. When you read it in Israel, you might as well have a jelly donut too.

PIETY AND PROPRIETY

Ask someone to translate into English the word מִצְוָה (*mits-vah*)—a word laden with the sense of obligation and commandment—and the definition you're most likely to encounter is a bland-sounding "good deed."

Curiously, there is a Hebrew word for good deed, חֶסֶד (*hesed*), and it is not bland at all. On the contrary, the word חֶסֶד (*hesed*) is so full of vigor that it has the power to mean both "goodness" and its opposite, "abomination." This phenomenon, called דָּבָר וְהִפּוּכוֹ (*davar ve-hippukho*), "the thing and its opposite," is not rare in Hebrew, where a word like בֵּרַךְ (*berakh*) can mean both "bless" and "curse." According to some scholars the two types of חֶסֶד (*hesed*) are of the same linguistic origin. As one medieval Hebraist explains it, a primary meaning of חֶסֶד (*hesed*) is excess; whether excess of kindness or excess of evil is up to us.

Overwhelmingly in Hebrew Scripture, the word retains its positive connotation. One of the thirteen attributes of God is רַב חֶסֶד (*rav hesed*), abundant goodness. The proverbial Woman of Valor is praised for the תּוֹרַת חֶסֶד (*torat hesed*), righteous learning, that is always on her tongue. When Israel's first prime minister, David Ben-Gurion, eulogized his wife Paula, he quoted Jeremiah's זָכַרְתִּי לָךְ חֶסֶד נְעוּרַיִךְ (*zakharti lakh hesed ne'uraikh*), "I remember the kindnesses of your youth." In *A Guest for the Night*, novelist S.Y. Agnon uses our root to express politeness: בְּחַסְדֵּךְ (*be-hasdekh*), "If you please." Do you see that dangerous driver? After failing his driving test four times, he finally passed בְּחֶסֶד (*be-hesed*), just barely, and thanks to the inspector's "kindness."

There is an expression, חֶסֶד שֶׁל אֱמֶת (*hesed shel emet*), literally, the righteousness of truth, that is applied specifically to the one good deed that cannot be repaid, accompanying a dead body to burial. Other specific terms using our root are somewhat tricky: גְּמִילוּת חֶסֶד (*gemilut hesed*), an interest-free loan, and גְּמִילוּת חֲסָדִים (*gemilut hasadim*), charity, philanthropy.

Everybody knows that, according to the Rabbis, the way to dance before the bride is to sing כַּלָּה נָאָה וַחֲסוּדָה (*kallah na'ah va-hasudah*), a beautiful and gracious bride. The Talmud asks why a stork is called a חֲסִידָה (*hasidah*). Because, the Rabbis answer, she does חֲסִידוּת (*hasidut*), acts of kindness, to her friends. And why, therefore, is the stork counted among the unclean animals? Because she is kind only to her own kind. There are times when one would rather receive a reward בִּזְכוּת וְלֹא בְּחֶסֶד (*bi-zekhut ve-lo be-hesed*), by right and not as a favor.

A חָסִיד (*hasid*) is one of the followers either of Judah he-Hasid (twelfth century) or Israel Ba'al Shem Tov (eighteenth century). A non-Jew can also be a hasid, specifically in the expression חֲסִידֵי אֻמּוֹת הָעוֹלָם (*hasidei ummot ha-olam*), Righteous Gentiles.

There is piety and then there is false piety, the latter called הִתְחַסְּדוּת (*hithasdut*), hyposcrisy. There is also foolish piety. A חָסִיד שׁוֹטֶה (*hasid shoteh*), foolish hasid, is one who, for seemingly religious reasons, fails to act humanely. It follows that a smart חָסִיד (*hasid*) is one who does gratuitous good deeds. That sounds like a good definition for a smart Jew as well.

HALF AND "HALF"

When do two halves make more then a whole? In Hebrew, the phenomenon occurs frequently, especially when the words חֲצִי (*hatsi*) and חֵצִי (*hetsi*), half, are used metaphorically. Take the case of former Chief of Staff of the Israel Defense Forces, Moshe Levy. He was so tall that he was called affectionately מֹשֶׁה וָחֵצִי (*moshe va-hetsi*), Moshe-and-a-Half. (In America, we would have called him Big Mo and been done with it.)

The noun חֵצִי (*hetsi*) derives from the root ח-צ-ה (*het, tsadi, heh*), which means both to divide in half and also to divide into several parts. In Scripture, the root can be found in many contexts, most prominently in the legal text dealing with property damage, where we are told that both the goring ox and the gored ox shall be divided equally between the owners, וְחָצוּ אֶת כַּסְפּוֹ וְגַם אֶת הַמֵּת יֶחֱצוּן (*ve-hatsu et kaspo ve-gam et ha-met yehetsun*). In the book of Esther, the Persian king indulges in a bit of hyperbole when he offers his queen עַד חֲצִי הַמַּלְכוּת (*ad hatsi ha-malkhut*), "up to half the kingdom," when she enters his chambers to ask for a royal favor. And then there is the מַחֲצִית הַשֶּׁקֶל (*mahatsit ha-shekel*), the half shekel, used as a means for taking the census.

One of the rituals of the Passover Seder is called יַחַץ (*yahats*), the dividing of the matzah into two unequal halves. We know that they are unequal from the instruction to take the bigger "half" and save it for the Afikoman. Anyone who has stepped into a synagogue has seen the מְחִיצָה (*mehitsah*) that divides the ritual space into a men's and women's section, also not exactly equally.

When you hear a little child cry out חֵצִי-חֵצִי (*hetsi-hetsi*), to his brother, look for the chocolate bar that he wants divided equally. Tell the truth, do you really believe the Hebrew proverb צָרַת רַבִּים חֲצִי נֶחָמָה (*tsarat rabim hatsi nehamah*), "The sorrow of others is a partial consolation"?

Even though midnight does not come at exactly the mid-point of night, it is nevertheless called in Hebrew חֲצוֹת הַלַּיְלָה (*hatsot ha-laylah*), literally, half the night. A period in a soccer match in Israel is a מַחֲצִית (*mahatsit*), since it takes up half the game. And the piece of clothing that covers half of a woman's body is called in Hebrew a חֲצָאִית (*hatsa'it*), "skirt." In math, a חוֹצֶה (*hotseh*) is a bisector, but a person who חוֹצֶה אֶת הַכְּבִישׁ (*hotseh et ha-kevish*) is merely crossing the street and only metaphorically cutting it in two. That report you have to present at the end of June is called דו"ח חֶצְיוֹן (*doch hetsyon*), a mid-year report. And if you are ambivalent about your findings, you have a לֵב חָצוּי (*lev hatsui*), a heart divided in half.

There are some who maintain that the noun חֵץ (*hets*), arrow, is related to our root. It is not at all difficult to imagine an arrow cutting through the air and cutting an apple in two. One modern scholar suggests that in ancient times one would divide a piece of property by casting arrows as lots. The use of an arrow for divining purposes may be what is going on in the story in I Samuel where Jonathan shoots arrows to warn David of imminent danger from King Saul. In more recent times, school children use a חֵץ וָקֶשֶׁת (*hets va-keshet*), bow-and-arrow, (notice the inversion in the English idiom) in their celebration of Lag ba-Omer, perhaps to commemorate a student uprising against the Romans in the time of Rabbi Akiva.

From Israeli generals to synagogue worshippers to student soldiers, the important thing is always to remain in the מְחִיצָה (*mehitsah*), domain, of good behavior.

I THINK, THEREFORE
I CALCULATE

When French philosopher René Descartes declared, in Latin, *Cogito, ergo sum*, "I think, therefore I am," a Hebrew lover might have speculated that what he was thinking about was the Hebrew root for thinking, ח-שׁ-ב (*het, shin, bet*). The uses of that root are so varied that, in Hebrew, thinking and being might be considered one and the same.

In Scripture we come upon the root in relation to Bezalel, the architect of the Tabernacle, credited with the talent לַחְשֹׁב מַחֲשָׁבֹת (*lahshov mahshavot*), not to think thoughts, but, to devise works of craftsmanship. The prophet Balaam implies that because the Israelite nation is "a people apart," לֹא יִתְחַשָּׁב (*lo yithashav*), "it will not be taken seriously," by other nations. When Judah saw his daughter-in-law Tamar pregnant, וַיַּחְשְׁבֶהָ לְזוֹנָה (*va-yahsheveha le-zonah*), "he mistook her for a harlot."

At Yom Kippur time we perform a חֶשְׁבּוֹן הַנֶּפֶשׁ (*heshbon ha-nefesh*), an accounting of the soul. On Shabbat we sing two songs using our root. In the synagogue, *Lekha Dodi* reminds us that Shabbat, though created last, was בְּמַחֲשָׁבָה תְּחִלָּה (*be-mahshavah tehillah*), in God's mind from the first. A table hymn reminds us we are not permitted לַחְשׁוֹב חֶשְׁבּוֹנוֹת (*lahshov heshbonot*), to do calculations, on Shabbat. The Rabbis warn against מְחַשְּׁבֵי קִצִּין (*me-hashvei kitsin*), those who try to calculate the time of the Messiah's coming.

79

This leads to today's most widely-used word having our root, the מַחְשֵׁב (*mahshev*), computer, which also gives us מַחְשְׁבוֹן (*mahshevon*), calculator or PDA. A person might want לְהַחְשִׁיב (*le-hahshiv*), to attach importance to, Ephraim Kishon's movie *Sallah!* It is from that movie that the expression רֶגַע, חוֹשְׁבִים (*rega, hoshvim*), "Wait a minute, I'm thinking," entered the Hebrew language.

The noun חֶשְׁבּוֹן (*heshbon*) is also חָשׁוּב (*hashuv*), important. You studied חֶשְׁבּוֹן (*heshbon*), arithmetic, in school. You might have used a סַרְגֵּל-חֶשְׁבּוֹן (*sargel heshbon*), slide rule, and before that, a חֶשְׁבּוֹנִיָּה (*heshboniyyah*), abacus. Today, you may have a חֶשְׁבּוֹן (*heshbon*), account, at the bank. At the restaurant, you signal the waitress, חֶשְׁבּוֹן, בְּבַקָשָׁה (*heshbon, be-vakashah*), Check, please. Your grocer will gladly put your purchase עַל הַחֶשְׁבּוֹן (*al ha-heshbon*), on your tab. When you buy something עַל חֶשְׁבּוֹן הַבָּרוֹן (*al heshbon ha-baron*), on the Baron's tab, you signal your intention not to pay. When you hand in the דִּין וְחֶשְׁבּוֹן (*din ve-heshbon*), report, of your business trip, ask the רוֹאֶה-חֶשְׁבּוֹן (*ro'eh heshbon*), accountant, at your firm to allow you to request a חֶשְׁבּוֹן עָגוֹל (*heshbon agol*), round number, for your expenses. His answer? לֹא בָּא בְּחֶשְׁבּוֹן (*lo ba be-heshbon*), bad idea.

There are many things לָקַחַת בְּחֶשְׁבּוֹן (*la-kahat be-heshbon*), to take under consideration, when you study מַחְשֶׁבֶת יִשְׂרָאֵל (*mahshevet yisrael*), Jewish philosophy and theology. One of these is the realization that, before Descartes did so, the One who called Himself "I am" was God. Completing the circle this way, this study of a Hebrew root turns out to be both philosophy and מְלֶאכֶת מַחֲשֶׁבֶת (*melekhet mahshevet*), artisanship.

IT'S GOOD TO GET
THE GOODS

There are two types of Jews in this world—those who see the good in everything, and those who see both the bad and the good. In both cases, the Hebrew root for good, ט-ו-ב (*tet, vav, bet*), gets a lot of use.

Those who see the good in those who see both bad and good believe that the טִיב (*tiv*), nature, of the Jewish people is לְבַקֵּר בֵּין טוֹב לָרַע (*le-vakker bein tov la-ra*), to make distinctions between good and bad. The medieval Hebrew poet Emmanuel of Rome saw good even in falsehood, using our root in his poem מֵיטַב הַשִּׁיר כְּזָבוֹ (*meitav ha-shir kezavo*), "The Best Part of a Poem Is Its Deceit," presumably because a poem is a work of the imagination.

The word טוֹב (*tov*) runs through Scripture, adding all sorts of colorful nuances to Jewish culture as it goes. How do we know that men are supposed to get married? From the expression in Genesis לֹא טוֹב הֱיוֹת הָאָדָם לְבַדּוֹ (*lo tov heyot ha-adam le-vado*), "it's not good for man to be alone." How do we know that it's good to have a friend? From a pronouncement in Kohelet that says טוֹבִים הַשְּׁנַיִם מִן הָאֶחָד (*tovim ha-shenayim min ha-ehad*), "Two are better than one." What happens when one tries, like Balaam, to curse Israel? What comes out instead is מַה טֹּבוּ (*mah tovu*), "How goodly [are thy tents, Jacob]." We know that Tuesday is a propitious day in Judaism because the Creation story tells that God looked on his handiwork on the third day and saw, not once, but twice, כִּי טוֹב (*ki tov*), "that it was good."

The root is also found in quirky contexts in Israel today. One way of saying hello today is ‏הַכֹּל טוֹב?‏ (*ha-kol tov?*), literally, Is everything good? A storekeeper who stands behind his goods might tell you ‏לֹא טוֹב לֹא כֶּסֶף‏ (*lo tov lo kesef*), Not good, no money, meaning, if you don't like it, don't buy it. In the pre-politically correct fifties, a recruiting slogan for the Israeli Air Force was ‏הַטּוֹבִים לַטַּיִס‏ (*ha-tovim la-tayiss*), "The good ones go to aviation."

A fringe benefit at work is a ‏הֲטָבָה‏ (*hatavah*), bonus, (interestingly, bonus is a Latin word for good), while a heated argument might end with ‏בְּלִי טוֹבוֹת‏ (*beli tovot*), "Don't do me any favors!" A goody-two-shoes is called in Israel a ‏יֶלֶד טוֹב יְרוּשָׁלַיִם‏ (*yeled tov yerushalayim*), equating Jerusalem with good behavior. Nostalgia buffs will remember the good old days when the border with Lebanon was called ‏הַגָּדֵר הַטּוֹבָה‏ (*ha-gader ha-tovah*), the good fence. The slogan of the Israeli food company, ‏זֶה טוֹב זֶה אֹסֶם‏ (*zeh tov zeh osem*), "It's good; It's Osem," still has resonance, as does Naomi Shemer's hit song ‏אֲנָשִׁים טוֹבִים בְּאֶמְצַע הַדֶּרֶךְ‏ (*anashim tovim be-emtsa ha-derekh*), "Good People in the Middle of the Road."

Can you ever get enough ‏בְּשׂוֹרוֹת טוֹבוֹת‏ (*besorot tovot*), good news? There are those who even see good in death, especially when one dies ‏בְּשֵׂיבָה טוֹבָה‏ (*be-seivah tovah*), in good old age. When optimistic Jews get bad news they will often deflect it by saying ‏גַּם זוֹ לְטוֹבָה‏ (*gam zo le-tovah*), This too is for the best.

The Hebrew way to express good wishes upon taking leave is ‏כָּל טוּב‏ (*kol tuv*), All the best. To be completely fair, though, the expression ‏שֶׁיִּהְיֶה לְךָ יוֹם טוֹב‏ (*she-yihyeh lekha yom tov*), You should have a good day, has started to make inroads in the spoken language. That's a good thing, isn't it?

KNOW IS KNOW

They say that a little knowledge is a dangerous thing. And a lot of knowledge isn't? Everyone will agree that it all depends on the use to which knowledge is put. For this reason, Jewish culture maintains that there is no possession more prized than יֶדַע (yeda), knowledge.

The root ע-ד-י (yod, dalet, ayin), to know, branches out into areas where knowledge is both more and less than itself. No sooner had Adam and Eve eaten from the עֵץ הַדַּעַת (ets ha-da'at), Tree of Knowledge, than they knew they were naked, וַיֵּדְעוּ כִּי עֵירֻמִּים הֵם (va-yed'u ki erummim hem). Once they became יוֹדְעֵי טוֹב וָרָע (yod'ei tov va-ra), able to discern between good and evil, it did not take long for another type of knowledge to set in: וְהָאָדָם יָדַע אֶת חַוָּה (ve-ha-adam yada et havah), "Adam had carnal knowledge of Eve."

Sometimes a willful lack of knowledge will lead to other forms of carnality. Folklore, יְדַע עַם (yeda am), teaches that Judaism's carnival, held at Purim time, is called an עַדְלוֹיָדַע (adloyada), because one is supposed to drink until one doesn't know the difference between Mordechai and Haman. When Potiphar's wife tries to seduce Joseph, one of the reasons he gives for refusing is that Potiphar trusts him so much that לֹא יָדַע אִתִּי מַה בַּבָּיִת (lo yada iti ma ba-bayit), "he does not know how I manage his household."

Hebrew makes subtle but important distinctions between forms of our root. דַּעַת (da'at), knowledge, should always be differentiated from דֵּעָה (de'ah), opinion. A יְדוּעָן (yedu'an) is a celebrity, a יַדְעָן (yad'an) is a connoisseur, a יִדְעוֹנִי (yid'oni), sorcerer, is one who knows—and apparently misuses his knowledge of—the secrets of the universe. Judaism's aversion to sorcery is יָדוּעַ (yadu'a), well known. Nowadays, זֶה לֹא יַעֲלֶה עַל הַדַּעַת (zeh lo ya'aleh al ha-da'at), one would not even think of doing it.

To one who knows that the English word "science" comes from the Latin verb for to know, it should not be a surprise that the Hebrew word for science is מַדָּע (madda). This word is not to be confused with מֵידָע (meida), information, something you learn at the מוֹדִיעִין (modi'in), information desk, or Israel's intelligence service. Were you מוּדָע (muda), aware, that the question מַדּוּעַ? (maddu'a?), why?, is a construction of the words מַה יָדוּעַ (ma yadu'a), what is known? Perhaps you gleaned it from a מוֹדָעָה (moda'ah), poster, or a הוֹדָעָה (hoda'ah), announcement. Or perhaps you learned it by studying מַדָּעֵי הָרוּחַ (madda'ei ha-ru'ah), humanities, in college or by reading one of Israel's daily newspapers, יְדִיעוֹת אַחֲרוֹנוֹת (yedi'ot aharonot), literally, latest news. Combining these two activities is one way to get both a little and a lot of knowledge.

Dangerous? מִי יוֹדֵעַ? (mi yode'a?), who knows? In my opinion, לְדַעְתִּי (le-da'ati), given the richness of our root, even יוֹדְעֵי סֵפֶר (yod'ei sefer), scholars, for whom חִלּוּקֵי דֵעוֹת (hillukei de'ot), differences of opinion, are at the center of their work, will never get to the end of their search for knowledge.

HAVE A GOOD GOOD DAY

Have you noticed lately, with so many people available "24/7," how life itself has come to seem like one fast-paced day? The many uses of the Hebrew word יוֹם (*yom*), day, help vary the notion of what constitutes a day.

The root י-ו-מ (*yod, vav, mem*) has given birth to the verb יָמַם (*yamam*), as in the sentence, "The fire מְיוֹמֶמֶת אֶת הַלַּיְלָה (*meyomemet et ha-laylah*), makes the night seem like day." This sense, if not the verb, comes from ancient times, יְמֵי הַקֶּדֶם (*yemei ha-kedem*): God calls the light he has created יוֹם (*yom*). The Scriptural verse widens the meaning of day by asserting, "There was evening, there was morning, יוֹם אֶחָד (*yom ehad*) one day." Since then, a Jewish day begins in the evening.

From the Passover Haggadah we learn that יְמֵי חַיֶּיךָ (*yemei hayyekha*), literally "the days of your life," is to be taken as a human life span. Add כָּל (*kol*), all, to *yemei hayyekha* and you get, say the Rabbis, יְמוֹת הַמָּשִׁיחַ (*yemot ha-mashiah*), the Messianic Era, sometimes known as אַחֲרִית הַיָּמִים (*aharit ha-yamim*), the End of Days. On Holidays, it's customary to say *Gut Yuntiff*, from יוֹם טוֹב (*yom tov*), forgetting perhaps that what we're really saying is "Have a good good day."

The talmudic tractate יוֹמָא (*yoma*), Aramaic for day, deals with the laws of Yom Kippur. A piece of wisdom taken from the Arabic reminds us that יוֹם עָסָל יוֹם בָּסָל (*yom asal yom basal*, accent on first syllable), some days are honey, some days are onions. If you want to use Hebrew, you can say לֹא כָּל יוֹם פּוּרִים (*lo kol yom purim*), not every day is Purim. A discussion of current events would deal with עִנְיָנֵי דְּיוֹמָא (*inyanei de-yoma*), events of the day. In Israel today, הַיּוֹם (*ha-yom*), some stores remain open twenty-four hours בִּימָמָה (*bi-yemamah*) a day. And of someone who works assiduously at a task, Israelis say עוֹשֶׂה לֵילוֹת כְּיָמִים (*oseh leilot ke-yamim*), he turns nights into days. Or is it the other way around? Even Israelis aren't sure.

In Hebrew one commemorates a יוֹם הַשָּׁנָה (*yom ha-shanah*), a parent's yahrzeit, by reciting kaddish בּוֹ בַּיּוֹם (*bo ba-yom*), on that very day. In Israel, the day before יוֹם הָעַצְמָאוּת (*yom ha-atsma'ut*), Independence Day, is יוֹם הַזִּכָּרוֹן (*yom ha-zikkaron*), Memorial Day. There is no English translation for one of the most solemn days in the Jewish calendar יוֹם הַשּׁוֹאָה (*yom ha-shoah*), the day set aside for commemorating the Holocaust. Ask a righteous person who is בָּא בַּיָּמִים (*ba ba-yamim*), advanced in age, how he feels and he will answer בָּרוּךְ הַשֵּׁם יוֹם יוֹם (*barukh ha-shem yom yom*), "Bless God every day." And don't forget to put a cake on the סֵדֶר הַיּוֹם (*seder ha-yom*), agenda, of someone celebrating a יוֹם הוּלֶדֶת (*yom huledet*), birthday. That is not the time to ask מַה יוֹם מִיּוֹמַיִם? (*ma yom mi-yomayim?*), why should this day be any different?

The last book of the Tanakh, Chronicles, is called in Hebrew דִּבְרֵי הַיָּמִים (*divrei ha-yamim*), an expression used today for history, including that of יְמֵי הַבֵּינַיִם (*yemei ha-beinayim*), the middle ages. Coming off her יְמֵי הַתּוֹם (*yemei ha-tom*), days of innocence, a teenager would begin her daily diary entries with יוֹמָנִי הַיָּקָר (*yomani ha-yakar*), "Dear Diary." While a daily newspaper might be called a יוֹמוֹן (*yomon*), the reporter's appointment book is his יוֹמַן פְּגִישׁוֹת (*yoman pegishot*), appointment book, and the weekly TV news program he appears on might be called יוֹמַן הַשָּׁבוּעַ (*yoman ha-shavua*), literally, the daily of the week.

And so, because יוֹם רוֹדֵף יוֹם (*yom rodef yom*), one day follows the other, we get back to 24/7.

RELATIVELY SPEAKING

Jews are "fraught with background," wrote Erich Auerbach in *Mimesis*, his landmark 1946 book on the literary representation of reality. Geneticists might argue that all humans come freighted with inherited characteristics. Nevertheless, Auerbach's point, that Jewish roots are particularly significant, is still well taken.

Take, for example, the Hebrew word for genealogy, יְחוּס (*yihus*), a word with its own pedigree. The root's more "noble" spelling, י-ח-שׂ (*yod, het, sin*), is the only one found in the Tanakh. With time, the שׂ (*sin*) was changed to a ס (*samekh*). With that latter spelling, the root began to take on an array of related meanings. The steps from family relations to other relations, and from there to relationships and relativity are short indeed.

True, the root still retains its original meaning. Parents do want their children to marry into a family with status, יְחוּס (*yihus*; in Yinglish, *yiches*). A distinguished Sefardi rabbinic family in Jerusalem is named מְיוּחָס (*meyuhas*), "from a good family." Status also produces arrogance, and that's where we get the often-pejorative term יַחְסָן (*yahasan*), one who puts on airs. Your mother will tell you לֹא לְהִתְיַחֵס אֵלָיו (*lo le-hityahes elav*), don't pay him any mind.

The word יַחַס (*yahas*) is found in a panoply of Hebrew idioms. When a husband and wife are also good friends, one can say יֵשׁ לָהֶם מַעֲרֶכֶת יְחָסִים יָפָה (*yesh lahem ma'arekhet yehasim yafah*), they have a good relationship. One shouldn't confuse יַחֲסֵי מִין (*yahasei min*), sexual relations, with יַחֲסֵי צִבּוּר (*yahasei tsibbur*), public relations, though יְחָסִים דִּיפלוֹמָטִיים (*yehasim diplomati'im*), diplomatic relations, might tempt us to do so.

87

Some countries have a יַחַס שְׁלִילִי (*yahas shelili*), negative attitude, בְּיַחַס לְיִשְׂרָאֵל (*be-yahas le-yisra'el*), in regard to Israel. In Hebrew grammar, the ב (*bet*) and the ל (*lamed*), together with כ (*kaf*) and נ (*nun*), are called אוֹתִיּוֹת יַחַס (*otiyyot yahas*), prepositional letters, while the words אֶל (*el*), עַל (*al*), בֵּין (*bein*), and מִן (*min*), which translate as to, on, between, and from, are מִלּוֹת יַחַס (*millot yahas*), prepositions. A preposition that is, יַחַסִית (*yahasit*), relatively, difficult to translate is אֶת (*et*).

Some families believe it is proper לְיַחֵס חֲשִׁיבוּת (*le-yahes hashivut*), to attribute importance, to a person who has achieved יִחוּס עַצְמִי (*yihus atsmi*), self-worth, without recourse to ancestors.

In a recent work of gentlemanly scholarship we find our root used subtly, in the expression פֵּרוּשׁ הַמְיוּחָס לְרַשִׁ"י (*perush ha-meyuhas le-rashi*), to show that a text commonly attributed to Rashi—a commentary on Chapter 6 of Pirkei Avot—was probably not written by him.

Speaking of scholars, some thirty years before Auerbach's book, Albert Einstein speculated that time and space were יַחֲסִיִּים (*yehasiyyim*), relative. He formulated this discovery in his famous תּוֹרַת הַיַּחֲסוּת (*torat ha-yahasut*), theory of relativity.

Many would conclude that there is יִחוּס (*yihus*) to be derived from the fact that both of these scholars were Jews. But if you don't believe in *yiches*, at least take a little *naches*.

BOOMER BABIES

One need not be a Pollyanna, or the author of a book on Hebrew roots, to recognize that the human spirit heals more readily than the body or the psyche. Nine months after the disaster of September 11 the birthrate was expected to be disproportionately high. To put it in a Hebrew context, they expected more תִּינוֹקוֹת (*tinokot*), infants—a word derived from the root ק-נ-י (*yod, nun, kof*), to be breast-fed—than in normal times.

In Scripture, the root appears most famously in the narrative of Abraham and Sarah and in the story of the birth of Moses. Told that she would give birth in old age, Sarah's embarrassed question ?הֵינִיקָה בָנִים שָׂרָה (*heinikah vanim sara?*), "Will Sarah suckle children?", betrays her amazement at the announcement. The hero of the Moses story is resourceful Miriam. She offers her mother as a מֵינֶקֶת (*meineket*), nursemaid, for the foundling child of Pharaoh's daughter and thereby saves Moses for the Hebrews.

The poetic Hebrew expression for first-graders, תִּינוֹקוֹת שֶׁל בֵּית רַבָּן (*tinokot shel beit rabban*), literally, "infants of the teacher's house," teaches a wider vocabulary lesson. Why infants? If they're in school, they have already passed the גִּיל יַנְקוּת (*gil yankut*), infancy, and they're certainly no longer nursing. Hebrew maven Avshalom Kor reminds us that תִּינוֹק (*tinok*) is merely the mishnaic version of the Biblical word *yeled*, which comes from a root meaning "newborn." Both words were once used for children of all ages, although now a *yeled* is older than a *tinok*.

Aramaic plays a major role in the spread of the root in Hebrew and Jewish culture. The child prodigy in novelist Aharon Appelfeld's masterpiece, *Badenheim 1939*, is called the יַנּוּקָא (*yannuka*), a term usually reserved in hasidic circles for one who has assumed the Rebbe's throne as a young child. A Jewish saying has it that the גִּרְסָא דְיַנְקוּתָא (*girsa de-yankuta*), i.e., what one learns at an early age, "with one's mother's milk," is not soon forgotten.

Back in school, we learn from a Hebrew proverb in the Talmud why one's college is called, in Latin, alma mater, nourishing mother. The rabbinic expression compares a teacher metaphorically to a cow nursing a calf: יוֹתֵר מִמַּה שֶּׁהָעֵגֶל רוֹצֶה לִינוֹק הַפָּרָה רוֹצָה לְהָנִיק (*yoter mi-ma she-ha-egel rotseh linok ha-parah rotsah le-hanik*), "The teacher is more anxious to teach than the pupil is to learn."

Biology may not be destiny but it does use our root to give us the Hebrew word for mammals, יוֹנְקִים (*yonkim*). This word is also used as a verb having more to do with theology than biology. All agree that both Christianity and Islam יוֹנְקִים (*yonkim*), are influenced by, draw their substance from, Judaism. Is that fact not a further cause for optimism?

SITUATIONAL POLITICS

Sometimes one word can express a historic moment in the annals of a nation. Take, for example, the Hebrew word מַצָּב (*matsav*), situation—from the root י־צ־ב (*yod, tsadi, bet*), to stand erect—uttered in virtually every Israeli conversation during the intifada.

The root is found in the Tanakh in connection with a long list of biblical characters. Among these are: Lot's wife, who turned into a נְצִיב מֶלַח (*netsiv melah*), pillar of salt; Jacob, whose ladder was מֻצָּב (*mutsav*), firmly planted, on earth; Rachel, at whose burial place Jacob erected a מַצֵּבָה (*matsevah*), tombstone; Joseph, in whose dream his sheaf נִצָּבָה (*nitsavah*), stood taller, than his brothers' sheaves; and the people of Israel, נִצָּבִים (*nitsavim*), standing ready, to enter into a covenant with God at Sinai.

A British subject always stands ready to serve his King. Sir Herbert Samuel served as the first נְצִיב עֶלְיוֹן (*netsiv elyon*), Lord High Commissioner, during the British Mandate. The אַרְמוֹן הַנְּצִיב (*armon ha-netsiv*), Commissioner's palace, is today the name given to the location of the Haas Promenade, overlooking the Old City of Jerusalem.

In geometry, the perpendicular line of a right angle, doubtlessly because it stands up straight, is called a נִצָּב (*nitsav*). Something that stands upright is perceived as true. On Shavuot, to introduce the haftarah, we recite the Aramaic formula יְצִיב פִּתְגָּם (*yetsiv pitgam*), "a true word." We proclaim the truth of the Shema by putting together from two different prayers their last and first words,

אֱמֶת וְיַצִּיב (emet ve-yatsiv), thus creating the modern idiom for "absolutely true."

On an El Al flight to Israel, the pilot will put on the fasten-seat-belt sign, announcing מֶזֶג אֲוִיר בִּלְתִּי יַצִּיב (mezeg avir bilti yatsiv), unstable weather conditions, as the reason. You'll feel comfortable on the long flight if you have יְצִיבָה נְכוֹנָה (yetsivah nekhonah), proper posture. Once in Israel, you'll be concerned with the יַצִּיבוּת (yatsivut), stability, of both the shekel and the government.

All conversations in Israel seem to return to the word מַצָּב (matsav), and so will we. According to hip-hop group Ha-Dag Nahash, Israelis always answer עֶשֶׂר (eser), ten, to the question מַה הַמַּצָּב? (mah ha-matsav?), How's it going? Will the government proclaim a מַצָּב חֵרוּם (matsav herum), emergency? When you get your צַו הִתְיַצְּבוּת לְמִלּוּאִים (tsav hityatsvut le-milu'im), orders to show up for army reserve duty, you go. Often the army will erect a מוּצָּב (mutsav), camp stationed in the border, to guard against enemy infitration. The expression מַצָּב רוּחַ (matsav ru'ah), which can describe both a good and a bad mood, has been taken so negatively lately that it has given birth to the adjective מְצוּבְרָח (metsuvrah), in a lousy mood.

When the director wants to film the crowd scene, he calls for all the נִצָּבִים (nitsavim), extras, to appear. Then there is the euphemism for a pregnant woman, said to be, simply, בְּמַצָּב (be-matsav), literally, in a situation, figuratively, in a family way.

Whatever the context, Jewish solidarity calls for the Jewish family to be at hand whenever there is a *matsav*. There's a word for that in Hebrew. It's called הִתְיַצְּבוּת (hityatsvut), being there.

RARE BIRDS / RARE WORD

Some words are so rich in the number of their meanings that they appear to land all over the linguistic map. Perhaps no root in the Hebrew language has more discrete connotations than ־ק-ר (*yod, kof, resh*), used to describe a wide range of contexts, including heavy, expensive, dear, noble, rare, esteemed, considerable, beautiful, and splendid, to name a few.

Take a letter, for example. You might begin your correspondence with חָבֵר יָקָר (*haver yakar*), Dear Friend, or גְּבֶרֶת יִצְחָקִי הַיְקָרָה (*geveret yitshaki ha-yekarah*), Dear Mrs. Yitshaki, and end with יְדִידְךָ וּמוֹקִירְךָ (*yedidkha u-mokirkha*), Your Friend and Admirer, or, somewhat more formally, בְּהוֹקָרָה וּבִבְרָכָה (*be-hokarah u-vivrakhah*), literally, With Esteem and Blessing.

A shopkeeper who charges high prices is called a יַקְרָן (*yakran*) because he contributes to the יֹקֶר הַמִּחְיָה (*yoker ha-mihyah*), high cost of living. But what can you do, except try לְהוֹצִיא יָקָר מִזּוֹלֵל (*le-hotsi yakar mi-zolel*), to make the best of a bad situation? That's what a נֶפֶשׁ יְקָרָה (*nefesh yekarah*), a noble soul, would do. If you have הוֹקָרָה (*hokarah*), admiration, for that person, you will yourself be worthy of יוּקְרָה (*yukrah*), a good reputation. Someone who has committed a marital gaffe might acknowledge זֶה עָלָה לִי בְּיֹקֶר (*ze alah li be-yoker*), I paid dearly for it. He might consider buying his wife a בֶּגֶד יוּקְרָתִי (*beged yukrati*), a classy coat, or a שְׁעוֹן יוּקְרָה (*she'on yukrah*), prestigious brand-name watch, to make up for it.

The book of Esther uses our root no fewer than ten times, proving, perhaps, the prominence of prestige among Persians. The pretext for the whole story is that Persian women, including Queen Vashti, are lax in giving יְקָר (yekar), honor, to their husbands. Later, King Ahashverosh asks מַה נַעֲשָׂה יְקָר? (mah na'aseh yekar?), "What honor was bestowed" on Mordechai for saving the King's life? Told that nothing was done, the King orders Haman to treat Mordechai to a procession through Shushan, announcing "Thus shall be done to the man whom the King חָפֵץ בִּיקָרוֹ (hafets bikaro), wishes to honor." Finally, Haman's downfall leads to a happy ending for the Jews, as they celebrate with light, happiness, rejoicing and, you guessed it, יְקָר (yekar), honor. Jeremiah uses our root to reassure the "remnant of Israel" that הֲבֵן יַקִּיר לִי אֶפְרַיִם (ha-ven yakkir li efra'im), "Truly, Ephraim is a dear son to me."

The Rabbis also had a predilection for our root, using it to reflect their values in ways that might seem off-beat. The hero of one talmudic tale is called יוֹסֵף מוֹקִיר שַׁבָּת (yosef mokir shabbat), "Joseph-Who-Honors-the-Sabbath." If one was מִיַּקִּירֵי יְרוּשָׁלַיִם (mi-yakirei yerushalayim), of Jerusalem's nobility, one conducted oneself with יַקְרוּת (yakrut), dignity. How do we know that the Rabbis considered phylacteries aesthetically splendid? They said, יְקָר, אֵלוּ תְּפִלִּין (yekar, elu tefillin) "Splendor, this means tefillin." They also used our word in Aramaic to describe a purported medical condition, cardiac asthma, יוֹקְרָא דְּלִבָּא (yokra de-liba), literally, heaviness of the heart.

Chaim Nachman Bialik, in his most famous poem אֶל הַצִּפּוֹר (el ha-tsippor), uses our root to evoke צִפּוֹרִי הַיְקָרָה (tsipori ha-yekarah), "my dear bird," that brings news of the Holy Land to his window in the Diaspora.

Today, you can find a whole school that made aliyah to Jerusalem. Called Yakar, London's esteemed contribution to Jewish adult education is adding new meaningfulness to what is already a word heavy with meaning.

STRAIGHT IS THE GAIT

So you walk into the office in Tel-Aviv for a job interview, looking to work for a no-nonsense company. When, on the interviewer's desk, you see prominently displayed a motto that reads, דַּבֵּר יָשָׁר וְלָעִנְיָן (dabber yashar ve-la-inyan), "Speak straight and to the point," you know you've found a home. Then, when, on your way to the bus station for your ride back to Jerusalem, you pass by a shop that sells sex toys and the sign on the storefront reads—wittily, you concede—יָשָׁר וְלָעִנְיָן (yashar ve-la-inyan), straight and to the point, you realize how supple Hebrew is.

The root י-שׁ-ר (yod, shin, resh) describes a physical quality, flatness, straightness. The concrete sense is found in the modern Israeli's ubiquitous answer to your request for directions, יָשָׁר יָשָׁר (yashar yashar), Go straight for a good bit [and then ask someone else]. The non-stop bus you took was the יָשִׁיר (yashir), the direct bus to Jerusalem. A while back, Jewish singer Enrico Macias appeared בְּשִׁדּוּר יָשִׁיר (be-shiddur yashir), in a direct broadcast, in a concert at Sultan's Pool. The מִישׁוֹר הַחוֹף (mishor ha-hof), coastal plain, stretching from Jaffa to Mount Carmel, is also called the שָׁרוֹן (sharon), a name which, missing its yod, derives from our root as well.

Most often, however, the root is found in abstract expressions, conveying the moral qualities of honesty and integrity. When Isaiah says יַשְּׁרוּ . . . מְסִלָּה (yashru . . . mesillah), "Make a straight path," he means a straight path to God. Moses Chaim Luzzatto, the eighteenth-century Italian mystic, adapts this expression for the title of his masterwork on Jewish ethics, מְסִלַּת יְשָׁרִים (mesillat *yesharim*), literally, *The Path of the Upright.* Twentieth-century novelist S.Y. Agnon borrows from Isaiah the title of one of his books, the figurative expression וְהָיָה הֶעָקֹב לְמִישׁוֹר (*ve-hayah he-akov le-mishor*), *And the Crooked Shall Be Made Straight.* Of an honest man one can say הוּא יָשָׁר כְּמוֹ סַרְגֵּל (*hu yashar kemo sargel*), He is straight as a ruler.

Sometimes, one person's straightforwardness is another's anarchy. That's the message one gets from the book of Judges, which tells us that because there was no king in Israel everyone would act according to what was הַיָּשָׁר בְּעֵינָיו (*ha-yashar be-einav*), "right in his own eyes," i.e., as he pleased.

The poetic name for Israel, יְשֻׁרוּן (*yeshurun*), also derives from the abstract use of our root, designating the Jews as "the righteous people." You can see the connection in the word לִנְהֹג בְּיֹשֶׁר (*li-nehog be-yosher*), to act fairly, and in the verse from Psalms declaimed before the performance of Kol Nidre on Yom Kippur eve, stating that "Light is sown for the righteous, and gladness for the יִשְׁרֵי לֵב (*yishrei lev*), upright in heart."

Probably the best known use of our root comes from the Hebrew expression for Congratulations, יְיַשֵּׁר כֹּחֲךָ (*ye-yasher kohakha*), literally "May your strength be made straight." In Hebrew-sprinkled, Yiddish-tinted English we transform the verb into a noun and give someone a יֹשֶׁר כֹּחַ (*yasher koah*). Either way, it's what you get when you speak יְשִׁירוּת (*yeshirot*), in a direct and plain manner.

THAT'S A WRAP

What do an eighteenth-century British nobleman and a first-century Jewish sage have in common? Both are credited with having invented the sandwich.

John Montagu, Fourth Earl of Sandwich, contributed his very title to the fast food industry. Hillel, adding to one of history's slowest meals, gave the Jewish people the Passover Seder ritual of כּוֹרֵךְ (korekh), wrapping the meat of the Passover sacrifice together with matzah and bitter herbs. From this we get the Hebrew word for sandwich, כָּרִיךְ (karikh).

To look at some of its other derivations, one might say that the root כ-ר-ך (kaf, resh, kaf), to bind, also lends itself to a כְּרִיךְ קוֹמוֹתַיִם (kerikh komotayim), a "double-decker" sandwich—and more.

The Mishnah, for example, tells us that at Passover if one drinks all four cups of wine בְּכֶרֶךְ אֶחָד (be-kherekh ekhad), all at once, one fulfills the mitzvah. Further, the Even-Shoshan Hebrew Dictionary is published in as many as שִׁשָּׁה כְּרָכִים (shishah kerakhim), six volumes. One uses our root here because each of the volumes is sent to the כְּרִיכִיָּה (kerikhiyyah), bookbindery, to be bound separately.

Kerikha is not only the binding of books. We also speak of כְּרִיכַת רְצוּעוֹת הַתְּפִילִין (kerikhat retsuot ha-tefillin), binding the tefillin straps on one's arm, as well as of putting a כְּרִיכָה עַל מְקוֹם הַפֶּצַע (kerikhah al mekom ha-petsa), binding a bandage on a wound. Perhaps because originally a burial shroud was wrapped around a dead body, the word for shroud in Hebrew is תַּכְרִיכִים (takhrikhim).

Sometimes it is important לִכְרוֹךְ דָּבָר בְּדָבָר (*li-khrokh davar be-davar*), to mix one subject inside another. For example, wrapping explains why, today, a city that has more than 100,000 inhabitants is called a כְּרַךְ (*kerakh*). This came about because large cities were usually surrounded by walls and could be said to be wrapped around by them. At any rate, large cities at some distance from Israel were called כְּרַכֵּי הַיָּם (*kerakei ha-yam*), literally, the cities of the sea, and someone who loves dwelling in urban settings is called a בֶּן כְּרַךְ (*ben kerakh*).

The adjective כָּרוּךְ (*karukh*), bound, as in חֶבֶל כָּרוּךְ סְבִיב הָעֵץ (*hevel karukh seviv ha-ets*), a rope tied around a tree, has many metaphorical meanings. Thus, one might ask בַּמֶּה הַדָּבָר כָּרוּךְ? (*bameh ha-davar karukh?*), What are the conditions? or say that a little boy is כָּרוּךְ אַחֲרֵי אִמּוֹ (*karukh aharei immo*), attached to his mother, or that a study fellowship in Israel is כָּרוּךְ בִּתְנַאי (*karukh be-tenai*), conditioned on the fellow's pledge to spend time in community service. Best-seller books often come in כְּרִיכָה קָשָׁה (*kerikhah kashah*), hardback, and כְּרִיכָה דַּקָּה (*kerikhah dakkah*), paperback.

Sometimes, the study of Hebrew root derivations is כָּרוּךְ בִּבְעָיוֹת (*karukh be-ve'ayot*), problematic. At other times, by helping us to understand how a sandwich can lead to that other food fashion, the wrap, it provides food for further thought.

HEART AND SOUL FOOD

It is not surprising that the Jewish people should have adopted as a rallying cry the expression לֵב אֶחָד (*lev ehad*), literally, one heart, alluding to the unity created under the marriage canopy.

The word לֵב (*lev*), together with its doublet לֵבָב (*levav*), is found more than 850 times in Scripture, in a wide variety of contexts. In the narrative of the Exodus from Egypt, God induces Pharaoh, for political reasons, to be stubborn and obstinate, by hardening לֵב פַּרְעֹה (*lev par'oh*), Pharaoh's heart. The enigmatic expression in Leviticus, לֵב עָרֵל (*lev arel*), uncircumcised heart, is used to describe someone who is incapable of understanding or feeling.

The lover in the Song of Songs muses out loud to his beloved לִבַּבְתִּנִי אֲחוֹתִי כַלָּה (*libavtini ahoti khallah*), "You have ravished my heart, my sister, my bride." In the terrible story of the sexual violence perpetrated by King David's son Amnon on his half-sister Tamar, a Freudian slip tied to our root rises to the surface. Amnon reveals subconsciously (or was it devilishly conscious?) that he is plotting to ravish Tamar against her will when he asks her to make him לְבִיבוֹת (*levivot*), pancakes, perhaps in the shape of a heart. *Levivot* is also the Hebrew word for the Jewish soul food eaten at Hanukkah, *latkes*.

Commercial enterprises in Jerusalem have adopted expressions containing the word לֵב (*lev*), in the sense of center, in their name. Take, for example, the apartment hotel on King George Street called לֵב יְרוּשָׁלַיִם (*lev yerushalayim*), Heart of Jerusalem, or the store a few meters down the street called לֵב הָעִיר (*lev ha-ir*), Center City, literally, heart of the city.

An insincere person is one who is אֶחָד בַּפֶּה וְאֶחָד בַּלֵּב (*ehad ba-peh ve-ehad ba-lev*), one thing in the mouth and quite another in the heart. When you send an important memo that you want the recipient to pay careful attention to, you add the words לִתְשׂוּמַת לִבְּךָ (*li-tsumat libkha*), literally, "for you to put your heart to." An elegant way of referring to philanthropy is נְדִיבוּת לֵב (*nedivut lev*), literally, nobility of the heart, metaphorically, generosity. On modern wedding invitations you will find the bride and groom called בְּחִירַת לִבּוֹ (*behirat libbo*) and בְּחִיר לִבָּהּ (*behir libbah*), the choice of his or her heart. And a good way to end a letter is with אִיחוּלִים לְבָבִיִּים (*ihulim levaviyyim*), cordial wishes.

And now it's time to sing, all together now, כָּל עוֹד בַּלֵּבָב פְּנִימָה (*kol od ba-levav penimah*), "As long as deep within our heart," the beginning of the Hatikvah. It's as good a way as any to show that we have לֵב אֶחָד (*lev ehad*), a sense of unity.

WHAT WHITE
HATH WROUGHT

If your best friend told you that white was black, would you believe her? Of course you would, especially if you were speaking Hebrew while shopping at Victoria's Secret. That's because, in the expression לְבָנִים שְׁחוֹרִים (levanim shehorim), literally, black whites, the word לְבָנִים (levanim), whites, is used for undergarments of any color.

When the root ל-ב-נ (lamed, bet, nun), to bleach, cleanse, make hot, clarify, appears in Scripture, it often refers to the לְבֵנִים (levenim), bricks, the Hebrew slaves made in Egypt. Some say they were made out of white clay, others that they were baked white-hot. (Today, like underwear, they may be red.) A מִלְבָּנָה (milbanah) is a brick kiln. The word מַלְבֵּן (malben) is used for rectangle, not because of the whiteness geometric forms don't have, but because it is brick-shaped.

Was לָבָן (lavan), Rebecca's brother Laban, so called because he was pale-faced? Is Lebanon called הַלְּבָנוֹן (ha-levanon) because of its snow-capped mountains?

The Rabbis, instituting the קִדּוּשׁ הַלְּבָנָה (kiddush ha-levanah) ceremony, the sanctification of the new moon, used our root to emphasize the moon's gleaming whiteness. The Talmud teaches that הַמַּלְבִּין פְּנֵי חֲבֵרוֹ (ha-malbin penei havero), one who shames his friend in public (whitening his face), is considered as if he shed his blood. It also teaches that you may begin saying the morning

Shema when it is light enough to distinguish between תְּכֵלֶת לְלָבָן (tehelet le-lavan), blue and white.

The word לָבָן (lavan), white, is found in spoken Hebrew in all sorts of contexts. The expression כָּחוֹל לָבָן (kahol lavan), blue and white, the colors of the Israeli flag, refers to goods manufactured or grown in Israel. The words סֵפֶר הַלָּבָן (sefer ha-lavan) call to mind the infamous White Paper issued by the British in 1939. A foreign resident said to have a מִסְפָּר לָבָן (mispar lavan), white-numbered license plate, owns a legally untaxed automobile. An Israeli may be a בַּעַל צַוָּארוֹן לָבָן (ba'al tsavaron lavan), white-collar worker, who pays taxes on his earnings and has כֶּסֶף לָבָן (kesef lavan), "clean" money. A celebrity may be put on a רְשִׁימָה לְבָנָה (reshimah levanah), A-list. A modern Israeli poet may disdain rhyme and write חֲרוּזִים לְבָנִים (haruzim levanim), blank verse. Many Israelis eat לֶבֶן (leben), coagulated sour milk, for breakfast, and some insist on eating בָּשָׂר לָבָן (basar lavan), pork.

To underscore his identification with Israel, Professor David Weiss, a leading American scholar skilled at לִבּוּן בְּעָיוֹת (libbun be'ayot), clarifying problems, in the Talmud, took a Hebrew translation of his family name and tacked it on as הַלִּבְנִי (ha-livni), to make his name Weiss-Halivni.

It has nothing to do with lingerie.

THE FIRE THIS TIME

When an Israeli novelist creates a character with a fiery personality—and a name to go with it—he has the opportunity also to teach an interesting Hebrew lesson about fire. In David Grossman's *The Zigzag Kid* (1993, English 1997) his heroes—father and son—are called Feuerberg, (in German, fire mountain, i.e., volcano). When Grossman finds it necessary to give a Hebrew version of the name Uncle Feuerberg to one of his peripheral characters, he is faced with an embarrassment of riches. Shall he use the common word אֵשׁ (*esh*), or shall he reach perhaps for דְּלֵקָה (*delekah*), or שְׂרֵפָה (*serefah*), or תַּבְעֵרָה (*tav'erah*)? He might also consider לַפִּיד (*lapid*), torch, or מְדוּרָה (*medurah*), campfire, or even, reaching back to the Latin word for hearth, פוֹקוּס (*focus*).

Grossman chooses to name his character דּוֹד שִׁלְהָב (*dod shilhav*), Uncle Shilhav, and to call his character's activity שִׁלְהוּב (*shilhuv*), "Shilhavization," meaning, in Grossman's fictional universe, to give a musar speech to a bar-mitzvah boy. These words come from the root ל-ה-ב (*lamed, heh, bet*), flame, and lead us to some interesting insights into the Hebrew language.

The first one is the revelation that the verbal form of the root quite likely originally meant to be thirsty. It is easy to see how that led to "to burn with thirst," and from there to "to blaze fiercely." It is also perhaps not too difficult, especially if you have a vivid imagination, to see how the word לַהַב (*lahav*), flame, came to mean, in addition, לַהַב חֶרֶב (*lahav herev*), the blade of a sword. Not surprisingly, a unit of the Israeli army, playing on this coincidence of vocabulary, has on its shield both a חֶרֶב (*herev*), sword, and a

לַהַב (*lahav*), flame. (That it also has an olive branch tells us not a little about Israeli culture.)

Speaking of weaponry, modern arsenals often come equipped with a piece of machinery whose Hebrew name is taken from our root. The word for flame-thrower, לַהַבְיוֹר (*lahavyor*), is made of two words, לַהַב (*lahav*), flame, and יוֹרֶה (*yoreh*), shoot.

Another word deriving from our root, שַׁלְהֶבֶת (*shalhevet*), torch, has two interesting extensions, one containing God's name and one doing God's work. The latter refers to an experimental Jewish Day High School in Los Angeles, California, Shalhavet, which carries a torch for encouraging and enabling students to make ethical choices independently. The other is the word for powerful flame, שַׁלְהֶבֶתְיָה (*shalhevetyah*), literally, a God-flame, a phrase that comes to us from the Song of Songs.

There is another way of burning that has nothing to do with physical fire. You will find this in an expression such as אֲנִי נִלְהָב מְאוֹד מֵהַתָּכְנִית הַחֲדָשָׁה (*ani nilhav me'od me-ha-tokhnit ha-hadashah*), I'm very enthusiastic about the new program. Or, a newspaper might report that the speaker at the convention הִלְהִיב אֶת שׁוֹמְעָיו (*hilhiv et shom'av*), fired the imagination of his audience.

If you're looking for novelists who can create הִתְלַהֲבוּת (*hitlahavut*), enthusiasm, among both readers and critics, you need look no further than some of Israel's masters of the Hebrew novel.

BREAD AND WAR

What can you say about a culture that uses the same root—ל-ח-מ (*lamed, het, mem*)—for both bread, לֶחֶם (*lehem*, accent on the first syllable) and war, מִלְחָמָה (*milhamah*)?

One of the first things one might say is: Do לֶחֶם (*lehem*) and מִלְחָמָה (*milhamah*) really come from the same root? It's a good question, and to answer it one must invoke a third use of the root. It seems that לָחַם (*laham*) means not only "he did battle" and "he ate bread" but also "he joined together." That sense is apparent in the verb לְהַלְחִים (*le-halhim*), to weld.

Using this third meaning, Ludwig Koehler, in his 1953 *Dictionary of the Hebrew Old Testament*, opines that our root generally had the connotation of "to be closely packed together" and that that meaning is the common denominator. In war, says Koehler, soldiers often engage in hand-to-hand combat in close quarters. Voilà for מִלְחָמָה (*milhamah*). Bread, he adds, suggesting perhaps that it is considered highly nutritious, is "compact food." Voilà for לֶחֶם (*lehem*).

In a different way, medieval Hebrew grammarian Rabbi David Kimhi (the Radak) offers a metaphorical explanation for the coincidence of bread and war in one root: War is called מִלְחָמָה (*milhamah*), he says, because "the sword eats up the belligerents on both sides."

As interesting as these conjectures may be, they do not begin to exhaust the fascinating developments of the Hebrew word for bread, לֶחֶם (*lehem*). Adam is banished from the Garden of Eden with the malediction בְּזֵעַת אַפֶּךָ תֹּאכַל לֶחֶם (*be-ze'at apekha tokhal* lehem), "You will eat *lehem* by the sweat of your brow." Obviously, since bread does not grow on trees (either of Life or of Knowledge), our word is used here in a general sense, to mean "food." After the recitation of the blessing הַמּוֹצִיא לֶחֶם מִן הָאָרֶץ (*ha-motsi lehem min ha-arets*), "who brings forth bread from the earth," one may eat a piece of bread and then partake of a whole meal.

Our word is found in a number of biblical contexts, like the לֶחֶם בִּכּוּרִים (*lehem bikkurim*), bread of first fruits, brought to the Temple on Shavuot and the לֶחֶם עַצְלוּת (*lehem atslut*), bread of laziness, that the proverbial Woman of Valor does not eat. The expression describing the double portion of manna provided on Fridays for the Israelites in the desert, לֶחֶם מִשְׁנֶה (*lehem mishneh*), accounts for the custom of putting two loaves of hallah on the table for Shabbat and holidays.

Not surprisingly, bread is a central theme of Jewish folk wisdom. The book of Numbers reminds us that לֹא עַל הַלֶּחֶם לְבַדּוֹ יִחְיֶה הָאָדָם (*lo al ha-lehem le-vaddo yihyeh ha-adam*), "Man does not live by bread alone." The book of Ecclesiastes observes that לֹא לַחֲכָמִים לֶחֶם (*lo la-hakhamim lehem*), "Don't expect to get rich if you're going to be a scholar."

Perhaps the greatest piece of Jewish wisdom having to do with bread is also the most poetic: שְׁלַח לַחְמְךָ עַל פְּנֵי הַמָּיִם (*shelah lahmekha al penei ha-mayim*), "Cast your bread upon the waters." If you do good deeds randomly, you'll receive a reward. A chant you'll hear at a rally of workers who have been laid off is לֶחֶם! עֲבוֹדָה! (*lehem! avodah!*), "Give us work so we can buy food!"

As Jewish folk hero Bontshe the Silent teaches us, a nice, warm roll—a לַחְמָנִיָּה (*lahmaniyyah*)—every morning wouldn't be a bad reward at all.

lamed kof het ל-ק-ח — 54

TAKING IT

Who says Hebrew is not in its ascendancy in the United States? There it is, for all to see, imprinted on a midtown Manhattan store window: Sy Syms, clothier extraordinaire, tells us, in perfectly modulated Hebrew, that the צָרְכָן הַמְחוּנָּךְ (*tsarkhan ha-mehunnakh*), his educated consumer, is הַלָּקוֹחַ הַטּוֹב בְּיוֹתֵר (*lakoah ha- tov be-yoter*), the best customer.

Syms is known for his astuteness is מִקָּח וּמִמְכָּר (*mikkah u-mimkar*), buying and selling. This chapter provides something else taken from the root ל-ק-ח (*lamed, kof, het*), to take, specifically לֶקַח (*lekah*), instruction.

The root appears some thousand times in Scripture, from Adam's rib which God לָקַח (*lakah*), took, to fashion Eve, to מַלְקוֹחַ (*malkoah*), spoils of war, to the Businesswoman of Valor in Proverbs, who considered a field וַתִּקָּחֵהוּ (*va-tikahehu*), and purchased it.

Given the business-like nature of ancient marriage (Did I hear someone whisper: What about today's prenuptial agreements?), it is not surprising that the biblical verse describing a falsely-accused wife reads כִּי יִקַּח (*ki yikkah*), when a man takes—i.e., acquires—a wife. Did you know that in addition to the Cohens and the Katzes, all people named Azoulay are from the Jewish priestly class? Their name comes from an anagram of a Biblical verse that says that priests לֹא יִקָּחוּ (*lo yikkahu*), may not marry, a defiled woman.

Jewish folk wisdom urges us לְעוֹלָם תִּקַּח (*le-olam tikkah*), which is perhaps best translated as If-it's-free-take-it-what-have-you-got-to-lose? Of course, if it costs more than you bargained for

107

in your מִקּוּחַ (*mikuah*), negotiation, then you may sue to annul the deal based on the Jewish legal principle of מְקַח טָעוּת (*mikah ta'ut*), a falsely advertised transaction.

A good grip is needed for taking, and that's why they invented tongs. In Israel today, your neighborhood electrician will have a מֶלְקַחַת (*melkahat*), pair of pliers, while your local obstetrician will be equipped with מֶלְקָחַיִם (*melkahayim*), forceps. Don't go in the ocean if you're afraid of sharks—they clamp down with their מַלְקוֹחַיִם (*malkohayim*), jaws. Also, אֲנִי אֲלַמֵּד אוֹתְךָ לֶקַח (*ani alammed otkha lekah*), I'll teach you a lesson or two: don't play with matches, lest something לָקִיחַ (*lakiah*), combustible, catch fire; and don't leave your door unlocked, lest a לַקְחָן (*lakhan*), petty thief, break in. If that happens, לֹא לָקַחַת לַלֵּב (*lo lakahat la-lev*), don't take it to heart.

The thief might steal all the nice clothing you, the לָקוֹחַ הַטּוֹב (*lakoah ha-tov*), good customer, bought at Syms. Even worse, he might take this copy of the book before you've had a chance to acquire all the לֶקַח (*lekah*), instruction, it contains.

On second thought, not to worry. In both Israel and America, you can learn Hebrew just by taking a walk in the street.

TO BE CONTINUED . . .

Go to any meeting of the organized Jewish community in North America these days and the one word you're most likely to hear is "continuity." What the word conveys is a fear that we have done precious little to transmit the attractiveness of the Jewish tradition to the next generation of Jews.

In Hebrew, the word continuity translates into הֶמְשֵׁכִיּוּת (hemshekhiyyut). The root of the word is מ-שׁ-ךּ (mem, shin, kaf), on the one hand, to pull, on the other, to attract. It is found in the Jewish textual tradition in the most poetic of circumstances. In the Song of Songs, for example, the beloved urges her lover, מָשְׁכֵנִי אַחֲרֶיךָ נָּרוּצָה (moshkheni aharekha narutsah), "Draw me after you, let us run." In the Psalm chanted before the Grace After Meals, the farmer who goes off in tears dragging after him a heavy "seed-bag," מֶשֶׁךְ הַזָּרַע (meshekh ha-zara), is reassured that he will return, carrying his sheaves, singing songs of joy. In a poem sung before the Kabbalat Shabbat service, Yedid Nefesh, the poet urges God, מְשׁוֹךְ עַבְדְּךָ אֶל רְצוֹנֶךְ (meshokh avdekha el retsonekha), "Draw your servant to your wishes."

The Jewish legal tradition teaches that one of the ways to acquire movable property is by מְשִׁיכָה (meshikhah), drawing it to oneself. The word מְשִׁיכָה (meshikhah) is used in Modern Hebrew to describe a withdrawal from one's bank account and is found in the term for gravity, כֹּחַ הַמְּשִׁיכָה (ko'ah ha-meshikhah), literally, the power of attraction, and in the expressions for attractiveness, מְשִׁיכָה (meshikhah), and sex appeal, מְשִׁיכָה מִינִית (meshikhah minit).

In its verb forms, the root is used both concretely—הוּא מוֹשֵׁךְ בַּמוֹשְׁכוֹת שֶׁל הַסּוּס (*hu moshekh ba-moshkhot shel ha-suss*), he pulls the horse's reins—and abstractly, as in הַשָּׂפָה הָעִבְרִית מוֹשֶׁכֶת אֶת הַלֵּב (*ha-safah ha-ivrit moshekhet et ha-lev*), The Hebrew language tugs at one's heart.

Perhaps continuity is less of a problem in Israel thanks to the Hebrew language itself. After all, does not every other door handle in the country tell us, מְשׁוֹךְ (*meshokh*), Pull? When you say that a speech נִמְשַׁךְ (*nimshakh*), you are complaining that it is dragging on too long, and perhaps also speculating that, during the speech, בְּמֶשֶׁךְ הַנְּאוּם (*be-meshekh ha-ne'um*), more than one listener will have dozed off. When a bureaucrat keeps putting you off, you can complain הוּא מוֹשֵׁךְ אוֹתִי (*hu moshekh oti*).

In a sarcastic reaction to all of those projects designed to promote הֶמְשֵׁכִיּוּת (*hemshekhiyyut*), Jewish continuity, Yaakov Kirschen, the *Jerusalem Post*'s Dry Bones cartoonist, has a community functionary announce a new movement for Jewish revival in America, a Judaism freed of its dependence on Torah, belief, and the land of Israel. Continuity without content. Harsh words, indeed, to which a diplomatic response seems appropriate. So why not just end this chapter, the way a סִפּוּר בְּהֶמְשֵׁכִים (*sippur be-hemshekhim*), serial, printed in a newspaper, ends—with the words הֶמְשֵׁךְ יָבוֹא (*hemshekh yavo*), To be continued.

THE CUSTOM
IS ALWAYS RIGHT

The Egged bus begins to pull away from the curb when all of a sudden, from the back of the bus, a shout rings out: נְהַג! הַדֶּלֶת! (*nehag! ha-delet!*). You panic for a second, fearing the worst, when you realize that it is merely a dilatory passenger who has just now remembered that this is her stop and is asking the נְהָג (*nehag*), driver, to open the rear door.

You can learn a lot about Israeli הִתְנַהֲגוּת (*hitnahagut*), behavior, simply by (1) riding the bus and (2) thinking of the shoresh נ-ה-ג (*nun, heh, gimmel*), related to an Aramaic word meaning "to lead" and to an Arabic word meaning "to go along the road."

The first sense is found in Isaiah's prophecy of an idyllic time when not only will the wolf dwell with the lamb but when נַעַר קָטוֹן נוֹהֵג בָּם (*na'ar katon noheg bam*)—a little boy leads them—a phrase that has been spun into a major tenet of Christian theology. The second sense is found in the book of Kings where the מִנְהַג (*minhag*), driving, of a certain leader, Yehu, is characterized thus: כִּי בְשִׁגָּעוֹן יִנְהָג (*ki be-shigga'on yinhag*), who drives like a madman—a phrase that describes many modern Israeli drivers as well.

Among the Rabbis, the word מִנְהָג (*minhag*) takes on a new coloration and is made to play a central role in Jewish theology. This is clear from the expression מִנְהַג יִשְׂרָאֵל—תּוֹרָה (*minhag yisrael—torah*), a custom that has been accepted by the Jewish community has the force of law. In the Talmud, the word נוֹהֲגִין (*nohagin*), signals a widely-accepted Jewish custom, like, during the

Grace After Meals, Jews נוֹהֲגִין (*nohagin*) are accustomed to place a cover on all knives.

Today, in certain rabbinical seminaries, it has become the custom to grant the title רַב וּמַנְהִיג (*rav u-manhig*) to a graduate who will be the leader and administrator of a religious community. In a democratic state, like Israel or the United States, it is נָהוּג (*nahug*), usual, for the citizens themselves to chose their own מַנְהִיגִים (*manhigim*), leaders.

The מִנְהָג (*minhag*) in America is to do so in November. At that time one hopes that the הֶגֶה (*hegeh*), steering wheel, of government will be entrusted to someone whose כֹּשֶׁר מַנְהִיגוּת (*kosher manhigut*), leadership ability, we're sure of. After all, unlike the inattentive bus passenger, we can't always shout נְהַג! הַדֶּלֶת! (*nehag! ha-delet!*), "Stop the world I want to get off."

MOVING RIGHT ALONG

From the Bible to the present day, Jews have always been in movement. That's what we learn from the Hebrew root נ-ו-ע (*nun, vav, ayin*), to move. In the Torah we find the story of the punishment meted out to Cain, that he will be נָע וָנָד (*na va-nad*), a wanderer. And in the twentieth century we find an end to wandering in the Zionist Movement, הַתְּנוּעָה הַצִּיּוֹנִית (*ha-tenu'ah ha-tsiyonit*).

The Hebrew language is like that. Often, the same root will provide both the plague and the cure. The book of Numbers tells us, וַיְנִעֵם בַּמִּדְבָּר אַרְבָּעִים שָׁנָה (*va-yeni'em ba-midbar arba'im shanah*), God caused the Israelites to wander in the desert for forty years. But, when the time came to give the Israelites the code by which all of Israel was to live, we are told in the book of Exodus, וַיַּרְא הָעָם וַיָּנֻעוּ (*va-yar ha-am va-yanu'u*), "The Israelites saw [the revelation at Mount Sinai] and they trembled."

The root has a prominent place in the story of the birth of the prophet Samuel. There, we are told, a barren Hannah goes up to Shiloh to pray for the birth of a child. But because רַק שְׂפָתֶיהָ נָעוֹת (*rak sefateha na'ot*), only her lips move, and not a sound is heard, the priest Eli thinks he is dealing with a drunkard.

Prayer and singing go together with our root in the rabbinic period, when we note two similarly constructed expressions, לְנַעֲנֵעַ בָּרֹאשׁ (*le-na'ane'ah ba-rosh*), to bow the head, and לְנַעֲנֵעַ בְּקוֹל (*le-na'ane'ah ba-kol*), to sing in a tremulous voice.

Grammatically, one can't speak about the Hebrew language without using our root. One of Hebrew's most useful contributions

113

to the International Phonetic Alphabet is the שְׁוָא (sheva), the mute e. The שְׁוָא נָע (sheva na), the mobile schwa, as the linguists call it, indicates that sometimes a "mute e" is not mute at all. Furthermore, the word תְּנוּעָה (tenu'ah) is used in Hebrew grammar to describe both a vowel and a syllable.

It is in modern Israeli Hebrew that our root is given full play. Just think of all the תְּנוּעוֹת נוֹעַר (tenu'ot no'ar), youth movements in Israel, with their branches abroad. The word תְּנוּעָה (tenu'ah) takes on a whole new meaning, associated with the development of Israel's cities into modern megalopolises. More and more often one hears on the radio the expression יֵשׁ הַרְבֵּה תְּנוּעָה בָּרְחוֹב הַיּוֹם (yesh harbeh tenu'ah ba-rehov ha-yom), "There is a great deal of traffic on the streets today." While some will blame this on the absence of שׁוֹטְרֵי תְּנוּעָה (shotrei tenu'ah), traffic cops, others will merely attribute the problem to the invention of the מָנוֹעַ (mano'a), motor, itself. Our מֵנִיעַ (menia), motive, in writing all this is to demonstrate how the vocabulary of Modern Hebrew is built.

For example, the makers of the language used our root in tandem with other words to name modern appliances that move. If אוֹפַן (ofan) is the classical Hebrew word for wheel, then אוֹפַנּוֹעַ (ofano'a) is a good modern word for motorcycle. When sound was added to the old silent movies, Hebraists took their linguistic invention רְאִינוֹעַ (re'ino'a), moving picture, and transformed it into קוֹלְנוֹעַ (kolno'a), moving sound. Today, קוֹלְנוֹעַ is the generic term for movies. When escalators were introduced, so was the word דְּרַגְנוֹעַ (deragno'a), itself soon replaced in common speech by מַדְרֵגוֹת נָעוֹת (madregot na'ot), moving stairs.

Now we know why they called us wandering Jews. Our vocabulary won't let us stay still.

LEANING ON MEANING

How do we know that Judaism is also a Humanism? From its attitude to human justice. The same expression in Exodus—אַחֲרֵי רַבִּים לְהַטֹּת (*aharei rabim le-hattot*), literally, to incline after the many—instructs us not to pervert justice by following the crowd; but it also teaches that, to have a society without chaos, the principle of "majority rules" must prevail.

Legal scholars use the root from which *le-hattot* derives, נ-ט-ה (*nun, tet, heh*), to bend, to lean, to stretch, in many different נְטִיּוֹת (*netiyyot*), grammatical conjugations. One legal expression, נָטָה אֶת הַדִּין (*natah et ha-din*), means he perverted justice; another, בֵּית דִּין נוֹטֶה (*bet din noteh*), designates a court with an odd number of judges, to assure that a verdict be rendered.

The root is found most famously in Scripture in God's promise to the Israelites to redeem them from Egypt בִּזְרוֹעַ נְטוּיָה (*bi-zero'a netuyah*), with an outstretched arm, i.e., with a great show of strength. The root is found more lyrically in Psalms where God is described as one who נוֹטֶה שָׁמַיִם כַּיְרִיעָה (*noteh shamayim ka-yeri'ah*), hangs up the heavens like a curtain. And who among our forefathers did not נָטָה אוֹהֶל (*natah ohel*), pitch a tent?

Nobel Prize-winning Hebrew novelist Shmuel Yosef Agnon borrows a phrase from Jeremiah, אוֹרֵחַ נָטָה לָלוּן (*ore'ah natah lalun*), for the title of his novel, *A Guest for the Night*. There our root is used because the weary traveler has deviated from his path to search out sleeping accommodations. Interestingly, the מִטָּה (*mittah*), bed, that the weary traveler will sleep on also comes from our root. That's because he will incline himself לְמַטָּה (le-matta), downward, to lay himself down to sleep.

There are several expressions using our root that have to do with other kinds of inclinations. "Don't ask, don't tell" means one should refrain from asking for a person's נְטִיָּה מִינִית (netiyyah minit), sexual orientation. The little girl with perfect pitch has a נְטִיָּה (netiyyah), inclination, toward music. Some people who can never lose weight נוֹטִים לְהַשְׁמָנָה (notim le-hashmanah), have a tendency to corpulence. Many architects will tell you that the tower in Pisa is נָטוּי עַל צִדּוֹ (natui al tsiddo), not only leaning but in position to fall. A person in old age is described picturesquely as being in his יְמֵי הַנְּטִיָּה (yemei ha-netiyyah), literallly, leaning days. Someone on his deathbed is נוֹטֶה לָמוּת (noteh la-mut), on the steep slope to decease.

And then there are those אוֹתִיּוֹת נְטוּיוֹת (otiot netuyot), slanting letters of italics you'll find here whenever a Hebrew word is transliterated into English. Some people נוֹטִים לְהַאֲמִין (notim le-ha'amin), are inclined to believe, that they add a certain human face to the otherworldly typeface of Hebrew.

NO TERGIVERSATING

W e've all had the experience at least once. The lecturer, after a forty minute speech, finally gets to the words "In conclusion, . . ." and then proceeds to speak for another thirty minutes.

In English, this failure to conclude is called, colorfully, ter-giversation (literally, turning one's back on). Hebrew has such straightforward terms for coming to a conclusion—among them, לְהַחְלִיט (le-hahalit), לְסַכֵּם (le-sakkem), לְסַיֵּם (le-sayyem) and, the most straightforward of them all, לְהַסִּיק מַסְקָנָה (le-hassik maskanah)—that no one speaking Hebrew would even think of tergiversating.

And that would be the end of it. And we ourselves could say, "In conlusion, . . ." and be on our way. Except that the root of מַסְקָנָה (maskanah), conclusion, is נ-ס-ק (nun, samekh, kof), meaning to rise, to go aloft. How does one rise to a conclusion? The answer lies, perhaps, in the imagination of those who love to ponder the roots, sources and derivations of Hebrew words and in basic theories of language.

Several scholars see a correlation between our root and one having Aramaaic and Arabic overtones ס-ל-ק (samekh, lamed kof), also meaning to go up. When the Talmud wants to to say "You might assume erroneously," it uses the Aramaic expression סָלְקָא דַּעְתָּךְ אָמִינָא (salka da'takh amina), literally, "it arises in your mind to say." In modern Hebrew, the root is used in less lofty contexts. When you pick something up, you remove it from its place. That's how we get to the slang expression הִסְתַּלֵּק מִפֹּה (histallek mi-poh), "get out of here." In the movies we might hear how a mobster סִלֵּק (sillek), got rid of, i.e., killed, a member of a rival gang. The word סְלִיק (selik) has nothing to do with a gangster's nickname. That word was used by the Hagannah for a place, removed form public view, to hide weapons.

The word appears in its primary meaning in Scripture in the Psalmist's vision of God's ubiquitousness. "Wherever I go, you are there," says the poet; even אִם אֶסַּק שָׁמַיִם (im essak shamayim), "if I ascend to heaven" (Psalms 139:8), there you are. Then there is the down-to-earth term that all Jerusalem dwellers in winter constantly have on their tongues, הַסָּקָה (hassakah), heating. When you light a fire, you cause the flame to go up. Metaphorically, one can then raise an idea, and logically thereafter, one מַסִּיק מַסְקָנָה (massik maskanah), rises to a rising, that is, a conclusion.

If the foregoing explanation—however מַסְקָנִי (maskani), as they used to say for logical, it may be—does not satisfy, then there is also the resource of creating a mind-picture with words. Take, for example, מַסָּק (massak), escalator, נְסִיקָה (nesikah), climbing, and נָסֵק (nassek), sharp (the musical notation which raises by a half-tone the pitch of a note). Think as well of מָסוֹק (massok), helicopter. As the helicopter rises and hovers above the earth, the observer inside is able to see all sides of a situation, all issues of a problem, and is able clearly to judge what is going on. It is only from these heights that one can come to a true conclusion.

With or without tergiversation.

VIRTUAL PATIENCE, AND OTHER WEIGHTY MATTERS

Patience is a virtue, they say. To judge by its virtual disappearance from modern life, one might say that patience is not only a virtue but a rare commodity. In Hebrew, the patience we all seem to lack is סַבְלָנוּת (*savlanut*), derived from סַבְלָן (*savlan*), long-suffering and סֵבֶל (*sevel*), both burden and pain.

The root ס-ב-ל (*samekh, bet, lamed*), to carry a heavy weight, is abundantly present in Jewish lore and life and brings us quite naturally to the story of the Exodus. In that story our root means one thing to Moses and two other things to Pharaoh. Moses decides to act when he sees his brethren בְּסִבְלֹתָם (*be-sivlotam*), in their suffering. Called on the carpet by Pharaoh, Aaron and Moses are told לְכוּ לְסִבְלֹתֵיכֶם (*lekhu le-sivloteikhem*), "mind your own business," and don't deter the Israelites מִסִּבְלֹתָם (*mi-sivlotam*), from what Pharaoh considers merely "their duties."

For the Rabbis, the Jews are מְסֻבָּלִים בְּמִצְווֹת (*mesubalim be-mitsvot*), laden with good deeds. The Talmud, the Siddur, and novelist S.Y. Agnon tell us that when a woman is betrothed she receives סִבְלוֹנוֹת (*sivlonot*), "weighty" presents. When a man observes a woman in childbirth, he is often amazed at her כֹּחַ סֵבֶל (*ko'ah sevel*), ability to endure pain.

In modern Israel, a person who carries heavy loads on his back is a סַבָּל (*sabbal*), porter, but you might also put the same word, סַבָּל (*sabbal*), on the back of your bicycle, so that you can carry your groceries home as you pedal. Let's face it, however, some things are—in the סָבִיל (*savil*), passive—בִּלְתִּי נִסְבָּלִים (*bilti-nisbalim*), intolerable, and when you really hate something you might catch yourself saying אֲנִי לֹא סוֹבֵל אֶת זֶה (*ani lo sovel et zeh*), "I can't stand such and such."

There is also סֹבֶלֶת (*sevolet*), the ability of a weight lifter, for example, to tolerete, endure a heavy burden. And then there is סוֹבְלָנוּת (*sovlanut*), tolerance, that other precious commodity that seems to have disappeared from our civil life. It's something a free people needs and a sovereign state can't do without. But we'll get there.

That's what סַבְלָנוּת (*savlanut*) is for.

I'M THINKING . . .

W hat's more important, the decision or the argument? In Jewish life, it all depends on whether one is—using the Aramaic spelling of the terms for the moment—a גְּמָרָא (*gemara*) or a סְבָרָא (*sevara*) person. The *gemara* person derives the law from a verse or a tradition; the *sevara* person—from a word using the Hebrew root ס-ב-ר (*samekh, bet, resh*), to think, to hold an opinion—derives the law from logical speculation.

There was a school of Rabbis for whom סְבָרָא (*sevara*), argumentation, was central. Following the Tanna'im of the Mishnah and the Amora'im of the Gemara, there existed a class of Rabbis called סָבוֹרָאִים (*savora'im*), who were adept at reasoning.

Our root, with its Aramaic tinge, exists almost not at all in Scripture. In a prophecy in the book of Daniel it is used to describe a king who will plot—יְסְבַּר (*yisbar*)—to change the laws and calendar of Judaism.

Let us try to explain it in simple terms, לְסַבֵּר אֶת הָאֹזֶן (*le-sabber et ha-ozen*), literally, to make it sound good. An early meaning of our root—in the verb סָבַר (*savar*), to brighten—can be found in the rabbinic dictum in Pirkei Avot that enjoins us to greet each other cordially, בְּסֵבֶר פָּנִים יָפוֹת (*be-sever panim yafot*), literally, "with the beauty of a shining countenance," in modern Hebrew לְהַסְבִּיר פָּנִים (*le-hasbir panim*), to greet cordially.

When a light shines brightly, it has a tendency to clarify what it is illuminating. That is the sense of another series of words derived from our root: לְהַסְבִּיר (*le-hasbir*), to interpret, הֶסְבֵּר (*hesber*), explanation, and the Zionist activity called הַסְבָּרָה (*hasbarah*), a presentation of the case for a Jewish State. Does that not have סְבִירוּת גְבוֹהָה (*sevirut gevohah*), a high degree of plausibility?

Two Aramaic words that introduce the Friday night Kiddush over the wine, סָבְרֵי מָרָנָן (*savrei maranan*) have a colorful history. This expression—meaning, "Have the gentlemen formed an opinion?"—was first used in legal circles as a polite way of asking the rabbis involved in a religious debate, "How do you vote?" In the Kiddush, סָבְרֵי מָרָנָן (*savrei maranan*) means, "Have those at the table agreed to allow me to say the blessing in their name?" That is one reason that, among the Sefardim (and in the Lowin household), those present answer לְחַיִּים (*le-hayyim*), which, in this context, means "Sure, go ahead, and may the wine we drink be for a happy occasion."

An Aramaic expression that has crept into everyday conversation has to do with entering a dissenting opinion, אִפְּכָא מִסְתַּבְּרָא (*ipkha mistabra*), "The opposite is likely to be true." In the store, a polite expression uses two forms of our root in one sentence, סָבוּר לִי שֶׁהַמְחִיר סָבִיר (*savur li she-ha-mehir savir*), I think the price is reasonable.

So, what's more important, גְמָרָא (*gemara*), the decision, or סְבָרָא (*sevara*), the argument? It's something that a severe person, one who is חָמוּר סֶבֶר (*hamur sever*), might contemplate with utter seriousness. One thing מִסְתַּבֵּר (*mistabber*), seems reasonable. Combining tradition with reasoning leads to the most interesting of conclusions.

(PARENTHETICAL REMARK)

Consider Hebrew poet Yehudah Amichai. The title of his last book of poetry, פָּתוּחַ סָגוּר פָּתוּחַ (*patu'ah sagur patu'ah*), *Open Closed Open*, suggests that opening and closing is not so open and shut.

In Scripture, the root ס-ג-ר (*samekh, gimmel, resh*), to close, is found in several dramatic stories. When Lot goes outside to protect his guests from his neighbors in Sodom, the text adds וְהַדֶּלֶת סָגַר אַחֲרָיו (*ve-ha-delet sagar aharav*), he makes sure to close the door behind him. After Moses's sister is cured of her skin disease, the text asserts וַתִּסָּגֵר מִרְיָם (*va-tissager miriam*), Miriam is sent out of the camp for a seven-day quarantine. (From here to the modern term applied to the "territories," סֶגֶר (*seger*), closure, is but a short distance.) Hannah prays for a child because, we are told, God סָגַר רַחְמָהּ (*sagar rahmah*), "closed her womb." (Let us add בְּסוֹגְרַיִם [*be-sograyim*], parenthetically, that Hannah's child will become the prophet Samuel.)

The root reveals a good deal about daily life in Israel. How do you add an extra room to your apartment? Most economically, אַתָּה סוֹגֵר מִרְפֶּסֶת (*atah soger mirpesset*), you enclose your porch. In Israel, חֲנוּיּוֹת סְגוּרוֹת (*hanuyyot segurot*) and מִשְׂרָדִים סְגוּרִים (*misradim segurim*), stores and offices are closed, on Shabbat, נְעוּלִים בְּסוֹגֵר וּבְרִיחַ (*ne'ulim be-soger u-veriah*), bolted shut.

An אָדָם סָגוּר וּמְסֻגָּר (*adam sagur u-mesuggar*) is an introverted person. One can only hope that one day soon יִפְתַּח סְגוֹר לִבּוֹ (*yiftah segor libbo*), he will open his closed-up heart.

The word מִסְגֶּרֶת (*misgeret*) is used not only for picture frames but also for frameworks. We know for example that in the 1940s Youth Aliyah הִרְחִיבָה אֶת מִסְגַּרְתָּהּ (*hirhivah et misgartah*), broadened its scope, to include children born in Palestine.

Sometimes the root takes unlikely leaps of meaning. Extradition is called הַסְגָּרָה (*hasgarah*), presumably so that the culprit can be locked up after he is given over. The expression זָהָב סָגוּר (*zahav sagur*) is used by jewelers for pure gold, ostensibly because impurities are locked out. While the word מַסְגֵּר (*masger*) is logically reserved for locksmiths, in rabbinic texts it sometimes means scholar. How so? Well, scholars do have a lock on knowledge. And then there is יוֹם סַגְרִיר (*yom sagrir*), a cold, persistently rainy day. How does that come from our root? According to medieval scholars David Kimhi and Jonah Ibn Jannah, on such a day one is likely to stay comfortably enclosed at home. And they didn't come to that decision בִּדְלָתַיִם סְגוּרוֹת (*be-delatayim segurot*), behind closed doors.

When the editor of a periodical calls to warn of the approaching סְגִירַת הַגִּלָּיוֹן (*segirat ha-gillayon*), press time, she is likely to suggest, אוּלַי תִּסְגֹּר עִנְיָן כְּבָר? (*ulai tisgor inyan kevar?*), Maybe you'll wrap up already?

Since Yehudah Amichai's title hints that all openings are closings too, we can confidently assert, in closing, that סָגַרְנוּ מַעֲגָל (*sagarnu ma'agal*), we've closed a circle, and now we can say הַנּוֹשֵׂא סָגוּר (*ha-noseh sagur*), "The issue is closed."

PAVING A ROAD TO PEACE

The road to peace is paved, not so much with good intentions, but with good values. That is a lesson learned from an examination of the Hebrew root ס-ל-ל (*samekh, lamed, lamed*), to pave.

You can find this lesson in the name of Israel's premier construction company, סוֹלֵל בּוֹנֶה (*solel boneh*), which paves the roads and builds the buildings of the modern Jewish state; in New York's UJA-Federation's "venture philanthropy" program, because their סוֹלְלִים (*solelim*) pave the way to new areas of Jewish giving; in the title of Moses Chaim Luzzatto's work of Jewish ethics, מְסִלַּת יְשָׁרִים (*mesillat yesharim*), *The Path of the Just,* and of Aharon Appelfeld's novel, מְסִלַּת הַבַּרְזֶל (*mesillat ha-barzel*), *The Railway.* In Scripture, the root is found in Isaiah's call (62:10), סֹלּוּ סֹלּוּ הַמְסִלָּה (*solu solu ha-mesillah*), "Clear a road," in which the root is used for removing obstacles on the road to God.

The Radak, Rabbi David Kimhi, speculates that "raising up" is at the heart of our root. It is thus connected to the word סֻלָּם (*sullam*), both סֻלָּם יַעֲקֹב (*sullam ya'akov*), Jacob's ladder, and סֻלָּם הַרמוֹנִי (*sullam harmoni*), musical scale. For Ahad Ha-Am, the Hebrew language is number one in the סֻלָּם הָעֲרָכִין (*sullam ha-arakhin*), the Zionist scale of values. To modern Israelis, the pound sign on the telephone looks like a ladder, so they call it a סֻלָּמִית (*sullamit*). Some speculate that the enigmatic biblical word סֶלָה (*selah*) is derived from our root because, when it appears in the chanted biblical text, the singer's voice, they say, rises.

It takes more imagination than you'll find here to jump from paved roads to סוֹלְלוֹת (*solelot*), batteries, but Hebrew makes that leap without pause. The word סוֹלְלָה (*solelah*), means "an abundance," even of human beings, for example סוֹלְלַת עוֹרְכֵי דִין (*solelat orkhei din*), a gaggle of lawyers. Batteries are made out of an abundance of סְלִילִים (*selilim*), coils, a word also applied to spools of thread, reels of film, and intrauterine devices. The adjective סְלִילִי (*selili*), spiral, helps us understand how our root is used in הַסְּלִיל הַכָּפוּל (*ha-selil ha-kaful*), the double helix coiled around itself in DNA.

One of the richest derivations of our root is the word מַסְלוּל (*maslul*), path, used in Hebrew camping for an obstacle course. It's always good, after an exotic vacation, לַחֲזוֹר לַמַּסְלוּל (*la-hazor la-maslul*), to return to normal life. The "fastest" route from Tel Aviv to Jerusalem is a כְּבִישׁ שֶׁל שְׁלוֹשָׁה מַסְלוּלִים (*kevish shel sheloshah maslulim*), three-lane highway. Some frustrated drivers think it still takes longer than a מַסְלוּל הַקָּפָה (*maslul hakkafah*), orbit of a star. Travelers to Israel often applaud when their flight reaches the מַסְלוּל נְחִיתָה (*maslul nehitah*), landing runway, of Ben-Gurion Airport. They know that the road to Israel, like the road to peace, is paved with good intentions, good values—and good pilots.

TRUST THYSELF

Sometimes, the slightest difference in nuance between similar expressions can point to a huge difference in worldview. Take the example of "Trust me," as compared with the Hebrew סְמוֹךְ עָלַי (*semokh alai*), "Rely on me." The first expression requires looking into one's character. Words that stem from the Hebrew root ס-מ-ך (*samekh, mem, kaf*) imply looking into someone's training.

Originally, the verb סָמַךְ (*samakh*) meant to lean, as in the verse in Amos, וְסָמַךְ יָדוֹ עַל הַקִּיר (*ve-samakh yado al ha-kir*), "He leaned his hand on the wall." That's also where we get the name for the fifteenth letter of the Hebrew alphabet, סָמֶךְ (*samekh*), which leans to the side, as in the action of a סֶמֶךְ (*semekh*), fulcrum. Eliezer Ben Yehudah is given credit for coining the word מִסְמָךְ (*mismakh*), a document in support of one's case. Today, one finds the root frequently in the adjective סָמוּךְ (*samukh*), close, nearby.

Twenty-five times in the Tanakh, our word is found in expressions denoting a ceremonious "laying on of the hands," for instance, וְסָמַךְ יָדוֹ עַל רֹאשׁ קָרְבָּנוֹ (*ve-samakh yado al rosh korbano*), "He placed his hand on the head of an animal to be sacrificed," thereby signaling ownership. When one "lays hands" on the head of a person, that action demonstrates a transfer of authority, as in סְמִיכָה (*semikhah*), rabbinic ordination, and in the words for a graduate of a rabbinical seminary or a university, a מוּסְמָךְ (*musmakh*), and for the הַסְמָכָה (*hasmakhah*), ordination. This usage implies sufficient training to have סַמְכוּת (*samkhut*), authority, or that the person is, in Aramaic, a בַּר סַמְכָא (*bar samkha*), an authority. Often, in pre-war days, a rabbinical student was סָמוּךְ עַל

שֻׁלְחָן (*samukh al shulhan*), taking his meals at a rich person's table, and, therefore, dependent on him.

Legal debates in the Talmud permit one to bring an אַסְמַכְתָּא (*asmakhta*), support for one's argument, by quoting a verse in the Torah that is not actually a source of the law in question. In other scholarly debates, one must also bring proofs and cite references, called in (mishnaic-style) Hebrew סְמוּכִין (*simmukhin*).

One of the most important keys to understanding the Hebrew language that stems from our root is the grammatical term סְמִיכוּת (*semikhut*), the construct state. By stringing together a series of nouns, one סָמוּךְ (*samukh*), near, to the other, one comes up with various expressions, from the two-noun מְדִינַת הַיְהוּדִים (*medinat ha-yehudim*), the Jews' State, (*der Judenstaat*, as Herzl had it) to the five-noun תּוֹרַת נֶגַע צָרַעַת בֶּגֶד הַצֶּמֶר (*torat nega tsora'at beged ha-tsemer*), the biblical "laws of leprosy in a wool garment."

While one may want to rely on an authority for one's sense of the Hebrew language, the אַסְמַכְתָּא (*asmakhta*), proof text, for actively building the Jews' State is the rabbinic dictum in Tractate Pesahim, אֵין סוֹמְכִין עַל הַנֵּס (*ein somkhin al ha-nes*), one must not rely on miracles. Sometimes, the best course is, after all, to trust oneself.

WORKERS OF
THE WORLD, UNTIE

Passover celebrates not only the "pass over" of the Angel of Death; it also celebrates the passage of the Israelites from עַבְדוּת (*avdut*), slavery, to freedom.

The Hebrew word for slavery comes from a root, ד-ב-ע (*ayin, bet, dalet*), originally meaning "to do." This root gives us the word עוּבְדָּה (*uvdah*), something that was done, a *fait accompli*, a fact.

In the Tanakh, where the root appears almost two thousand times, its verb form quickly took on two separate meanings: to work and to worship. Thus, Adam is put into the Garden of Eden and subsequently driven from it, לַעֲבוֹד אֶת הָאֲדָמָה (*la'avod et ha-adamah*), to work the land. In the Ten Commandments we are told that a six-day work week is a mitzvah: "Six days תַעֲבוֹד (*ta'avod*), shall you work."

Using the second meaning of the root, we are told לְעָבְדוֹ בְּכָל לְבַבְכֶם (*le-ovdo be-khol levavkhem*), "To worship Him with all your hearts." In Psalms we are enjoined to do so joyfully, עִבְדוּ אֶת ה' בְּשִׂמְחָה (*ivdu et ha-shem be-simhah*), "Worship God with joy." What should be avoided at all costs is עֲבוֹדַת אֱלִילִים (*avodat elilim*), idol worship, or עֲבוֹדָה זָרָה (*avodah zarah*), paganism.

Some eight hundred times in the Tanakh, we find our root as a form of the word עֶבֶד (*eved*), slave. Modern Israeli argot gives us עֶבֶד נִרְצָע (*eved nirtsa*), a person hopelessly enslaved to his appetites. This term was applied to an Israelite slave who chose lifetime servitude by having his ear screwed to a doorpost with a

מַרְצֵעַ (martse'a), awl. The Tanakh also speaks of Isaac's עֲבֻדָּה רַבָּה (avuddah rabbah), great household, (Genesis 26:14) when he had acquired riches. At the Passover Seder we remind ourselves עֲבָדִים הָיִינוּ (avadim hayinu), we were once slaves. The book of Proverbs also warns against עֶבֶד כִּי יִמְלוֹךְ (eved ki yimlokh), a slave who becomes a king.

In modern times, a scientist who goes into her מַעְבָּדָה (ma'badah), laboratory, to prove a theory, may end up accepting an unanticipated result בְּדִיעֲבַד (be-di'avad), after the fact. A scriptwriter is often called upon לְעַבֵּד (le-abbed), to adapt, a novel into a film. Once the music is written, the מְעַבֵּד (me'abbed), arranger, arranges it for performance. At home you would use your מְעַבֵּד מָזוֹן (me'abbed mazon), food processor, to lighten your burden. Because there are often conflicts between the מַעֲבִיד (ma'avid), employer, and the עוֹבֵד (oved), employee, about שְׁעוֹת עֲבוֹדָה (she'ot avodah), office hours, or עֲבוֹדָה שְׁחוֹרָה (avodah shehorah), scut work, one sometimes needs a הִסְתַּדְרוּת עוֹבְדִים (histadrut ovdim), labor union, or an עוֹבֵד סוֹצְיָאלִי (oved sotsiali), social worker, to resolve the problem. This is especially necessary where one person is convinced that the other עָבַד עָלַי (avad alai), "put something over on me."

In Modern Hebrew, the word עֲבוֹדָה (avodah) has taken on many new meanings, such as "work of art" or "written assignment." And let's not forget the דַּת הָעֲבוֹדָה (dat ha-avodah), religion of work, promulgated by Zionist thinker A.D. Gordon and the ideology that called for עֲבוֹדָה עִבְרִית (avoda ivrit), Jews working the land.

Let us also not forget the saying in Ecclesiastes that, however arduous the work, מְתוּקָה שְׁנַת הָעוֹבֵד (metukah shenat ha-oved), "The sleep of the worker is sweet indeed."

ALL WORK AND NO WORD PLAY?

Work is drudgery, we know. And yet, if we look hard at words derived from the Hebrew root ע-מ-ל (*ayin, mem, lamed*), to toil, we learn that work leads to some pretty good things.

The original sense appears frequently in the Bible. Why did God liberate the Hebrews from Egypt? Because, according to Deuteronomy, he saw עֲמָלֵנוּ (*amalenu*), our misery, as slaves. Not surprisingly, the root is a staple in Wisdom Literature. Job tells us that misery is man's lot, כִּי אָדָם לְעָמָל יוּלָד (*ki adam le-amal yullad*), "for man is born to misery." The Preacher in the book of Kohelet asks despairingly, "What profit has mankind בְּכָל עֲמָלוֹ שֶׁיַּעֲמוֹל (*be-khol amalo she-ya'amol*), for all the labor he does under the sun?" And yet, both the Rashbam and Robert Gordis suggest that at times in Kohelet our root means also the fruit of labor, wealth.

In Modern Hebrew our root gives us הִתְעַמְּלוּת (*hitamlut*), calisthenics, turning work into healthful exercise. That meaning is found in an interesting story in rabbinic literature. It seems that Hillel the Elder once bought a horse for a formerly wealthy man who, we are told ambiguously, הָיָה מִתְעַמֵּל בּוֹ (*hayah mitamel bo*). Did Hillel give the poor man a horse so that he might earn his living through work, as one might expect? Or was the unfortunate man rather, as the story's context hints, to resume horseback riding, as he once did, for pure exercise?

On Erev Shabbat, in preparation for baking hallah, one might use our root לְעַמֵּל (le-ammel), to knead, the dough. Whether or not this is a drudgery, a Shabbat table hymn tells us לְעַמֵל קִרְאוּ דְרוֹר (le-ammel kir'u deror), on Shabbat we are to proclaim liberty from toil. When early Zionist pioneers despaired of seeing the fruits of their labor, Chaim Nachman Bialik wrote a resoundingly supportive poem reminding them, עֲמַלְכֶם לֹא לַשָּׁוְא (amalkhem lo la-shav), "Your labor is not in vain." People with much life experience will tell you that those things are most worth having that are acquired בְּעָמָל רַב (be-amal rav), with a great deal of work.

In the politically incorrect sixties, the root was used in a catchy slogan, יוֹתֵר חַשְׁמַל, פָּחוֹת עָמָל (yoter hashmal, pahot amal), "More electricity, less work." Today, it's found at the bank, where דְמֵי עֲמָלָה (demei amalah), a commission fee, is tacked on to your trans-action; in the import/export business, when one hires what is called technically an עָמִיל מֶכֶס (amil mekhes), customs agent; in politics, where תַּעֲמוּלָה (ta'amulah), propaganda, is used to get a message across; and in the manufacture of honey, where an עֲמֵלָה (amelah), worker bee, bears the brunt of the process.

And what about learning Hebrew? Is it not a form of עַמְלָנוּת (amlanut), education through practical work? It all depends on how hard you look at our root.

THE PROPHECY OF LANGUAGE

Who was the true prophet of the Jewish State? Theodor Herzl? David Ben-Gurion? Did you realize that we would not have a ‏יוֹם הָעַצְמָאוּת‏ (*yom ha-atsma'ut*), Israel Independence Day, at all, without Itamar Ben-Avi* (d. 1943)? Years before the 1948 declaration of independence, he coined the word ‏עַצְמָאוּת‏ (*atsma'ut*) in the phrase, ‏הָעַצְמָאוּת הָעִבְרִית בְּכֹל תִּפְאַרְתָּהּ‏ (*ha-atsma'ut ha-ivrit be-khol tifartah*), "Hebrew independence in all its glory."

Ben-Avi derived his coinage from the Hebrew root ‏עַ-צַ-מ‏ (*ayin, tsadi, mem*), which gives us the noun ‏עֶצֶם‏ (*etsem*), bone, and the verb ‏עָצַם‏ (*atsam*), to be strong and numerous. (The verb also means "to close," as in "to close one's eyes," but that comes from a different root altogether.)

Was he thinking of another meaning, as in ‏עֶצֶם הָעִנְיָן‏ (*etsem ha-inyan*), the core of the matter, subtly intuiting that national independence is essential to Judaism? Certainly, he did not foresee that the income tax people in Israel would be interested in knowing whether you were a salaried worker or ‏עַצְמָאִי‏ (*atsma'i*), self-employed. It could be that ‏בְּעֶצֶם‏ (*be-etsem*), as a matter of fact, Ben-Avi was thinking of ‏הָעֲצָמוֹת הַיְבֵשׁוֹת‏ (*ha-atsamot ha-yeveshot*),

---

*Itamar Ben-Avi. The journalist son of Hebrew prophet Eliezer Ben Yehudah also coined (and punned) his own last name. Taking the Hebrew word for my father, ‏אָבִי‏ (*avi*), he added a "double chupchik" to form ‏אָבִ"י‏, the initials of ‏אֱלִיעֶזֶר בֶּן יְהוּדָה‏.

the dry bones prophecy of Ezekiel in which the Jewish people is reborn.

Elsewhere in Scripture, when Laban wants to reassure Jacob of his good will, he reminds him that they are kin, saying, "You are עַצְמִי (atsmi), my bone." We know that the Israelites flourished in Egypt from the verse that tells us וַיַּעַצְמוּ (va-ya'atsmu), they grew greatly in number. Speaking of numbers, when you have enough signatures, that is the time לְהַגִּישׁ עֲצוּמָה (le-haggish atsumah), to submit a petition.

A prominent passage in the Haggadah uses our root to assert that, not an emissary, but God himself, בִּכְבוֹדוֹ וּבְעַצְמוֹ (bikhvodo u-ve-atsmo), in person, redeemed his people from Egypt. The Talmud takes a psychological turn when it reminds us that people do not ordinarily point out their own deficiencies, because, אָדָם קָרוֹב אֵצֶל עַצְמוֹ (adam karov etsel atsmo), "man is close to himself."

In Israel today stores encourage their customers to use שֵׁרוּת עַצְמִי (sherut atsmi), self-service. In America, Project Otzma takes its name from a Hebrew word for strength, עָצְמָה (otsmah), a meaning which also gives us מַעֲצָמָה (ma'atsamah), Great Power.

A language lover, coming upon a newly-coined שֵׁם עֶצֶם (shem etsem), noun, is likely to shout, עָצוּם! (atsum!), "Terrific!" an interjection that is as appropriate for Ben-Avi's innovation as it is for יוֹם הָעַצְמָאוּת (yom ha-atsma'ut) itself.

ROOT, ROOT, ROOT
FOR THE MAIN THING

In Hebrew—as almost anyone familiar with the language will tell you—it all begins with the root. But what happens when the word for "root" is not שֹׁרֶשׁ (*shoresh*), but comes from ע-ק-ר (*ayin, kof, resh*)?

One of the things that happen is semantic pyrotechnics, an explosion of words expressing at one and the same time: barrenness and a balabusta, a scholar and the Yigdal prayer, the P.S. at the end of a letter and the denial of the existence of God, pulling a tooth and moving to a new apartment.

How all these meanings come together is a fascinating tale. The main noun derived from our root is עִקָּר (*ikkar*), the main thing, the essence. And the thing is to distinguish בֵּין עִקָּר לְתָפֵל (*bein ikkar le-tafel*), the essential from the unimportant.

Pirkei Avot tells us that לֹא הַמִּדְרָשׁ הָעִקָּר (*lo ha-midrash ha-ikkar*), study is not the main thing, but rather action. Maimonides, seeking to express the essence of Judaism, comes up with Thirteen Principles of Faith, י"ג עִקָּרִים (*yod gimmel ikkarim*), transposed poetically into the Yigdal prayer. A person who is כּוֹפֵר בָּעִקָּר (*kofer ba-ikkar*) denies the existence of God.

As a verb, our root means to uproot. Kohelet teaches us that there is a time to plant and a time לַעֲקוֹר נָטוּעַ (*la-akor natu'a*)—an expression used by Naomi Shemer in her song עַל כָּל אֵלֶּה (*al kol eleh*)—to pull up what has been planted. The Haggadah asserts that Laban wanted לַעֲקוֹר אֶת הַכֹּל (*la-akor et ha-kol*), to destroy Jewish civilization at its root. A person who pulls up roots and moves to a new apartment עוֹקֵר דִּירָה (oker dirah). That Jewish scholarship is labor intensive comes across when you call a scholar an עוֹקֵר הָרִים (oker harim), a "mover" of intellectual mountains. A dentist עוֹקֵר שֵׁן (oker shen), pulls a tooth out by its roots.

Our root appears in the Bible as a noun for a person who cannot have children, עָקָר (akar) or עֲקָרָה (akarah). The Midrash, trying to tie this word to our root, asserts that Rachel, even when infertile, was the עִקָּר (ikkar), essence, of Jacob's household. Others theorize that barrenness has to do with biological "uprooting" in the reproductive system. To prevent puppies, one goes to the veterinarian לְעַקֵּר (le-akker), to sterilize, the female dog. And how do we get the Modern Hebrew term עֲקֶרֶת בַּיִת (akeret bayit), female family manager, *balabusta*, from our root? We get there from a popular misreading of Psalm 115:9, where a barren housewife, *akeret ha-bayit*, becomes "a happy mother of children."

An Israeli whose Hebrew grammar leaves a lot to be desired will tell you that even though he has expressed himself incorrectly, הָעִקָּר שֶׁהֵבַנְתָּ אוֹתִי (ha-ikkar she-hevanta oti), The main thing is that you understood me. At the restaurant, the waiter suggests the stuffed chicken as the מָנָה עִקָּרִית (manah ikkarit), main course.

At the end of a Hebrew letter a P.S. is not a mere afterthought, but rather the main thing, or, as they say, עִקָּר שָׁכַחְתִּי (ikkar shakhahti), I forgot the essence. In conversation, בְּעִקָּר (be-ikkar), especially, among Ashkenazim, you'll hear a word with a Yiddish lilt, הָעִיקֶּר (ha-ikker), instead of הָעִיקָּר (ha-ikkar), the main thing. Most Jews of a certain age who can trace their roots to the Yiddish of *Abi Gezunt* will agree that הָעִקָּר הַבְּרִיאוּת (ha-ikkar ha-beri'ut), Health is the main thing.

DOING, DOING, DONE

There are two types of good Jew in this world: הַמְצֻוֶּה וְעוֹשֶׂה (*ha-metsuvveh ve-oseh*), one who is commanded to do a good deed and does it, and מִי שֶׁאֵינוֹ מְצֻוֶּה וְעוֹשֶׂה (*mi she'eino metsuvveh ve-oseh*), a person who is not commanded to do a good deed and does it. Also, as recorded in the Sayings of the Fathers, לֹא הַמִּדְרָשׁ עִקָּר אֶלָּא הַמַּעֲשֶׂה (*lo ha-midrash ikkar elah ha-ma'aseh*), "The chief thing is not learning, but doing." Obviously, what these three phrases have in common is the Hebrew root ע־שׂ־ה (*ayin, sin, heh*).

The verb's most significant use can be found in the book of Exodus where, in response to the giving by Moses of the laws of the Torah, the Israelites answer, נַעֲשֶׂה וְנִשְׁמַע (*na'aseh ve-nishma*), rabbinically, "First we will do, then we will understand." This response emphasizes, at the earliest stages of its peoplehood, the Jewish nation's high regard for action. The verb also appears in the story of the Creation (and subsequently in the Friday night Kiddush), in the line, אֲשֶׁר בָּרָא אֱלוֹקִים לַעֲשׂוֹת (*asher bara elokim la'asot*), literally, "which God created to do." The infinitive לַעֲשׂוֹת (*la'asot*) here has a connotation of human continuity, of both Shabbat and Creation.

Yiddish also uses our root, as in *bubbe mayseh*, a tall tale, and *mayselakh*, little stories. In Modern Hebrew, a מַעֲשִׂיָּה (*ma'asiyyah*), is a tale, and a מַעֲשֶׂה שֶׁהָיָה (*ma'aseh she-hayah*), is a true story. A criminal can be caught תּוֹךְ כְּדֵי מַעֲשֶׂה (*tokh kedei ma'aseh*), *in flagrante delicto*. Don't cry over spilt milk, they say, or אֶת הַנַּעֲשָׂה אֵין לְהָשִׁיב (*et ha-na'asah ein le-hashiv*), What's done is done. In kabbalistic literature, our root is used to denote both the mystery of creation, מַעֲשֵׂה בְּרֵאשִׁית (ma'aseh be-reishit) and the mystery of God's chariot, the prophet Ezekiel's מַעֲשֵׂה מֶרְכָּבָה (ma'aseh merkavah). On a note somewhat more מַעֲשִׂי (ma'asi), practical, the proverbial Woman of Valor is praised not only by her husband and children but also by מַעֲשֶׂיהָ (ma'aseha), her own deeds.

A generous person לֹא עוֹשֶׂה חֶשְׁבּוֹן (lo oseh heshbon), doesn't pay attention to money when he invites a guest to lunch. The modern Israeli six-day work week, playing on the expression for the Six Days of Creation, is called, in popular parlance, שֵׁשֶׁת יְמֵי הַמַּעֲשֶׂה (sheshet yemei ha-ma'aseh). Although Shabbat was created only on the last day, it's primacy is emphasized in the expression סוֹף מַעֲשֶׂה בְּמַחְשָׁבָה תְּחִלָּה (sof ma'aseh be-mahshavah tehillah), at the end of God's deeds but first in His thought. Nowadays, one can be invited לַעֲשׂוֹת שַׁבָּת (la-asot Shabbat), to spend Shabbat, at the home of a friend or relative. One way to ask someone how he earns a living is to say מַה מַעֲשֶׂיךָ? (ma ma'asekha?), literally, what are your doings? In the Old Country, the answer might have been, shnaider (tailor), or shuster (shoemaker). When Israel's economy is booming, everyone is at least—again, using our root—a תַּעֲשִׂיָּן (ta'asiyyan), an industrialist.

In conversation, a woman's best friend might tell her: עֲשִׂי חַיִל (asi hayil), "Be successful," עֲשִׂי לִי טוֹבָה (asi li tovah), "Do me a favor," or עֲשִׂי חַיִּים (asi hayyim), "Enjoy yourself." An אֵשֶׁת מַעֲשֶׂה (eshet ma'aseh), a woman of action, is one who gets things done. For this type of woman, as for all good Jews, the best start for any מַעֲשֶׂה (ma'aseh), deed, is its עֲשִׂיָּה (asiyyah), doing.

138

ADDING INJURY TO INSULT

Not long ago—like Israelis—American Jews were beginning to use, even in English, the word *matsav* to describe the political, economic, and military situation in Israel. To our misfortune, the subsequent Hebrew nonce word—a word seemingly created for this particular occasion—is פִּגּוּעַ (*piggu'a*), applied to an Arab terrorist attack on Jews.

If the word פִּגּוּעַ (*piggu'a*) is relatively new (found only in recently published dictionaries), the thing it describes is not. Nevertheless, the root ע-ג-פ (*peh, gimmel ayin*), to meet, begins life in a much more benign context.

After Jacob takes leave of Laban's home in Haran, we are told, וַיִּפְגְּעוּ בּוֹ מַלְאֲכֵי אֱלוֹקִים (*va-yifge'u bo malakhei elokim*), angels of the Lord came to meet him. Earlier, the story of Jacob's ladder-dream also uses our root, telling us וַיִּפְגַּע בַּמָּקוֹם (*va-yifga ba-makom*), "He arrived at the place," which some translate as "He encountered the Lord in prayer." This sense is echoed in the prophecy of Jeremiah when God tells him אַל תִּפְגַּע בִּי (*al tifga bi*), "Don't pray to me," for this sinning nation.

There are good encounters and evil encounters. To avoid the latter, Jews, in their morning prayers, repeat a phrase formulated by Rabbi Judah the Prince that God should protect them from a פֶּגַע רַע (*pega ra*), an encounter with a harmful spirit. In some religious circles, several verses of Psalm 91, called by the Rabbis the שִׁיר שֶׁל פְּגָעִים (*shir shel pega'im*), the song of evil occurrences, are recited as a charm.

In the talmudic parable of the Four Sages Who Entered the Orchard (by studying esoteric literature), our root takes on a slightly different coloring. One of the four, Ben-Zoma, הֵצִיץ וְנִפְגַּע (hetsits ve-nifga), "looked and went mad." This passive form is found in another rabbinic expression with a completely different sense, אֵין שׁוֹטֶה נִפְגַּע (ein shoteh nifga), "No fool feels insulted."

Today, if someone insults another, it is said that he פָּגַע בִּכְבוֹדוֹ (paga bi-khevodo), literally, harmed his honor, figuratively, insulted him. Amos Oz, in his majestic autobiography, describes Hebrew poet Saul Tchernikhovski's arrival at Oz's grandmother's literary salon. This sensitive man, he says, was פָּגִיעַ כְּמוֹ פַּרְפַּר אַךְ גַּם פּוֹגְעָנִי (pagi'a kemo parpar akh gam pog'ani), as delicate as a butterfly yet also hurtful.

An incident of the hit-and-run variety, literally translated from the English, is called in Hebrew a פְּגַע וּבְרַח (pega u-verakh). When it is not an accident but an attack, the evildoer is called a פַּגְעָן (pag'an), the act is called, as even English-speakers say, a פִּגּוּעַ (piggu'a), and all lovers of peace are פְּגוּעִים (pegu'im), wounded, by it.

'SWONDERFUL

It happened during a concert at the Jerusalem Theatre. Rita, Israel's dynamic pop vocalist, suddenly cries out to a woman sitting in the first row, מַה זֶה, פֶּלֶא-פוֹן? (*ma zeh, pele-fon?*). Rita is laughing because the woman is pointing a cell phone at the stage so that the person on the other end may "attend" the performance without taking the trouble to buy a ticket. That theatrical moment teaches us a great deal about the ease with which Israeli culture reaches back to its classical linguistic roots. The construction פֶּלֶא-פוֹן (*pele-fon*)—a cell-phone brand-name—plays on the fact that the ancient Hebrew word for miracle, פֶּלֶא (*pele*), rhymes with the "tele" of telephone. There was even a children's television program called טֶלֶ-פֶּלֶא (*tele-pele*), an Israeli *Wonderama*.

It is fascinating to follow the curious meanderings of the root פ-ל-א (*peh, lamed, alef*) in Scripture and rabbinic literature. When Sarah laughs at the announcement that at her advanced age she is to bear a child, God asks, הֲיִפָּלֵא מֵה' דָּבָר? (*ha-yipale me-hashem davar?*), "Is anything impossible for God?" When Moses, in his valedictory address, reviews Israel's obligations, he reassures the nation לֹא נִפְלֵאת הִיא מִמְּךָ (*lo niflet hi mimekha*), "[The Torah] contains no secrets beyond your grasp." Despite Moses's disclaimer, the Rabbis expressed awe at all the unexplainable things in the Torah, saying פֶּלֶא הִיא הַתּוֹרָה (*pele hi ha-torah*). And yet they warned us בְּמֻפְלָא מִמְּךָ אַל תִּדְרֹשׁ (*be-mufla mimmekha al tidrosh*), "Do not seek to understand what is beyond your grasp." And what of לְפַלֵּא נֶדֶר (*le-falle neder*), to make a vow? It is a way for ordinary human beings to reach beyond the ordinary. But then, the Rabbis

141

did insist that both גְּאוּלָה (*ge'ulah*), redemption, and פַּרְנָסָה (*par-nasah*), earning a living, have the status of פֶּלֶא (*pele*), miracle.

In modern times, Hebrew writers have used the archaic-sounding נִפְלֵאתִי (*nifleti*), to express "I have always wondered why. . . ." Aharon Appelfeld calls his 1981 novel, תּוֹר הַפְּלָאוֹת (*tor ha-pela'ot*), *The Age of Wonders.* The סִיר פֶּלֶא (*sir pele*), Wonder Pot, you'll find on Israeli stove-tops is a utensil for baking cakes without an oven. And שׁוֹקוֹ-פֶּלֶא (*shoko pele*) is used to market instant chocolate milk powder. When a student does work that the teacher considers נִפְלָא (*nifla*), outstanding, parents may be excused for boasting that their child is succeeding in school לְהַפְלִיא (*le-hafli*), marvelously. But when an Israeli speaks of a יֶלֶד פֶּלֶא (*yeled pele*), boy wonder, it's not always a compliment.

Do you doubt it? Just eavesdrop on a conversation in Hebrew during intermission at the Jerusalem Theater and תִּתְפַּלֵּא (*titpalle*), you'll be surprised at what you hear. Some call it the reborn language of a reborn Jewish nation; others call it something much much more, נִסִּים וְנִפְלָאוֹת (*nissim ve-nifla'ot*), truly a miracle.

GIVE ME A BREAKTHROUGH

Is rhetorical overstatement a particularly Jewish trait? We all have cousins who, having not eaten for two hours, are "dying" of hunger, or who, having nicked a finger, are "bleeding all over." On a different register of hyperbole—ironic or prophetic—Israelis might tell you that in 1948, פָּרְצָה הַמְּדִינָה (*partsah ha-medinah*), the State of Israel "burst" on the scene, or that, in 2008, יִפְרוֹץ הַשָּׁלוֹם (*yifrots ha-shalom*), peace will suddenly "erupt."

The root פ-ר-צ (*peh, resh, tsadi*), with its multiple meanings of breaking through, spreading out and overflowing, lends itself to such hyperbole.

When, in the Tanakh, our forefather Jacob becomes wealthy in Laban's house, we are told, וַיִּפְרֹץ הָאִישׁ מְאֹד מְאֹד (*va-yifrots ha-ish me'od me'od*), "The man increased exceedingly." The Rabbis tell us that even God, speaking of Jacob, used our verb. They quote Him as saying, פָּרַצְתִּי גְדֵרוֹ שֶׁל עוֹלָם מִפְּנֵי יַעֲקֹב (*paratsti gedero shel olam mipnei ya'akov*), "I ruptured the boundary of the world for Jacob's sake," meaning, I reversed the natural order of things so that Jacob's flock would be extremely fertile. And doesn't the angel tell Jacob in his dream, וּפָרַצְתָּ (*u-faratsta*), you and your seed will spread far and wide, to the west, east, north, and south? Subsequently, when Judah's twin sons are born, the one who tries to jump out of Tamar's womb ahead of the legitimate first-born is named פֶּרֶץ (*perets*), one who jumps in front. The biblical expression (Exodus 1:12) כֵּן יִרְבֶּה וְכֵן יִפְרֹץ (*ken yirbeh ve-khen yifrots*) teaches us that the more you oppress the people of Israel, the greater they grow.

The root has taken on both negative and positive shadings over the centuries. The overstepping of the boundaries of sexual modesty is called פְּרִיצוּת (peritsut). A burglary is termed a פְּרִיצָה (peritsah), break-in. Were wealthy Polish landowners at times lawless, violent men? That's the impression one gets from the works of Yiddish writer Y.L. Peretz (there goes our root again), where a nobleman is called a פָּרִיץ (parits).

Without overstating the case, one can say פָּרְצָה הַמִּלְחָמָה (par-tsah ha-milhamah), "the war broke out." After a battle, no announcement is more welcome than the sentry's call, אֵין פֶּרֶץ וְאֵין צְוָחָה (ein peresz ve-ein tsevahah), literally, "There is no breach and no outcry," idiomatically, "All's quiet." Then there is the "hero" who מִתְפָּרֵץ לְדֶלֶת פְּתוּחָה (mitparets le-delet petuhah), breaks down open doors.

Not all derivations imply a major rupture, however. Look at the expression פִּרְצָה קוֹרֵאת לַגַּנָּב (pirtsah kor'et la-gannav), the slightest opening beckons the burglar. Nor are they all pejorative. Kohelet, ever philosophical, teaches עֵת לִפְרוֹץ וְעֵת לִבְנוֹת (et li-frots ve-et li-vnot), "There is a time to break down and a time to build up." Is a פֶּרֶץ עָנָן (perets anan), cloudburst, good or bad? The expression לַעֲמוֹד בַּפֶּרֶץ (la-amod ba-perets), to be in the vanguard, is used for heroes of war and of ideas. Neither good nor bad, a gulf or a bay is called a מִפְרָץ (mifrats), because that's where the sea breaks through toward the shore. On the decidedly positive side, a scientific or medical advance is often called a פְּרִיצַת הַדֶּרֶךְ (peritsat ha-derekh), breakthrough. And the battalion of the Palmach that ran over obstacles to break through to Jerusalem in 1948 is commemorated reverently with a street name, הַפּוֹרְצִים (ha-portsim).

Whatever treatment we give it, we can deduce from the foregoing that our root is indeed בְּשִׁמּוּשׁ נִפְרָץ (be-shimmush nifrats), in widespread use. And that's no hyperbole.

DOING WHAT COMES JUDICIALLY

If you were to ask David Letterman to name the top ten things Jews are good at, he would easily come up with fields like medicine, business, bridge, and cooking foods high in cholesterol. But is Letterman enough of an insider to put צְדָקָה (*tsedakah*), commonly translated as charity, near the top of his list of things that Jews are good at?

A look at words derived from the root צ-ד-ק (*tsadi, dalet, kof*), to be in the right, reveals that *tsedakah* is much more than charity.

First of all, there is the notion of צִדְקוּת (*tsidkut*), righteousness, from which we get צַדִּיק (*tsaddik*, feminine צַדֶּקֶת, *tsaddeket*), a righteous person. From the Flood Story we learn that a צַדִּיק תָּמִים (*tsaddik tammim*) is a uniformly righteous person. Knowing that righteousness too often leads to self-righteousness, Ecclesiastes warns אַל תְּהִי צַדִּיק הַרְבֵּה (*al tehi tsaddik harbeh*), "Don't be too much of *tsaddik*." The Talmud tells us that there are ל"ו צַדִּיקִים (*lamed vav tsaddikim*), 36 just men, in every generation. For the Rabbis, the observation צַדִּיק וְרַע לוֹ (*tsaddik ve-ra lo*), "He is righteous yet he suffers," becomes a question of theodicy, an inquiry into God's justice.

The root finds its way into judicial proceedings in daily life in the word צֶדֶק (*tsedek*), justice. The Torah leads the way by ordaining firmly צֶדֶק צֶדֶק תִּרְדֹּף (*tsedek tsedek tirdof*), "Justice, justice shall you pursue." That justice also means morality we learn from both the biblical injunction to keep מֹאזְנֵי צֶדֶק (*moznei tsedek*), honest

145

scales, and the existence of Israel's בֵּית דִּין גָּבוֹהַ לְצֶדֶק (*beit din gavo'ah le-tsedek*), High Court for moral justice, called familiarly בַּגָ"ץ (*bagats*). A non-Jew who converts to Judaism out of conviction is praised with the epithet גֵּר-צֶדֶק (*ger tsedek*), a convert of virtue.

In modern Israel, you don't have to go to court to give your הֵן צֶדֶק (*hen tsedek*), word of honor, and a child on the street may be heard complaining to a stern parent זֶה לֹא בְּצֶדֶק (*zeh lo be-tsedek*), "That's not fair." Have you heard the Jewish joke in which the Rabbi tells his wife הַצֶּדֶק גַּם עִמָּךְ (*ha-tsedek gam immakh*), "You're also right"? An important hospital in Jerusalem is called שַׁעֲרֵי צֶדֶק (*sha'arei tsedek*), gates of righteousness, for obvious reasons. At a Jewish funeral, the bereaved is asked to recite a formula called the צִדּוּק הַדִּין (*tsidduk ha-din*), a justification of God's judgment. That's also where you'll hear a collector of alms cry out צְדָקָה תַּצִּיל מִמָּוֶת (*tsedakah tatsil mi-mavet*), "Charity will save you from death."

The verb forms of the root are also used in judicial proceedings. In what is probably the most humanistic moment in the Torah, when Judah learns that he has falsely accused Tamar of harlotry, he admits, צָדְקָה מִמֶּנִּי (*tsadkah mimmeni*), "She is more in the right than I." Later, answering an accusation of stealing by his highly-placed brother Joseph, the same Judah asks, מַה נִּצְטַדָּק? (*mah nits'taddak*), How can we clear ourselves of these charges?

A store-owner will do well to teach his employees הַלָּקוֹחַ תָּמִיד צוֹדֵק (*ha-lakoakh tamid tsodek*), the customer is always right. And to the reader who complains that there is much more to be learned from our root, we can only answer אַתָּה צוֹדֵק בְּהֶחְלֵט (*atah tsodek be-hehlet*), "you're absolutely right."

146

JUST(LY) DO IT

An attribute of American English is its ability to turn a noun into a transitive verb. Surely all of us have heard, or said, sentences like: "I just e-mailed my brother"; "She paused the VCR"; or "There's the rabbi who bat-mitzvaed me."

In Judaism, curiously enough, nobody really needs a ceremony in which one is bar- or bat-mitzvaed. All one really needs is to come of age; at that point one is obligated to observe ‎מִצְווֹת‎ (*mitsvot*), commandments.

The word ‎מִצְוָה‎ (*mitsvah*), comes from the root ‎צ-ו-ה‎ (*tsadi, vav, heh*), to command. This also gives us the term for the imperative form of a verb, the ‎צִוּוּי‎ (*tsivvu'i*), as in ‎קוּם‎ (*kum*), "Get up!" and the verb ‎צִוָּה‎ (*tsivah*), he ordained, as in ‎תּוֹרָה צִוָּה לָנוּ מֹשֶׁה‎ (*torah tsivvah lanu moshe*) "Moses ordained that we observe [the laws of] the Torah."

According to Maimonides, in his ‎סֵפֶר הַמִּצְווֹת‎ (*sefer ha-mitsvot*), *Book of Commandments,* there is a total of ‎תַּרְיַ"ג מִצְווֹת‎ (*taryag mitsvot*), 613 commandments. Fewer than half of these are effective today—if you do twenty, you're considered ultra-Orthodox—and a significant number of the rest can function only in the Land of Israel. There are, however, seven commandments, the ‎שֶׁבַע מִצְווֹת בְּנֵי נֹחַ‎ (*sheva mitsvot benei no'ah*), the Seven Noahide Laws, that are incumbent on all humanity, at all times and in all places.

So strong is the concept of commandment in Judaism that our Sages were wont to de-emphasize gratuitous acts of loving-kindness, affirming that ‎גָּדוֹל הַמְצֻוֶּה וְעוֹשֶׂה מִמִּי שֶׁאֵינוֹ מְצֻוֶּה וְעוֹשֶׂה‎ (*gadol ha-metsuvveh ve-oseh mi-mi she-eino metsuvveh ve-oseh*),

"One who acts righteously because he is so commanded is 'greater' than one who does so voluntarily."

This thinking does not at all exclude the idea of voluntarism. The rabbinic equivalent of "virtue is its own reward," שְׂכַר מִצְוָה מִצְוָה (*sekhar mitsvah mitsvah*), is "the reward for doing one mitzvah is the opportunity to do another."

There is a beautiful tradition in Judaism stemming from our root. Parents with wisdom to impart will often leave their children a צַוָּאָה (*tsavva'a*), a last will and testament, in which they "command" their children to follow a certain ethical path. This sense is found in the somber but moving statement pronounced at memorial ceremonies in Israel, בְּמוֹתָם צִוּוּ לָנוּ אֶת הַחַיִּים (*be-motam tsivvu lanu et ha-hayyim*), "Through their deaths they have bequeathed to us life."

Because a very old meaning of our root has to do with erecting fortresses, a minority of scholars associate our root with צִיּוּן (*tsiyyun*), landmark, and consequently with צִיּוֹן (*tsiyyon*), Zion, the Landmark, with a capital L, of the Jewish people. Just as a landmark tells you how to get to a desired physical destination, so too doing a mitzvah gets you to a desired ethical goal.

After all, one of the greatest מִצְווֹת (*mitsvot*) in Judaism is to dwell in Zion. And that's also where you'll find the greatest number of opportunities to do a מִצְוָה (*mitsvah*).

"BEFORE YOU"

It's an old joke, but true to life. The guest speaker, duly introduced, steps up to the microphone and says: "Before I begin my speech, I'd like to say a few words." This need to explain "where one is coming from" is apparently universal. Perhaps that's why the Hebrew root ק-ד-מ (*kof, dalet, mem*), to precede, has such a wide variety of uses, in both time and space.

First of all, קוֹדֶם כֹּל (*kodem kol*), in the Tanakh, the noun קֶדֶם (*kedem*) means both "ancient times" and "east." The biblical story of the early years of the universe places mankind in a garden מִקֶּדֶם (*mi-kedem*), in the east, because that's where human time—the day—conventionally begins. One of the most popular chants in the liturgy, taken from Scripture, asks God to חַדֵּשׁ יָמֵינוּ כְּקֶדֶם (*haddesh yameinu ke-kedem*), "renew our days as of old." The Rabbis used the root to deal with the sticky problem of biblical historicity, affirming אֵין מֻקְדָּם וּמְאֻחָר בַּתּוֹרָה (*ein mukdam u-me'uhar ba-torah*), "There is no chronological order (literally earlier or later) in the Torah." And then there is אָדָם קַדְמוֹן (*adam kadmon*), prehistoric man.

In modern times, a good administrator will return calls as soon as possible, בְּהֶקְדֵּם הָאֶפְשָׁרִי (*be-hekdem ha-efshari*); a good lawyer will know how to manipulate תַּקְדִּימִים (*takdimim*), precedents, to her client's advantage; and a good businessman will require customers to leave a מִקְדָּמָה (*mikdamah*), down payment, on all orders. And many popular songs in Israel come from the קְדַם-אֵרוֹוִיזְיוֹן (*kedam-irovizyon*), Pre-Eurovision Contest.

The plain meaning of the verb is evident in the proverbial כָּל הַקּוֹדֵם זוֹכֶה (*kol ha-kodem zokheh*), "First come, first served."

Thanks to the malleability of Hebrew roots, the expression הוּא הִקְדִּים לָצֵאת (*hu hikdim la-tset*), He left early, (i.e., before the meeting was over) is clearly different from הוּא יָצָא מֻקְדָּם (*hu yatsa mukdam*), He left early (i.e., before sunrise). During the prophet Jonah's explanation of his flight from God's service, he concludes, "That's why I hastened, קִדַּמְתִּי (*kiddamti*), to flee to Tarshish."

In the army, the sergeant can often be heard to bellow, קָדִימָה! (*kadimah!*), forward march. On the road, Israeli drivers are enjoined לָתֵת זְכוּת קְדִימָה (*latet zekhut kedimah*), to yield the right-of-way. Your television screen will present a קְדִימוֹן (*kedimon*), promo, to tell viewers what's coming up next. One thing people in the twenty-first century understand very well is אִי אֶפְשָׁר לַעֲצוֹר אֶת הַקִּדְמָה (*i efshar la-atsor et ha-kidmah*), you can't stop progress. Sometimes a visionary is not understood by the people of his generation. Later on people will say that he הִקְדִּים אֶת זְמַנּוֹ (*hikdim et zemano*), was ahead of his time.

All this, of course, is just an introduction, הַקְדָּמָה (*hakdamah*), to a value system based on the expression זְרִיזִים מַקְדִּימִים לְמִצְוָה (*zerizim makdimim le-mitsvah*), "The diligent strive to be first to do a good deed."

When a group of tourists came to visit a development town in Israel recently, the local newspaper reported that the mayor קִדֵּם אוֹתָם בִּבְרָכָה (*kiddem otam bivrakhah*), welcomed them courteously.

It didn't say whether he prefaced his speech with a few words.

A GATHERING FOR
MODERN TIMES

One of the advantages of Hebrew is its ability to keep up with the times. Take the example of the root ק-ל-ט (*kof, lamed, tet*), to gather, absorb, as it is manipulated and molded into a vocabulary for the latest technologies.

It all started with תַּקְלִיט (*taklit*), the vinyl record popular a generation ago, spun by your local discothèque's תַּקְלִיטָן (*taklitan*), disk jockey. Later, when the mode changed to tape cassettes, Hebrew adapted itself quite nicely and came up with קַלֶּטֶת (*kaletet*), as in קַלֶּטֶת וִידֵאוֹ (*kaletet vide'o*), video cassette. With the arrival of the computer, the root hurried into the future and came out as תַּקְלִיטוֹן (*takliton*), a floppy disk inserted into the A: drive. With the development of laser technology, Hebrew performed a light show of its own, combining תַּקְלִיט (*taklit*) with אוֹר (*or*), light, to form תַּקְלִיטוֹר (*taklitor*), a compact disk, or CD. And let us not forget that technological marvel that permits us to live in a worldwide intellectual wasteland, the מַקְלֵט טֶלֶוִיזְיָה (*maklet televiziah*), television set.

Because the root appears only infrequently in Scripture, its origin is somewhat shrouded in mystery. Two theories that are קְלִיטִים (*kelitim*), easy to understand, present themselves. One theory says the root originally meant to stop or prevent, as a filter prevents the dregs from being decanted with the wine. The other says the root was applied to the shrinking of a limb, and therefore gathered it together.

The root appears twenty times in the Tanakh applied to the six עָרֵי מִקְלָט (*arei miklat*), Cities of Refuge, where an accidental killer might seek sanctuary. The word מִקְלָט (*miklat*), meaning underground shelter, is ubiquitous on signs posted on outdoor walls in modern Israel.

A more peaceful use of the root describes that uniquely Israeli institution, the מֶרְכַּז קְלִיטָה (*merkaz kelitah*), absorption center, where new *olim* acclimate themselves before moving into Israeli society. That's where one learns לִקְלוֹט (*li-klot*), to understand, Israeli jokes and to make sense of a הוֹדָעָה מוּקְלֶטֶת (*hoda'ah mukletet*), recorded announcement, on the telephone. And when you look at the roof of your new apartment building you will surely see the ubiquitous קוֹלְטִים (*koltim*), solar panels, for your ecological heater.

The Talmud tells us כְּשֵׁרִים שֶׁבְּבָבֶל אֶרֶץ יִשְׂרָאֵל קוֹלְטָתָן (*kesherim she-be-vavel, erets yisrael koltetan*), loosely, the Land of Israel absorbs well "kosher" Babylonians, i.e., Diaspora Jews prepared for living there (by learning Hebrew, etc.).

On this score, to judge by the use it makes of our root, modern Western technology is glatt kosher. So, now, ?אַתָּה קוֹלֵט אוֹתִי (*atah kolet oti?*), Do you see what I'm saying?

152

SHUT MY MOUTH AND CALL ME CHEAPSKATE

Question: What is the name of the "earliest" introduction to the Hebrew vowel system?

Answer: *Oyfn Pripetshik*. In this Yiddish folksong the teacher instructs his little pupils that when one places the Yiddish-accented vowel *kometz* under an *alef*, the latter is pronounced "aw."

Follow-up Question: Where does one learn why the Hebrew-accented vowel is called **קָמָץ** (*kamats*)?

Answer: Here.

It all has to do with the lips. The *patah*, related to many Hebrew words that mean opening, is a vowel pronounced "ahhh," with the mouth wide open. The *kamats* is a vowel reserved for the sound produced with the lips somewhat more closed. When we learn that **קָמַץ פִּיו** (*kamats piv*) means "he closed his mouth," we understand that the name of the vowel means what the mouth does when it pronounces it, i.e., it closes.

The "small" *kamats* one sometimes encounters has nothing to do with the size of the written vowel. Rather, it too has to do with making the mouth smaller. This vowel is pronounced "oh," with the lips fully rounded and foreshortened. Thus, the word for wisdom, **חָכְמָה**, is enunciated as though it were spelled **חוֹכְמָה** (*hokhmah*).

The verb **קָמַץ** (*kamats*), related to a word having to do with fingertips, means to grasp, to enclose with the hand. It is not without interest that the word for ring finger in Hebrew is **קְמִיצָה** (*kemitsah*), important for understanding the use of our root in

Scripture. In Leviticus we are told that, when a meal offering is made, one of the priests scoops out מְלֹא קֻמְצוֹ (*melo kumtso*), a threefingersful, of the flour.

The question is: Is that a lot or a little? We are told in Genesis that when Joseph, as viceroy in Egypt, gathered food during the seven good years, he did so לִקְמָצִים (*li-kmatsim*), by the handfuls, that is, in abundance.

And yet, as the Talmud teaches us, אֵין הַקֹּמֶץ מַשְׂבִּיעַ אֶת הָאֲרִי (*ein ha-komets masbia et ha-ari*), a small amount does not satisfy the lion. The Talmud also uses our root to mean small-minded, as in the story it tells about two men, named sarcastically קַמְצָא (*kamtsa*) and בַּר-קַמְצָא (*bar-kamtsa*), whose pettiness leads to the baseless hatred for which the Temple was destroyed.

The root ק-מ-צ (*kof, mem, tsadi*) is highly malleable. A recipe will often call for a קֹמֶץ מֶלַח (*komets melah*), a pinch of salt. One way to control anger is לְקַמֵּץ אֶגְרוֹפִים (*le-kammets egrofim*), to clench one's fists. It's rarely a bad idea לְקַמֵּץ בְּמַשְׁאַבִּים (*le-kammets be-mash'abim*), to preserve one's (and the world's) resources. Sometimes, when your stock portfolio מִתְקַמֵּץ (*mitkammets*), shrinks, it is necessary לְקַמֵּץ (*le-kammets*), to economize, but one must be careful not be become a קַמְצָן (*kamtsan*), cheapskate, the same word used in the Hebrew translation of Molière's comedy, *L'Avare*.

Remember, it is always good to face life with a little pinch—a קַמְצוּץ (*kamtsuts*), as it were—of good humor.

BE THE ENVY *FOR* YOUR NEIGHBORHOOD

Christian theology views Envy as one of the Seven Deadly Sins, to be avoided at all costs. Judaism sees Envy as an emotion that, on the one hand, demonstrates the weakness and vulnerability of human character and, on the other, can be beneficial to humankind's development.

The Hebrew root for envy is ק-נ-א (*kof, nun, alef*). According to Wilhelm Gesenius, the nineteenth-century father of Modern Hebrew lexicography, our root was probably originally tied to an Arabic word meaning to become intensely red with dye. In Hebrew, by a facile linguistic leap, the word came to be used for the color produced on the face by a deep emotion and then for the emotion itself. Nowadays, to show how languages are influenced by English, one can be יָרוֹק מִקִּנְאָה (*yarok mi-kin'ah*), green with envy.

The word קִנְאָה (*kin'ah*), is today commonly translated as jealousy, envy, and even suspicion of adultery on the part of one's spouse. In Genesis, the root is used to move the narrative along by describing a universal human trait, sibling rivalry. We are told that foremother Rachel feared that she might remain barren in the face of her sister Leah's fertility and that therefore וַתְּקַנֵּא רָחֵל בַּאֲחוֹתָהּ (*ve-tekanne rahel ba-ahotah*), Rachel was jealous of her sister. Later on, the same root is used in connection with Rachel's son, Joseph, about whose coat of many colors Joseph's brothers were jealous indeed, וַיְקַנְאוּ בוֹ אֶחָיו (*va-yekan'u vo ehav*).

Sometimes the root is used to express not jealousy but zealotry, another extreme emotion. Take for example its use in connection with the story of Moses and the rebellion of Eldad and Medad (Numbers 11:29). When Joshua suggests that Moses put down the rebellion harshly, Moses responds הַמְקַנֵּא אַתָּה לִי? (*ha-mekanne atah li?*), "Why are you being so zealous for my sake?" Moses would rather, he explains, that all Israelites were prophets.

There is zealotry, and then there is Zealotry. During the revolt against Rome in Second Temple times, there arose a political party, the קַנָּאִים (*kanna'im*), who were against any compromise with Rome. The same expression is used in modern times to describe those whose love for the Hebrew language is exclusive, קַנָּאִים לַשָּׂפָה הָעִבְרִית (*kanna'im la-safah ha-ivrit*), zealots for the Hebrew language.

The language of the *Yalkut Shim'oni* (a popular thirteenth-century compilation of *midrashim*) sounds like that of a football coach speaking of the competitive spirit. There it is written, אִלְמָלֵא הַקִּנְאָה אֵין הָעוֹלָם עוֹמֵד (*ilmale ha-kin'ah, ein ha-olam omed*), "If it weren't for jealousy (i.e., competitiveness), the world could not exist." According to the Rabbis of the Talmud (Baba Batra 21a), this idea applies specifically to writers, קִנְאַת סוֹפְרִים תַּרְבֶּה חָכְמָה (*kin'at soferim tarbeh hokhmah*), "Jealousy among writers increases wisdom." This is ostensibly because the urge to outdo one's fellow writer leads to even deeper insights.

What are we to say, finally, of the expression אֵל קַנָּא (*el kanna*), a form of the root reserved exclusively for God? Christian theology has turned this attribute into something terrible and terrifying, even deadly. But Jewish theology does not view God pejoratively. The word *kanna* describes not an emotion against the "other" but rather the passion of God for his people. That subtlety makes all the difference in the world.

THE KINDEST CUT

When looking up a word in the dictionary, you sometimes find more than you were expecting: not only the meaning of a word, but also an insight into a people. In the English-Hebrew volume of the Alkalay dictionary, for example, the entry "cut" leads to more than fifty verbs and almost thirty nouns. A close look at the Hebrew-English volume reveals that four verbs—קָצָה (katsah), cut, קָצַץ (katsats), chop, קָצַר (katsar), harvest, and קָצַב (katsav), slice—have in common what might be an ancient two-letter root, ק-צ (kof, tsadi). These variations show not only that cutting was an important occupation for Hebrew-speakers, but that verbal precision was a preoccupation for them too.

In Scripture, the root ק-צ-ב (kof, tsadi, bet), for example, has meaning beyond the physical act of cutting. The two olivewood cherubs adorning King Solomon's Temple, we are told in the book of Kings, are to have קֶצֶב אֶחָד (ketsev ehad), "one form." In insisting that these two pieces of sculpture must have the exact same shape, the text conveys to us the religious importance of esthetic sensibility. There are further esthetic contexts for our root. In music, the word קֶצֶב (ketsev) means rhythm. And even more strikingly, when the lover in the Song of Songs compares the teeth of his beloved to an עֵדֶר הַקְּצוּבוֹת (eder ha-ketsuvot), his metaphor portrays the dual picture of a flock of "smooth-looking" sheep who have just had their wool shorn and of a flock of sheep arrayed precisely in a row.

For the Rabbis of the Talmud, the root had a both an esthetic and a didactic use. Tractate Shabbat tells the story of a wealthy man whose Sabbath table was the height of opulence. When asked by his rabbinical guest to what his wealth was due, he replies, קַצָּב הָיִיתִי (*katsav hayyiti*), "I was once a butcher," and he explains that he set aside all the "pleasant-looking" animals in his shop for Shabbat. Does Israeli president Moshe Katsav, who has the power לִקְצוֹב עֳנָשִׁים שֶׁל אֲסִירִים (*li-ketsov onashim shel asirim*), to shorten prisoners' sentences, come from a family of butchers? In Tractate Beitsa we are told that all of the coming year's expenses are קְצוּבִים (*ketsuvim*), allotted, on Rosh ha-Shanah, except what is to be spent on Shabbat and on one's children's education. In those instances, we are assured, the more one spends, the more one receives.

This last sense of our root, to set aside money, is reflected in the modern words תַּקְצִיב (*taktsiv*), budget, הַקְצָבָה (*haktsavah*), allocation (of both time and money), and קִצְבָּה (*kitsbah*), pension.

In these cases, one rarely gets more than one expected.

IN BRIEF

There are a lot of good things to say about brevity—and people will say so at substantial length. The Hebrew root encompassing brevity, for example, ר-צ-ק (*kof, tsadi, resh*), to cut short, leads us far and wide into the social and religious life of the Jews.

The agricultural roots of the Israelites can be deduced from one of the early names of the Shavuot holiday, חַג הַקָּצִיר (*hag ha-katsir*), the Feast of Reaping. The root appears frequently in the book of Ruth where the most dramatic action takes place among the קוֹצְרִים (*kotsrim*), reapers, of Boaz. And it is quite possible that King David—proclaiming in Psalms 126:5 הַזֹּרְעִים בְּדִמְעָה, בְּרִנָּה יִקְצֹרוּ (*ha-zor'im be-dim'ah, be-rinnah yiktsoru*), "They who sow in tears will reap in joy"—is alluding metaphorically to the tale of his ancestors Ruth and Boaz.

The prophet Isaiah (28:20) uses our root eloquently in tongue-tying Hebrew to describe the tragic side of the human condition, saying קָצַר הַמַּצָּע מֵהִשְׂתָּרֵעַ וְהַמַּסֵּכָה צָרָה כְּהִתְכַּנֵּס (*katsar ha-matsa me-hishtare'a ve-ha-massekhah tsarah ke-hitkannes*), "The couch is too short for stretching out, and the cover too narrow for curling up."

The Rabbis of Pirkei Avot are poetically succinct in admonishing their fellow Jews to get down to the work of Torah. After all, they said, הַיּוֹם קָצָר וְהַמְּלָאכָה מְרֻבָּה (*ha-yom katsar ve-ha-melakhah merubbah*), "The day is short and the work is great."

If brevity is such a value why do Jewish stories tend to go on and on? Perhaps because Jewish narrators like to talk "of this and that," in Hebrew, אֲרֻכּוֹת וּקְצָרוֹת (*arukot u-ketsarot*), literally, longs and shorts. In a story that might spin itself out at length, the narrator will eventually announce that the end is approaching, using either the literary expression בְּקִצּוּר נִמְרָץ (*be-kitsur nimrats*), with utmost brevity, or the Yiddish-Hebrew clip הַקִּצֵּר (*ha-kitser*), to make a long story short.

The root appears frequently in Modern Hebrew in the Israeli office. A slangy way to say I'm in a hurry is אֲנִי קָצָר בִּזְמָן (*ani katsar bi-zeman*), I'm short in time. Don't worry about reading the full report; sooner or later a תַּקְצִיר (*taktsir*), synopsis, will appear on your desk. And don't fret about your tendency to dictate long-winded memos; the office has a קַצְרָן (*katsran*), a stenographer, on its staff. In office politics, you'll frequently find someone who cuts a colleague down—מְקַצֵּר אוֹתוֹ (*mekatser oto*)—with a word or a gesture. And when there is a controlling boss who diminishes your autonomy, you might complain הוּא מַחֲזִיק אוֹתִי קָצָר (*hu mahazik oti katsar*), He holds me [on a] short [leash]. But don't worry, the time will come when you'll be able לִקְצוֹר אֶת הַפֵּרוֹת (*li-ketsor et ha-perot*), to reap the fruits of what you've sown.

Perhaps that's why when you're having another one of your attacks of קַצֶּרֶת (*katseret*), asthma, you have קֹצֶר נְשִׁימָה (*kotser neshimah*), shortness of breath. And when the computer crashes due to an electrical קֶצֶר (*ketser*, accent on the first syllable), short-circuit, perhaps it's time to run out to your local café for a small cup of coffee.

Just go in and ask the waiter for a קָצָר (*katsar*), a "short" shot of espresso.

HEAD 'EM UP,
ROLL 'EM OUT, BEGIN

With all the recent hoopla surrounding the beginning of the secular century, some Jews may have overlooked the new beginnings that are the stuff of Jewish culture. To begin at the beginning, רָאשֵׁי מֵרֹאשׁ לְהַתְחִיל (le-hathil me-rosh), let's have רָאשֵׁי פְּרָקִים (rashei perakim), an outline, of a Hebrew root intimately associated with new beginnings, ‏רֹ-אֹ-שֹׁ‎ (resh, alef, shin).

First of all, בְּרֹאשׁ וָרִאשׁוֹנָה (be-rosh va-rishonah), let us not forget that in January 2000, on 15 Shevat, Jews celebrated one of four Jewish New Years, רֹאשׁ הַשָּׁנָה לָאִילָנוֹת (rosh ha-shanah la-ilanot), the New Year for Trees. In Tishre's New Year we pray to be לְרֹאשׁ וְלֹא לְזָנָב (le-rosh ve-lo le-zanav), at the head and not at the tail.

The Biblical story of creation, מַעֲשֵׂה בְּרֵאשִׁית (ma'aseh bereishit), tells of the division of a primordial river into אַרְבָּעָה רָאשִׁים (arba'ah rashim), four streams. The book of Esther relates that Haman, forced to honor Mordechai, walked about חֲפוּי רֹאשׁ (hafui rosh), depressed. In the Jewish Pledge of Allegiance, taken from Psalms, we swear to place Jerusalem עַל רֹאשׁ שִׂמְחָתִי (al rosh simhati), "above my greatest joy."

Jewish sovereignty means that no Jew need walk about on figurative tiptoes, עַל רָאשֵׁי אֶצְבָּעוֹת (al rashei etsba'ot), and may henceforth enter the seat of power through the כְּנִיסָה רָאשִׁית (kenisah rashit), main entrance. Israeli democracy is assured by its free press, including a freely functioning רְשׁוּת הַשִּׁדּוּר (*rashut ha-shiddur*), broadcast authority.

A Jewish State will have many "heads," from a רֹאשׁ מֶמְשָׁלָה (*rosh memshalah*), prime minister, to a רֹאשׁ הָעִיר (*rosh ha-ir*), mayor, and from a רֹאשׁ יְשִׁיבָה (*rosh yeshivah*), head of a talmudical academy, to a רַב רָאשִׁי (*rav rashi*), chief rabbi.

Our root is used as well to denote abbreviations, רָאשֵׁי תֵּיבוֹת (*rashei teivot*). The chairperson of a Jewish organization, יוֹשֵׁב / יוֹשֶׁבֶת רֹאשׁ (*yoshev/yoshevet rosh*), will take up his or her duties בְּכֹבֶד רֹאשׁ (*be-khoved rosh*), with utmost seriousness, as does the רִאשׁוֹן לְצִיּוֹן (*rishon le-tsiyyon*), the Sefardi chief Rabbi, literally the "First in Zion."

A Modern Hebrew-speaking society will have to invent new words, even for the smallest things. An Israeli soldier, for example, who seeks to avoid responsibility is called a רֹאשׁ קָטָן (*rosh katan*), little head. A small creature with a big head is a רֹאשָׁן (*roshan*), tadpole. Soccer enthusiasts call the act of hitting the ball with one's head a רֹאשִׁיָּה (*roshiyyah*). A stupid person may be called a רֹאשׁ כְּרוּב (*rosh keruv*), cabbage head, and a stubborn person is considered as having a רֹאשׁ אֶבֶן (*rosh even*), head made of stone. A good hiker will strive to reach רֹאשׁ הָהָר (*rosh ha-har*), the top of the mountain, or רֹאשׁ הַנִּקְרָה (*rosh ha-nikrah*), the northernmost coastal town in Israel.

All you need is a רֹאשׁ טוֹב (*rosh tov*), good head—in a good body.

TIME *CAUSES* ALL WOUNDS

What is it about small units of time—seconds, minutes, moments—that they often feel primed for danger? For example, a clock was discovered not long ago bearing the menacing Latin legend, *Omnia vulnerant; ultima necat,* "They all wound; the last one kills." A similar emotion was displayed by medieval Hebrew poet Yehudah ha-Levi when he rhymed אֵין רֶגַע בְּלִי נֶגַע (*ein rega beli nega*), "There is no instant without a wound [in it]."

What is curious about the Hebrew root ע-ג-ר (*resh, gimmel, ayin*) is that, according to some scholars, it exemplifies once again the not uncommon Hebrew phenomenon of דָּבָר וְהִפּוּכוֹ (*davar ve-hipukho*), the "thing and its opposite." The verb רָגַע (*raga*) means both to be at rest and to set in motion.

The first meaning is the more prevalent in Modern Hebrew, giving us the expressions בֵּית מַרְגּוֹעַ (*bet margo'a*), rest house or sanatorium, תְּרוּפַת הַרְגָּעָה (*terufat harga'ah*), anti-anxiety medication, וּלְקָן רָגֵעַ (*vulkan raghe'a*), a dormant volcano, רַק רֶגַע (*rak rega*), just a minute, and the exclamation תֵּרָגַע (*tiraga*), relax!

Scholars point out that just as the word "moment" derives from "movement" (think of the hands of that clock), so too the word רֶגַע (*rega*) comes from a Hebrew word for motion. A רֶגַע (*rega*), supposedly a minute, is a "twinkling of an eye," so fast that you hardly even notice the movement. When the Palestinian Talmud speaks of a תִּינוֹק הַמַּרְגִּיעַ (*tinok ha-margia*), it refers to an infant zipping around on all fours. The Rabbis of both Talmuds ask, "How long indeed is a רֶגַע (*rega*)? They answer, רֶגַע כְּמֵימְרֶה (*rega ke-*

memreh), as long as it takes to say רֶגַע (*rega*). Israel radio presents רֶגַע שֶׁל עִבְרִית (*rega shel ivrit*), the Hebrew "spot."

The most popular use of our root in modern Israeli culture is totally silent. It involves bringing together the five fingertips of one hand and raising them—back of hand facing the "listener"—to eye level. The listener invariably understands this gesture to mean רֶגַע! (*rega!*), Wait a minute! (This motion has been known to stop traffic in Israel. It is not, however, recommended for that purpose to tourists or new olim.) You don't always want to say "There's never a dull moment", אֵין רֶגַע דַּל (*ein rega dal*), playing on "dull" to say, literally, there is not a "poor" moment. A person waiting impatiently for the doctor to arrive is told by the receptionist that the doctor צָרִיךְ לְהַגִּיעַ כֹּל רֶגַע (*tsarikh le-hagi'ah kol rega*), should be here any moment.

The second most popular use comes from the iconic Hebrew film *Sallah!* When hurriedly asked to make a fateful decision, the film's hero consistently responds רֶגַע, חוֹשְׁבִים (*rega, hoshvim*), "Wait a minute, I'm thinking." So deeply ingrained is that expression in Israeli Hebrew—almost like Catch-22 in English—that you find the phrase הוּא עָשָׂה רֶגַע חוֹשְׁבִים (*hu asah rega-hoshvim*) to describe someone who asks for, and takes, the time to ponder his answer.

When the word רֶגַע (*rega*), moment, is linked thus to the word חוֹשְׁבִים (*hoshvim*), we're thinking, it obviously takes a little longer to say. In that brief moment, it also changes its menacing character to the possibility of a happier outcome.

AT THE CENTER

Most people, when the conversation turns to borrowing and lending, think first of banking and commerce and then, perhaps, of Shakespeare's Polonius, who advised his son, "Neither a borrower nor a lender be."

Borrowing and lending are also central to the development of languages. Think of the word מֶרְכָּז (*merkaz*), center. The story of how it usurped the place of the biblical word צִיר (*tsir*), fulcrum, is almost as dramatic as the story of Hamlet.

According to Eliezer Ben Yehudah, the Father of Modern Hebrew, the word מֶרְכָּז (*merkaz*) entered the Hebrew language around the turn of the twelfth century in Spain when mathematician Rabbi Abraham Bar Hiyya and Hebrew translator Rabbi Samuel Ibn Tibbon needed a precise Hebrew expression for "center of the universe" and turned to an Arabic word, *markaz*. Since then, the Arabic word has gone on to make its fortune in Hebrew, displacing almost completely its biblical synonym, צִיר (*tsir*).

The word מֶרְכָּז (*merkaz*), can be found in the Zionist writings of Ahad Ha-Am, who envisioned the future State of Israel as a מֶרְכָּז רוּחָנִי (*merkaz ruhani*), spiritual center, for the Jewish people. The word מֶרְכָּז (*merkaz*), is found in the name of the Center Party that pushed for the election of General Yitshak Mordechai as prime minister. It is found also in מֶרְכַּז קְלִיטָה (*merkaz kelitah*), the expression for an Absorption Center for new *olim* to Israel. And in the United States, Merkaz USA is the Zionist organization for Conservative Judaism. The word is also in the name of the National

Center for the Hebrew Language, הַמֶּרְכָּז לַלָּשׁוֹן הָעִבְרִית (*ha-merkaz la-lashon ha-ivrit*).

The three-letter root ר-כ-ז (*resh, kaf, zayin*) was created (in what linguists call a back-formation) out of the noun מֶרְכָּז (*merkaz*). As the root took root in Hebrew, it took on meanings as disparate as מְרַכֵּז (*merakkez*), organizer, מֶרְכָּזִיָּה (*merkaziyyah*), telephone switchboard, and מַעְגָּלִים מֶרְכָּזִיִּים (*ma'galim merkaziyyim*), concentric circles. The hero of a novel or play is its דְּמוּת מֶרְכָּזִית (*demut merkazit*), central figure. The person who mans a "desk" at an Israeli newspaper is called a רַכָּז מַעֲרֶכֶת (*rakaz ma'arekhet*). The eighteen men and women in the United States who are in charge of Hebrew programs in their communities are called רַכָּזֵי עִבְרִית (*rakazei ivrit*). In Israeli kindergartens, when all physical activity is stopped for a break, you have a שְׁעַת רִכּוּז (*she'at rikkuz*), quiet time. The root is also found in a twentieth-century emotion-laden expression, מַחֲנֵה רִכּוּז (*mahaneh rikkuz*), concentration camp, and in the more intellectually satisfying verb לְהִתְרַכֵּז (*le-hitrakkez*), to concentrate. Hebrew national poet Chaim Nachman Bialik claimed that the Hebrew language was part of a רַעְיוֹן עֶלְיוֹן וּמֶרְכָּזִי (*ra'yon elyon u-merkazi*), a "supreme and central concept," of Jewish peoplehood.

In Israel's cities, if you start out from the תַּחֲנָה מֶרְכָּזִית (*tahanah merkazit*), central bus station, you will often find signs pointing to מֶרְכַּז הָעִיר (*merkaz ha-ir*), city center.

One might say that the Jewish people have taken the advice of Polonius in at least one of his dicta. Not the one about borrowing and lending, to be sure, but the one that enjoins: "This, above all: To thine own self be true." In its way, Hebrew will do that, even when it borrows.

ON THE MEND

The idea of repair is so ingrained in the Jewish value system—*tikkun olam*, and all that—that it is not at all surprising to find tailoring prevalent among the Jewish occupations. Curiously, the Semitic root that our Arabic-speaking cousins use for "to mend, patch, darn, sew up," Hebrew-speakers use for "to heal." And that's how we get from tailors to doctors.

The root ‏ר-פ-א‏ (*resh, peh, alef*) meanders throughout the Bible in a multitude of contexts. The most verbally economical Hebrew prayer in recorded Jewish history, ‏רְפָא נָא לָהּ‏ (*refa na lah*), "Please cure her," was uttered by Moses for the healing of his sister Miriam from a leprosy-like illness.

In the Torah, God is quoted as saying ‏אֲנִי ה' רֹפְאֶךָ‏ (*ani ha-shem rof'ekha*), "I, God, am your healer," but the Rabbis made sure to find a biblical text permitting human intervention in illness. They extrapolate, from the doubling of our root in the expression ‏רַפֹּא יְרַפֵּא‏ (*rapo yerapeh*), "Surely shall you heal," that human beings are enjoined to become doctors. Because religious Jews believe that everything, including illness and doctors, comes from God, they remind us proverbially that God ‏מַקְדִּים רְפוּאָה לַמַּכָּה‏ (*makdim refu'ah la-makkah*), "creates the cure before the plague." Ecclesiastes teaches that "for everything there is a season," and then goes on, in his list of opposites, to contrast ‏עֵת לַהֲרֹג וְעֵת לִרְפֹּא‏ (*et la-harog ve-et lirpo*), "a time to kill and a time to heal." What this says, if anything, about doctor-assisted suicide we'll leave to medical ethicists.

In the Siddur, the eighth of the nineteen blessings of the daily Amidah prayer is referred to as the רְפוּאָה (*refu'ah*) blessing, the blessing of healing. This brief supplication for health and healing uses our root no fewer than five times. The מִרְפָּאָה (*mirpa'ah*), infirmary, is one of the places where you'll hear the expression רְפוּאָה שְׁלֵמָה (*refu'ah shelemah*), used for "Get well soon." Nowadays a growing branch in medicine is רְפוּאָה מַשְׁלִימָה (*refu'ah mashlimah*), complementary medicine. An injured laborer is often prescribed a series of sessions of רִפּוּי בְּעִסּוּק (*rippui be-issuk*), occupational therapy.

There are doctors, and then there is not exactly. Only a רוֹפֵא (*rofeh*), doctor, is authorized to issue a prescription for a תְּרוּפָה (*terufah*), medication. A specialist is called a רוֹפֵא מוּמְחֶה (*rofeh mumheh*), literally, an expert doctor. A non-diplomaed medical practitioner is called a רוֹפְאָן (*rof'an*) or a מְרַפֵּא (*merapeh*). A medical charlatan, i.e., a quack, is a רוֹפֵא אֱלִיל (*rofe elil*), literally, an idol doctor.

There are three words that appear to share our root: one does, one might, and one does not. The angel רְפָאֵל (*refa'el*), Raphael, is so-called because he is the angel of healing. The רְפָאִים (*refa'im*), a tribe of giants who dwelt on the east bank of the Jordan, might have been big and strong because they had doctors who knew about herbal "steroids." Finally, the ghosts who populate Sheol, the underworld, are also called רְפָאִים (*refa'im*). All scholars agree that they have nothing to do with our root. Then again, if there is such a thing as repairing the world, might there not be such a thing as repairing the underworld? And wouldn't one need רְפָאִים (*refa'im*), doctors, for that as well?

PRAISE THE PRAISE,
. . . AND PASS THE DONUTS

Hanukkah is the Festival of Lights, all agree. But a good case can be made for also calling it the Festival of Song.

As part of the candle-lighting ceremony we sing the hymn Ma'oz Tzur, "Rock of Ages." When we come to the line לְךָ נָאֶה לְשַׁבֵּחַ (*lekha na'eh le-shabe'ah*), "To You it is pleasant to give praise," we encounter the root שׁ-ב-ח (*shin, bet, het*), whose many meanings provide oil-soaked food for thought.

Among these meanings is "to praise," of course. But also, we find, "to repair," "to improve," "to be superior," "to grow," "to be bright," "to increase in value," and, according to some, "to quiet," "to calm."

We also find the meaning "to sing," albeit somewhat tortuously. It appears that in the Song of the Sea in Exodus 15:1, the Aramaic Targum translates the first words, *az yashir moshe,* as בְּכֵן שַׁבַּח מֹשֶׁה (*be-khen shabbah moshe*), "Then Moses sang," using our root for the Hebrew word "he sang."

Someone who buys or inherits land would do well לְהַשְׁבִּיחַ אֶת הַקַּרְקַע (*le-hashbi'ah et ha-karka*), to make improvements on the property. When you tell someone that יַיִן יָשָׁן מִשְׁתַּבֵּחַ (*yayin yashan mishtabe'ah*), you are affirming that wine improves with age. When you smack your lips over a particularly delicious morsel of food, you don't have to praise it; you just say that its taste is שְׁבַחֵי שְׁבָחִים (*shivhei shevahim*), the best. The expression שְׁבָחָה שֶׁל אֶרֶץ יִשְׂרָאֵל (*shevahah shel erets yisra'el*) proclaims the superiority of the Land

169

of Israel. The Psalmist tells us that God's power מַשְׁבִּיחַ שְׁאוֹן יַמִּים (*mashbi'ah she'on yammim*), "calms the roar of the sea." What is praised is good, indeed very good, like יַיִן מְשֻׁבָּח (*yayin meshubbah*), superior wine. On Passover we proclaim that those who speak at length of the story, הֲרֵי זֶה מְשֻׁבָּח (*harei ze meshubbah*), "That is praiseworthy."

Of course, there are other instances where our root means just praise. The Israeli Army, known for its penchant for abbreviations, will hand out a צַלַ"שׁ (*tsalash*), a צִיּוּן לְשֶׁבַח (*tsiyyun le-shevah*), commendation, for praiseworthy action in the field.

One way to damn someone with faint praise in Hebrew is to use the expression לִשְׁבְחוֹ יֵאָמֵר (*le-shivho ye'amer*), which means: despite-all-the-bad-things-one-might-say-about-him-this-one-little-point-could-nevertheless-be-said-in-his-favor.

A punctilious Hebrew maxim states מִקְצַת שִׁבְחוֹ בְּפָנָיו (*miktsat shivho be-fanav*), One may say to a person's face only a portion of the praise due him.

Alternatively, just sing a Hanukkah ditty.

ALL THE BREAKS

We envy those who always seem to get all the "breaks"; but did we ever stop to think why "brokenness" should be a good in the first place? An answer lies perhaps in the lexico-graphic conjecture that these "breaks" are also "brakes," limits on misfortune. In Hebrew, both breaking and braking can be seen in expressions tied to the root ש-ב-ר (shin, bet, resh), to break.

The biblical Joseph was the man in charge of breaking and braking the famine by the distribution of שֶׁבֶר (shever), provisions. The מַשְׁבִּיר לַצַּרְכָן (mashbir la-tsarkhan), literally, provider to the consumer, is the name of a department store chain in Israel. Joseph came to his position because of his talent at another form of שֶׁבֶר (shever), breaking things down through the interpretation of dreams.

The breaking of the first set of the Tablets by Moses gives us שִׁבְרֵי לוּחוֹת (shivrei luhot), fragments. The שְׁבָרִים (shevarim), tremolo, sound of the shofar on Rosh ha-Shanah mimics the wail-ing of a broken heart. And did not Rabbi Nachman of Bratslav teach us to sing that there is nothing more whole than a לֵב שָׁבוּר (lev shavur), broken heart?

An archeologist will tell you that pottery is שָׁבִיר (shavir), breakable. But so is light, not only as it breaks into rays of שַׁבְרִירִים (shavririm), sunbeams, but also, in the lens trade, in its שְׁבִירוֹת (shevirot), refractions. A legal "rip-off" is a שׁוֹבֵר (shover), voucher.

And let's not forget שְׁבִירַת הַכֵּלִים (shevirat ha-kelim) the kabbalistic Breaking of the Vessels. When an Israeli child is dissatis-fied with the way a game is going he stops it by yelling שׁוֹבְרִים אֶת

הַכֵּלִים (*shovrim et ha-kelim*), we're not playing any more. "Breaking down" the wizardly word *Shabriri* into *briri, riri, iri, ri* gives Jewish magicians a Hebrew incantation as effective as abracadabra. In math there are whole numbers and there are שְׁבָרִים (*shevarim*), fractions. When something is really broken it is נִשְׁבַּר לִרְסִיסִים (*nishbar li-rsisim*), broken to bits. And someone who falls off a ladder is likely to get a שֶׁבֶר (*shever*), fracture, in his leg. A person who has undergone a traumatic situation is often called a שֶׁבֶר כְּלִי (*shever keli*), broken vessel.

Probably because of the turmoil of Israel's political-sociological-religious situation, one of the most frequently used words in Modern Hebrew is מַשְׁבֵּר (*mashber*), crisis. In Isaiah, the term means womb or birthing chair. What to do, laments the prophet metaphorically, when the fetus arrives at the מַשְׁבֵּר (*mashber*), mouth of the womb, and there is no strength left to complete the delivery?

Modern Israeli metaphors, reflecting both Hebrew slang and inner agitation, are even more cinematographic. Pan to the *tayyelet* in Tel Aviv where a sad-faced citizen stares out at the שׁוֹבְרֵי גַּלִּים (*shovrei gallim*), breakers, jutting out into the sea. Fed up with life—נִשְׁבַּר לוֹ מֵהַחַיִּים (*nishbar lo me-ha-hayyim*)—our hero glimpses a beautiful apparition and falls madly in love. Suddenly, in a שַׁבְרִיר שְׁנִיָּה (*shavrir sheniyyah*), fraction of a second, a crack Israeli driver, to avoid an oncoming car, שׁוֹבֵר יְמִינָה (*shover yeminah*), swerves right, onto the *tayyelet*, and brings us back into reality.

Give me a brake.

ERROR, ERROR ON THE WALL

After several months in Ulpan, the new oleh boasts: אֲנִי מְדַבֵּר עִבְרִית מְצֻיֶּנֶת, כִּמְעַט בְּלִי שְׁגִיאִים (*ani medabber ivrit metsuyyenet, kim'at beli shegi'im*), I speak an excellent Hebrew, almost without mistakes. Unfortunately, our enthusiastic student mistakes the gender of the word for mistake, שְׁגִיאָה (*shegi'ah*), not recognizing its feminine ending.

It's easy to make mistakes about Hebrew, especially when it comes to the root שׁ-ג-ה (*shin, gimmel, heh*), to err. The first thing to note is that our three-letter root derives perhaps from a more primitive two-letter root, שׁ-ג (*shin, gimmel*), meaning "to go wrong." According to at least some scholars this ancient root has given birth not only to שָׁגָה (*shagah*), he erred, but also to its sisters שָׁגַע (*shaga*), he went mad, and שָׁגַג (*shagag*), he commited a sin inadvertently.

In Scripture, our root has several meanings. The Torah, very sensitive to the plight of the unsighted, declares, in Deuteronomy, אָרוּר מַשְׁגֶּה עִוֵּר בַּדָּרֶךְ (*arur mashgeh ivver ba-derekh*), "Cursed be he who misleads a blind man on the road." The Psalmist, who realizes that it's difficult enough to understand why one sins, asks שְׁגִיאוֹת מִי יָבִין? (*shegi'ot mi yavin?*), "Who can understand (and therefore avoid) errors?"—and prays, אַל תַּשְׁגֵּנִי מִמִּצְוֹתֶיךָ (*al tashgeni mi-mitsvotekha*), "Let me not stray from Your commandments."

There is a use of our root that puzzles the scholars. It comes in the opening words of Psalm 7, שִׁגָּיוֹן לְדָוִד (*shiggayon le-david*). Because the root has the sense of to swerve, to stagger, to reel, to be intoxicated, some speculate that this title refers to a literary genre

173

akin to the Greek dithyramb, a "frenzied hymn." Proverbs takes our word to that level as well, blessing the fortunate husband with the words בְּאַהֲבָתָהּ תִּשְׁגֶּה (*be-ahavatah tishgeh*), "May you be ravished with her love ((of the wife of your youth)."

These senses are very close to the meaning of the sister root שׁ-ג-ע (*shin, gimmel, ayin*), to be in a frenzy, to wander about, to rave. In Modern Hebrew, one will hear expressions like מַה אַתָּה, מְשֻׁגָּע (*ma atah, meshugga?*), Are you nuts? The other sister root heard most frequently is שׁ-ג-ג (*shin, gimmel, gimmel*), especially in the Jewish legal expression בְּשׁוֹגֵג (*be-shogeg*) or בִּשְׁגָגָה (*bi-sh-gagah*), used for committing a sin unintentionally.

As with שְׁגִיאוֹת דְּפוּס (*shegi'ot defuss*), typos, this happens most often when one is שָׁגוּי בַּחֲלוֹמוֹת (*shagui ba-halomot*), engrossed waywardly in dreams, or, like any Hebrew student, מְשֻׁגָּע לַדָּבָר (*meshugga la-davar*), completely devoted to the cause.

When it comes to love of Hebrew, there is much to recommend the slang expression שִׁגָּעוֹן! (*shigga'on!*), That's great!

MATCHMAKER, MATCHMAKER

If, as they say, אֵין זִווּגוֹ שֶׁל אִישׁ אֶלָּא מִן הַקָּדוֹשׁ בָּרוּךְ הוּא (*ein zivugo shel ish ella min ha-kadosh barukh hu*), "A person's marriage partner comes from Heaven alone," where does the Jewish institution of matchmaking, שַׁדְכָנוּת (*shadkhanut*), come from? Perhaps from Jewish folklore, where lively, talkative שַׁדְכָנִים (*shadkhanim*) and שַׁדְכָנִיּוֹת (*shadkhaniyyot*), marriage brokers, a purely human invention, also have a role to play.

The Hebrew root שׁ-ד-כ (*shin, dalet, kaf*), can be traced to an Aramaic verb meaning to quiet, to calm, to appease. Targum Yonatan translates into Aramaic the biblical word וַתִּשְׁקֹט (*va-tishkot*), literally, became quiet, by using our root. The root exists in other Bible commentaries as well, where it also retains one of its original Aramaic meanings. How do we know, for example, that God, though not explicitly named, is nevertheless present in the book of Esther? The Midrash on Esther tells us, using our root, that it is God who מַשְׁדִּיךְ אֲחַשְׁוֵרוֹשׁ (*mashdikh ahaverosh*), appeases the Persian King.

There are those who believe that Abraham's servant Eliezer, charged with finding a wife for Isaac, was the first to act as a matchmaker. Nevertheless, the astute reader has already guessed that the root itself is nowhere to be found in Hebrew Scripture. All the same, it is not difficult to imagine—even though it took several centuries—how the meaning of the root moved from the appeasement of the Midrash to negotiating an agreement, to negotiating a marriage contract.

A medieval hymn chanted at the Sabbath table draws up a chart of actions that are either prohibited or permitted on Shabbat. Thus, while crunching numbers is forbidden on the Sabbath, it is more than appropriate, says the song, לְשַׁדֵּךְ הַבָּנוֹת (*le-shaddekh ha-banot*), to arrange marriages for the maidens of the community—presumably with all the numbers-crunching that implies.

As long as we're on the financial side, let us not forget the matter of דְּמֵי שַׁדְכָנוּת (*demei shadkhanut*), the marriage broker's fee. Nowadays, in Israel, to avoid these fees, one can turn to a Hebrew newspaper to read the often-colorful מוֹדָעוֹת שִׁדּוּכִים (*moda'ot shiddukhim*), personal ads in the singles columns.

Probably the most vivid instance of our root in Modern Hebrew has nothing to do with marriage. It is the flamboyant use of the word שַׁדְכָן (*shadkhan*) to designate a stapler, the office utensil that binds two sheets of paper tightly together.

If you're looking for a good *shadkhan* of this type, go to the store that advertises, "Yeah, we've got that." If they do, indeed, have everything, it could also be a place where one might find a good שִׁדּוּךְ (*shiddukh*), marriage partner, as well.

A DEPOSIT, A RETURN

When Gertrude Stein asked "What is the question?" she was ostensibly mocking those who think they have all the answers. Uncannily perhaps, she intuited that a תְּשׁוּבָה (teshuvah) is more than an "answer;" it is also a "return" to one's people. That's the sense given to the word by Hebrew poet Chaim Nachman Bialik in his poem בִּתְשׁוּבָתִי (be-seshuvosi, in Bialik's Ashkenazic pronunciation, accent on the penultimate syllable) "Upon My Return."

Of course, Bialik was also playing on the more prevalent religious sense of the word תְּשׁוּבָה (teshuvah), repentance. In the month of Tishrei there are the עֲשֶׂרֶת יְמֵי תְשׁוּבָה (aseret yemei teshuvah), Ten Days of Penitence; and in the Ohr Somayach Yeshivah a בַּעַל תְּשׁוּבָה (ba'al teshuvah) is a person who returns to the Jewish religion.

The root of our word is שׁ-ו-ב (shin, vav, bet), to return. If you make frequent deposits and withdrawals, your bank account is called a חֶשְׁבּוֹן עוֹבֵר וָשָׁב (heshbon over va-shav); when you fly round-trip to Israel, your ticket is called a כַּרְטִיס הֲלוֹךְ וָשׁוֹב (kartis halokh va-shov). A recuperated patient has שָׁב לְאֵיתָנוֹ (shav le-eitano), returned to his strength. Don't you get annoyed when your neighbor's cell phone rings שׁוּב וְשׁוּב (shuv ve-shuv), over and over? Are you going to have to tell him שׁוּב פַּעַם (shuv pa'am), once again, to turn it off? He can always rely on his מְשִׁיבוֹן (meshivon), answering machine, for a message.

Significantly, the root also means to return to the Land for good, as in the refrain of a popular Yemenite song celebrating four generations in Israel, שַׁבְנוּ שַׁבְנוּ הַבָּנִים וְהַבָּנוֹת (*shavnu shavnu ha-banim ve-ha-banot*), "We have truly returned, boys and girls." Another song taken from Scripture, proclaims joyfully, וְשָׁבוּ בָּנִים לִגְבוּלָם (*ve shavu banim li-gvulam*), "The children have returned to their borders." The prophet Jeremiah adds another sense to the root when, in a play on words, he calls out שׁוּבוּ בָּנִים שׁוֹבְבִים (*shuvu banim shovevim*), "Return, rebellious children." The word שׁוֹבָב (*shovav*)—naughty child in Modern Hebrew—designates a backslider, one who has "returned" in the other direction, away from his people. Speaking of puns, Israeli writer A.B. Yehoshua plays on our root bilingually in his novel, הַשִׁיבָה מֵהוֹדוּ (*ha-shivah me-hodu*), which could mean "The Return from India" or "The Indian Shiva."

A rich vein of words and expressions can be mined from לְהָשִׁיב (*le-hashiv*), to return, as in the Jewish mitzvah, הָשָׁבַת אֲבֵדָה (*hashavat avedah*), returning lost property. It is also a mitzvah to be learned enough to be able to answer the questions of scoffers and proselytizers, וְדַע מַה שֶׁתָּשִׁיב (*ve-da ma she-tashiv*), "Know what to answer." The last word of Jewish prophecy calls for the reconciliation of the past and the future, וְהֵשִׁיב לֵב אָבוֹת עַל בָּנִים (*ve-heshiv lev avot al banim*), "The hearts of the parents shall be returned to the children."

The Rabbis of Pirkei Avot believed that מֵשִׁיב כַּהֲלָכָה (*meshiv ka-halakhah*), giving direct answers to direct questions, was an ethical matter. Organizers of events often ask their audience for מָשׁוֹב (*mashov*), feedback. And when the book of Proverbs said, Dantesquely, כָּל בָּאֶיהָ לֹא יְשׁוּבוּן (*kol ba'eha lo yeshuvun*), "None that go to her return," was it talking of that writer who asked a question about a question? It all depends on the meaning you assign to תְּשׁוּבָה (*teshuvah*).

EQUAL TIME

One of the lessons of Jewish history is that the notion of "worth"—in Hebrew, שׁוִֹי (*shovi*, accent on the first syllable)—has very little to do with money. Take the case of evil Haman, of Purim infamy. Although he has been given power, glory, and riches by his Persian master, he nevertheless complains to his wife and friends that וְכָל זֶה אֵינֶנּוּ שׁוֶֹה לִי (*ve-khol zeh einenu shoveh li*), "all this is worth nothing to me [as long as I see Mordechai the Jew sitting at the King's gate]."

One of the original meanings of the root שׁ-ו-ה (*shin, vav, heh*), is evenness, smoothness. Today, in Israel, one inclined to use metaphor in his speech will say בָּאוּ לְעֵמֶק הַשָּׁוֶה (*ba'u le-emek ha-shaveh*), They arrived at a compromise, alluding both textually and linguistically to a peace offering made to forefather Abram in an important battle early in his career.

The most popular use of our root is probably the most difficult to fathom. It is found in a phrase taken from the Psalms and put on plaques found on the eastern wall of many places of Jewish worship: שׁוִּיתִי ה' לְנֶגְדִּי תָמִיד (*shiviti ha-shem le-negdi tamid*), "I have placed God before me always." Perhaps if David is placing himself on a level with the Deity, it is only the better to worship Him.

Many fields of Jewish endeavor have the צַד הַשָּׁוֶה (*tsad ha-shaveh*), common characteristic, of using our root. One of the building blocks of poetry is הַשְׁוָאָה (*hashva'ah*), comparison, while a principle of talmudic textual analysis is the גְּזֵרָה שָׁוָה (*gezerah shavah*), analogy. A lover of democracy will call for שׁוְּיוֹן זְכוּיוֹת

179

(*shivyon zekhuyyot*), equal rights, while a geographer will want to pinpoint the קַו הַמַּשְׁוֶה (*kav ha-mashveh*), equator, on his maps. Every year, on March 21, someone will remind us that we have הַיּוֹם הַשָּׁוֶה (*ha-yom ha-shaveh*), the vernal equinox. We all know that a carpenter without tools—especially a מַשְׁוִית (*mashvit*), plane—is no carpenter. And you'd better believe that a tightrope walker needs שִׁוּוּי מִשְׁקָל (*shivvui mishkal*), equilibrium, to remain successful. A good report is שָׁוֶה מִילְיוֹנִים (*shaveh milyonim*), worth a lot to you, while that kitschy souvenir you bought on a vacation לֹא שָׁוֶה גְרוּשׁ (*lo shaveh gerush*), is not worth a penny. In tennis, before you get to "game," you often get to שִׁוְיוֹן (*shivyon*), deuce. Some players who are usually שְׁוֵי נֶפֶשׁ (*shevei nefesh*), calm, get agitated at this point.

Probably the most colorful use of our root—in which evenness of gait is seen to encourage one to go slowly—is not in Hebrew but in Arabic. A billboard sign in Cairo recently proclaimed, "*shwayeh shwayeh, bibsi gayeh*" meaning "Take it easy, Pepsi's coming." In Israel today, when you want your friend to contain his enthusiasm, you hold up your hand in a gesture that means "stop" and say שְׁוַוִיֶה שְׁוַוִיֶה (*shwayeh shwayeh*), "Slow down." And so, let's stop here.

SURFACE MATTERS

There are two types of people in this world, those who delve deeply and those who are content to accept the exterior aspect of things. In Hebrew, these are called, on the one hand, the עֲמְקָנִים (*amkanim*), the profound ones, and, on the other, the שַׁטְחָנִים (*shathanim*), the superficial ones. Let's not be too prompt, however, to disdain שִׁטְחִיּוּת (*shit'hiyyut*), superficiality. After all, concern for the surface has not only everyday applications but also national ones.

The root ש-ט-ח (*shin, tet, het*), which gives us the noun שֶׁטַח (*shetah*), area, comes to us from geometry (i.e., land measurement), where multiplication of length by width yields the שֶׁטַח (*shetah*), area, of a parcel of land. Curiously, geometry itself is a שֶׁטַח (*shetah*), inasmuch as it is a "field" of inquiry.

The Torah (Numbers 11:32) tells us that when the Israelites in the desert demanded that Moses provide meat, God sent so many quails that וַיִּשְׁטְחוּ לָהֶם שָׁטוֹחַ (*va-yishtehu lahem shato'ah*), "They carpeted the camp with the quail" (Cassuto), or (Rashi) "they greedily piled the quail into several layers." The Psalmist (88:10) asks God why He hides His face from him; after all, does he not say daily, שִׁטַּחְתִּי אֵלֶיךָ כַפָּי (*shittahti eleikha khappai*), "I have spread out my hands to you [in prayer]?" Another way our root is used in religious ritual is at the grave of a saintly rabbi, where one מִשְׁתַּטֵּחַ (*mishtatte'ah*), prostrates oneself .

In modern Israel, the word שֶׁטַח (*shetah*) and its derivations are found strewn all over the semantic field. Will the מִשְׁטַח עֲבוֹדָה (*mishtah avodah*), work space, in your kitchen be large enough

181

for gourmet cooking? A carpet is called a שְׁטִיחַ (shati'ah) and the smaller welcome mat you put on the floor at your door is a שְׁטִיחוֹן (shetihon). Jewelers say that the more שְׁטָחוֹת (shithot), facets, a diamond has the more sparkle it is likely to have.

One of the more successful tactics adopted by the Israeli army is to create עוּבְדוֹת בַּשֶּׁטַח (uvdot ba-shetah), facts on the ground. Civilians are warned not to enter a שֶׁטַח אֵשׁ (shetah esh), a place where guns are being fired. What are called the "territories" on the West Bank, whether conquered or liberated depending on one's politics, are known in popular Hebrew parlance as the שְׁטָחִים (shetahim). In soccer, a low-flying pass that grazes the ground is called a כַּדּוּר שָׁטוּחַ (kaddur shatu'ah).

In 1492, in the days of Columbus, there were two types of people in the world: those who argued the Earth was round, עָגוֹל (agol), and those who contended it was flat, שָׁטוּחַ (shatu'ah). A deep question like this is all too often answered in a שִׁטְחִי (shithi), superficial, manner. "O.K.! Let it be your way." A philosopher of the surface, after all.

WHEN IT FLOWS IT FLOODS

What does it take to be a prophet in Israel? Is a prophet merely someone who can foretell the future? Or is it also someone who sees things the way others do not and has the linguistic power to describe them in a creative way? That's the impression one gets from a look at the way Isaiah and Jeremiah, for example, use the Hebrew root שׁ-ט-פ (*shin, tet, peh*), to rinse, flow, inundate.

The root appears in the Pentateuch only in Leviticus where we are told, prosaically, that an unclean vessel יִשָּׁטֵף בַּמַּיִם (*yishatef ba-mayim*), shall be rinsed in water. When Isaiah uses our root, it is to envision the cleansing of sin as a נַחַל שׁוֹטֵף (*nahal shotef*), raging torrent. Jeremiah takes the metaphorical use of our root even further; he sees a wicked sinner and describes him as a סוּס שׁוֹטֵף בַּמִּלְחָמָה (*sus shotef ba-milhamah*), a galloping horse in battle. When the book of Proverbs gets into the act, it warns against שֶׁטֶף אָף (*shetef af*), an overflowing of the nose, i.e., anger.

The Talmud uses our root in the reflexive form, לְהִשְׁתַּטֵּף (*le-hishtattef*), to describe concretely those who rinse themselves off by taking a cold shower after a shvitz. The Midrash uses the passive form, לְהִשָּׁטֵף (*le-hishatef*), for those who are "carried away," as if by a torrent, into infidelity. The Rabbis would not have approved of our passionate television judges either. If, said our Sages, יֵשׁ שֶׁטֶף בְּדִינוֹ (*yesh shetef be-dino*), there is fury in his judgment, the verdict is suspect.

In modern Israel, the radio announces that there is a שִׁטָּפוֹן (*shittafon*), inundation, in the Aravah. An internal wound can lead to שֶׁטֶף דָּם (*shetef dam*), hemorrhaging.

The root can be used in its concrete sense as well when one has cleaning chores, as in שְׁטִיפַת כֵּלִים (*shetifat kelim*), washing dishes, or שְׁטִיפַת רִצְפָּה (*shetifat ritspah*), washing the floor. This form of the root is also used abstractly, but nefariously, in שְׁטִיפַת מֹחַ (*shetifat mo'ah*), brainwashing. When a parent scolds a teenager for staying out too late, הוּא שׁוֹטֵף אוֹתוֹ (*hu shotef oto*), he dresses him down, by flooding him with words.

Not uncommonly, a young Tel-Avivian will suggest to his friend to go down to the beach לִשְׁטוֹף אֶת הָעֵינַיִם (*lishtof et ha-eynaim*), literally, to rinse their eyes. The observer who speaks עִבְרִית שׁוֹטֶפֶת (*ivrit shotefet*), fluent Hebrew, will understand that these young men are merely intent on scoping out the pretty girls. It's a colorful expression, but no one is a prophet in his own city—or at his city's beach.

FUHGEHDAHBOUDIT

We all know that Rosh ha-Shanah, the Jewish New Year, is a time for introspection. It is also a time for retrospection. Indeed, one of its earliest names is יוֹם הַזִּכָּרוֹן (*yom ha-zikkaron*), a day for remembering. But what of שִׁכְחָה (*shikhehah*), forgetting? The root שׁ-כ-ח (*shin, kaf, het*) comes at us with so many surprising twists and inversions that it, too, is worth investigating.

One of the earliest forms of charity has to do with forgetting. In the book of Deuteronomy we find a strange agricultural law. Should you have "forgotten" somehow to reap some sheaves in your field—וְשָׁכַחְתָּ עֹמֶר בַּשָּׂדֶה (*ve-shakhahta omer ba-sadeh*)— these sheaves, in a law called in the Talmud שִׁכְחָה (*shikhehah*), belong automatically to the poor. For your charitable forgetfulness, the verse continues, you will be rewarded "in all the work of your hands."

Sometimes, forgetting is used to add a psychological nuance to not remembering. Pharaoh's wine steward did not remember the good that Joseph had done him in prison; in fact, וַיִּשְׁכָּחֵהוּ (*va-yishkahehu*), he blotted him out from his memory. To blot out the memory of arch-enemy Amalek, the Jewish people is told לֹא תִשְׁכָּח (*lo tishkah*), essentially, "Do not forget not to remember." For the Rabbis, astute observers of the ways of mankind, forgetting is sometimes a positive good. After all, יוֹם טוֹבָה מְשַׁכֵּחַ יוֹם רָעָה (*yom tovah meshake'ah yom ra'ah*), "A day of good things chases away the memory of a day of bad things."

The Jewish people's pledge of allegiance to Jerusalem (Psalms 137:5) takes us into metathesis, the linguistic playfulness in which

a word's syllables are inverted. The first half of the pledge, אִם
אֶשְׁכָּחֵךְ יְרוּשָׁלָיִם (*im eshkakheh yerushalayim*), "If I forget thee,
O Jerusalem," is straightforward enough. The second half, תִּשְׁכַּח
יְמִינִי (*tishkah yemini*), literally, "may my right hand forget," makes
no sense. Forget what? One scholar suggests that we switch the
syllables of שָׁכַח (*shakah*) to form כָּחַשׁ (*kahash*), which means to
wither. We now have a perfectly familiar oath, "If I forget you, O
Jerusalem, may my right hand lose its cunning." A town that has
become rundown can be called a מָקוֹם שְׁכוּחַ אֵל (*makom shekhu'ah
el*), a godforsaken place.

Is senility a neurological or a linguistic phenomenon? Edward
Horowitz, an American Hebraist of a past generation, takes syllable-
switching metathesis to a frightening place. He tells us to look inside
the חֹשֶׁךְ (*hoshekh*), darkness, of the mind, to find, by changing the
order of the syllables of that word, a chilling doublet that gives us
שָׁכַח (*shakhah*), He forgot.

Aramaic uses what looks like our root (but may not be) in
the word שְׁכִיחָא (*shekhiha*), everyday, common, to express an idea
semantically at odds with its Hebrew meaning. One doesn't forget
everyday occurrences. That sense has nevertheless entered Hebrew
in the adjective שָׁכִיחַ (*shakhi'ah*), common, and in the noun
שְׁכִיחוּת (*shekhihut*), frequency. Something לֹא שָׁכִיחַ (*lo shakhi'ah*)
is rare indeed.

In modern Israel, a forgetful person is a שַׁכְחָן (*shakhehan*), and
may be suffering from שַׁכַּחַת (*shakahat*), amnesia.

To tell someone "No," just say תִּשְׁכַּח מִזֶּה (*tishkah mi-zeh*). It's
not quite as juicy as the New Yorkism "fuhgehdahboudit," but it
does the job quite nicely.

PAYBACK TIME

The trouble with ascribing a system of beliefs to Judaism is that theology often clashes with reality. Take, for example, the fundamental Jewish tenet of שָׂכָר וָעֹנֶשׁ (*sakhar va-onesh*), reward and punishment. Not every righteous deed receives its just שָׂכָר (*sakhar*), reward.

The root שׂ-כ-ר (*sin, kaf, resh*), nevertheless, can be found in several biblical contexts where the subject is both lack of reward and proper payback. On the one hand, our forefather Jacob complains that Laban, on a mere whim, has changed מַשְׂכֻּרְתִּי (*maskurti*), "my salary." On the other, our foremother Leah names her son יִשָּׂשׂכָר (*yissakhar*), because, as she says gratefully, נָתַן אֱלוֹקִים שְׂכָרִי (*natan elokim sekhari*), "God has given me my reward."

The Midrash has a similar polarity. In one story, Moses is permitted to see in the future both the holy life and the martyr's death of Rabbi Akiva. Moses cannot refrain from blurting out accusingly at God: זוֹ תוֹרָה וְזֶה שְׂכָרָהּ? (*zo torah ve-zeh sekharah?*), "This is Torah, and this is its reward?" The Rabbis of the Talmud were not comfortable with the teaching that suffering in this life is rewarded with a diminution of suffering in the world to come. We learn this from the answer to the question "Are your sufferings dear to you?" The answer is לֹא הֵן וְלֹא שְׂכָרָן (*lo hen ve-lo sekharan*), "neither the sufferings nor their reward." And yet, the Rabbis did teach that the main reason the Israelites were redeemed from Egypt was בִּשְׂכַר נָשִׁים צִדְקָנִיּוֹת (*bi-skhar nashim tsidkaniyyot*), "as a reward for the righteous women" of that generation.

Hebrew translation of certain English sayings will often seem to stand the Hebrew expression on its head. Thus the descriptive "Crime does not pay" becomes in prescriptive Hebrew אֵין הַחוֹטֵא נִשְׂכָּר (ein ha-hoteh niskar), A sinner ought not to profit from his sin. An English expression whose meaning is not transformed by its Hebrew equivalent is "The game is not worth the candle"; in Hebrew, יָצָא שְׂכָרוֹ בְּהֶפְסֵדוֹ (yatsa sekharo be-hefsedo), The profit was cancelled by the loss.

The Talmud makes a neat ethical distinction between someone who does a favor and someone who charges for his services. A שׁוֹמֵר שָׂכָר (shomer sakhar), who charges to watch your property, is held more liable for its loss or damage than someone who performs the same service without a fee.

In modern Israel, the poet Leah Goldberg made a famous children's story from a real estate sign, דִּירָה לְהַשְׂכִּיר (dirah le-haskir), "Room for Rent." Be careful, don't confuse le-haskir, to rent "out" with לִשְׂכּוֹר (liskor), to rent. Unless you are the boss, as most Israelis are, there are several ways of earning your מַשְׂכֹּרֶת (maskoret), salary. You can be a שָׂכִיר (sakhir), a regular salaried worker, or a שְׂכִיר יוֹם (sekhir yom), a daily worker. Our culture frowns upon becoming a שְׂכִיר חֶרֶב (sekhir herev), mercenary. We all know that a student at the university pays שְׂכַר לִמּוּד (sekhar limmud), tuition, and that a publisher pays writers שְׂכַר סוֹפְרִים (sekhar soferim), royalties or authors' fees. But did you know that God pays his worshipers שְׂכַר הֲלִיכָה (sekhar halikhah), a reward for walking great distances to synagogue? Of course, once at the synagogue, you'll be able to contemplate at your leisure the knotty Jewish problem of שָׂכָר וָעֹנֶשׁ (sakhar va-onesh).

YOU SEND ME

For high-tech e-commerce to succeed, a mundane system to deliver the goods is a necessity. In Judaism, the Hebrew root שׁ-ל-ח (*shin, lamed, het*), to send, teaches that delivery, like deliverance, is a commandment. That's what we learn from the Purim custom of מִשְׁלוֹחַ מָנוֹת (*mishlo'ah manot*), the delivery of prepared foods to neighbors, and from the demand of Moses to Pharaoh, שַׁלַּח אֶת עַמִּי (*shalah et ami*), "Let my people go."

The biblical phrase שַׁלַּח לַחְמְךָ עַל פְּנֵי הַמָּיִם (*shallah lahmekha al penei ha-mayim*), "Cast thy bread upon the waters, [and it will return two-fold]" is used by fund-raisers to encourage donations, even by the מְשֻׁלָּח (*meshullah*), fund-raiser, who rings your doorbell. The charming custom of sending charity money along with a traveler to Israel stems from a rabbinic dictum, שְׁלוּחֵי מִצְוָה אֵינָן נִזּוֹקִין (*sheluhei mitsvah einan nizzokin*), "People sent on a good deed come to no harm." Personal responsibility for one's actions is emphasized in the saying, אֵין שָׁלִיחַ לִדְבַר עֲבֵרָה (*ein shaliah li-devar averah*), "There is no such thing as a 'courier' for a sinful act."

In a synagogue that doesn't have a cantor, a layperson may be asked to serve as שְׁלִיחַ צִבּוּר (*sheliah tsibbur*), the emissary of the congregation. In internal Jewish politics today, there is some tension about the funding of Israeli שְׁלִיחִים (*shelihim*), emissaries, sent to America. No one will argue, however, that they do not have הַרְגָּשַׁת שְׁלִיחוּת (*hargashat shelihut*), a sense of mission. If you want to send a package across town you call up חֶבְרַת שְׁלִיחוּיּוֹת (*hevrat shelihuyyot*), messenger company, to make the delivery. Every Zionist summer camp will agree, however, that the מִשְׁלַחַת (*mishlahat*), delegation, it receives is programmatically outstanding.

Did you know that Haifa University was once a שְׁלוּחָה (*sheluhah*), branch, of the Hebrew University? The word *sheluhah* also denotes a telephone extension and this meaning—to extend— may have led some scholars to believe that the word שֻׁלְחָן (*shulhan*), table, a spreading out, may come from our root. If you are a hiker you will definitely want to climb the Hermon or one of the שְׁלוּחוֹת (*shelu'hot*), hills of its range. It's very dangerous to hike with a partner whose behavior is שְׁלוּחַת רֶסֶן (*sheluhat resen*), unbridled.

A questionnaire may ask for your מִשְׁלַח יָד (*mishlah yad*), occupation, but be careful with similar-sounding expressions. A newspaper may report that someone שָׁלַח יָד בְּנַפְשׁוֹ (*shalah yad be-nafsho*), committed suicide. And then there is the שׁוֹלֵחַ יָדַיִם (*shole'ah yadayim*), a slang expression that teenage American girls of another generation might have translated as "a guy who has Roman hands."

Hebrew is like a שֶׁלַח (*shelah*), missile, isn't it? How else could you go from the Persia of Purim to the Egypt of the Exodus to the Rome of a bad pun in one easy lesson?

CONTROL YOURSELF

In an era when even intimate relationships are looked on as power struggles, it is no wonder that possession of something as trivial as the remote control for the family TV should often be considered a victory over the "other." So, when the time came for technologically sophisticated Israelis to choose a Hebrew word for "remote control," they dug deep into classical Jewish culture and came up with the neologism שַׁלָּט (*shallat*), whose root means to rule, master, dominate, control.

The biblical narrative of Joseph and his brothers records that Joseph was the שַׁלִּיט (*shallit*), master, over Egypt. Ecclesiastes remarks philosophically that no man has שִׁלְטוֹן (*shilton*), power, over the day of his death. Throughout the sixteenth chapter of Ezekiel, Jerusalem is personified as a harlot and, in one instance, as an אִשָּׁה זוֹנָה שַׁלָּטֶת (*ishah zonah shallatet*), a strong-willed harlot.

In Modern Hebrew the word שֶׁלֶט (*shelet*) is used for the sign hung at the entrance of a store. In the Bible, the word שֶׁלֶט (*shelet*) is applied to instruments of war, as in the narrative of David's many conquests, שִׁלְטֵי הַזָּהָב (*shiltei ha-zahav*), "the golden shields," or, as in one of Jeremiah's exhortations, מִלְאוּ הַשְּׁלָטִים (*mil'u ha-shelatim*), "Fill the quivers." Notice the similarity of sound between the Hebrew word שֶׁלֶט (*shelet*) and the English word shield. That the German word *Schild*—like שֶׁלֶט (*shelet*)—means both shield and sign might indicate a Semitic origin for the German word.

The Rabbis of the Palestinian Talmud often use our root to discuss domestic issues. They inquire what is to be done when one's hand cannot "handle" the hot handle of a pan, אֵין הַיָּד שׁוֹלֶטֶת

בוֹ (*ein ha-yad sholetet bo*). They also discuss issues raised when a man's wife מְשַׁלֶּטֶת עַל נְכָסָיו (*meshalletet al nekhasav*), has "power of attorney" over her husband's property. The Rabbis also make a distinction between a מֶלֶךְ (*melekh*), king, and a שִׁלְטוֹן (*shilton*), governor. If you listen to the sound of שִׁלְטוֹן (*shilton*), you will certainly hear its near homophony with the Turkish/Arabic word Sultan. Interestingly, both words come from an Aramaic source.

In modern Israel, the goal of some military actions is לְהִשְׁתַּלֵט עַל הַשֶּׁטַח (*le-hishtalet al ha-shetah*), to take over an area, and an army officer might report back from his מֶרְכַּז שְׁלִיטָה (*merkaz shelitah*), control station in the field, to headquarters that אָנוּ שׁוֹלְטִים בַּמַּצָּב (*anu sholtim ba-matsav*), We're in control of the situation. A student who has gained mastery over the course material can be said to be שׁוֹלֵט בַּחֹמֶר (*sholet ba-homer*). And of one who has become proficient in Hebrew one says הוּא שׁוֹלֵט בְּעִבְרִית (*hu sholet be-ivrit*).

As laudable as these last may be, perhaps the best control is שְׁלִיטָה עַצְמִית (*shelitah atsmit*), self-control, where one can be said לִשְׁלֹט בַּיֵּצֶר (*li-shlot ba-yetser*), to control his inclination. And, speaking of self control, stay away from the TV set, with or without the remote.

THE WHOLE PEACE

If, as they say, variety is the spice of life, then Jerusalem must be the spiciest city in the world. And we're not even talking about the population. What we're talking about are words attached to the city's name.

One of the roots from which the name יְרוּשָׁלַיִם (yerushalayim), Jerusalem, comes, שׁ-ל-מ (shin, lamed, mem), is a model of pluralism. At least a dozen proper names derive from it. These include שָׁלוֹם (shalom), as in the name of Israeli pop singer Shalom Hankoh; שְׁלֹמֹה (shelomo), the wise King who built the Temple; שׁוּלַמִּית (shulamit), from the Song of Songs; מְשׁוּלָּם (meshullam), a medieval poet of the Kalonymos family; and שְׁלוּמִיאֵל (shelumiel), a prince of the Biblical tribe of Simon, from whose name we get our beloved Yinglish word, schlemiel.

To no one's surprise, our word abounds in religious contexts. We sing שָׁלוֹם עֲלֵיכֶם (shalom aleikhem) on Friday eve to welcome the Sabbath angels. The Hebrew Sabbath greeting is שַׁבָּת שָׁלוֹם (shabbat shalom). One speaks gently of the departed by adding עָלָיו הַשָּׁלוֹם (alav ha-shalom) or עָלֶיהָ הַשָּׁלוֹם (aleha ha-shalom), "Rest in peace." One of the highest Jewish values is שְׁלוֹם בַּיִת (shelom bayit), peace in the home. The standard Hebrew greeting is שָׁלוֹם עֲלֵיכֶם (shalom aleikhem), literally "Peace be unto you," to which the formulaic response is עֲלֵיכֶם שָׁלוֹם (aleikhem shalom), "Unto you, Peace." One's inner circle is referred to as אַנְשֵׁי שְׁלוֹמוֹ (anshei shelomo).

Even when the word שָׁלוֹם (shalom) means "peace," it is often something else as well, including one of the names of God.

To inquire about another's health, one asks, idiomatically, מַה שְׁלוֹמְךָ? (*mah shelomkha?*), "How are you?" To send greetings via an intermediary, one says דְּרִישַׁת שָׁלוֹם (*derishat shalom*), or דַּ"שׁ (*dash*), in short, "Regards." When an outcome is particularly dreaded, one hears the interjection חַס וְשָׁלוֹם! (*has ve-shalom!*), "Heaven forbid!" And to friends going on a trip—and to the departing angels on Friday night—one says, צֵאתְכֶם לְשָׁלוֹם (*tsetkhem le-shalom*), "Bon voyage."

Another derivative of our root is לְשַׁלֵּם (*le-shallem*), to pay, to pay in full, to complete the transaction. The word תַּשְׁלוּם (*tashlum*) means both payment and completion; a debt paid in full is marked שֻׁלַּם (*shullam*). In Israel it's common for purchases to made בְּתַשְׁלוּמִים (*be-tashlumim*), in instalments. Sometimes, זֶה לֹא מִשְׁתַּלֵּם (*zeh lo mishtallem*), it's not worth it. In the news, there are discussions of שִׁלּוּמִים (*shillumim*), Holocaust reparations.

The original sense of our root is שָׁלֵם (*shalem*), whole or complete. To be in one piece is to be at peace. One wishes an ill person a רְפוּאָה שְׁלֵמָה (*refu'ah shelemah*), complete recovery. When doing math problems, it's always easier to deal with מִסְפָּרִים שְׁלֵמִים (*misparim shelemim*), whole numbers. Want to perfect your skills? Sign up for הִשְׁתַּלְּמוּת (*hishtalmut*), professional development. Whatever you do, do it בְּלֵב שָׁלֵם (*belev shalem*), wholeheartedly. According to Rabbi Nachman of Bratslav, however, there is nothing שָׁלֵם יוֹתֵר (*shalem yoter*), more complete, than a broken heart.

And, if we are able לְהַשְׁלִים עִם הַמַּצָּב (*le-hashlim im ha-matsav*), to be at one with, current events, we will have real שְׁלֵמוּת (*shelemut*), a sense of wholeness similar to the inner peace one feels just by being in Jerusalem.

NAMING THE NAME

In Judaism, nothing is more complex than the subject of names. Although God, for example, has many names, these are replaced in conversation by הַשֵּׁם (*ha-shem*), the Name, as a sign of reverence.

The word שֵׁם (*shem*) is found in virtually every area of Jewish life, most familiarly in its Aramaic form in the Kaddish, יְהֵא שְׁמֵהּ רַבָּא מְבָרַךְ (*yehei shemeh rabbah mevorakh*), "Blessed be His Great Name." The second book of the Pentateuch, Exodus in English, is called שְׁמוֹת (*shemot*), Names, in Hebrew. This is not to be confused with שֵׁמוֹת (*shemot*), tattered pieces of paper bearing the name of God, which must be disposed of respectfully, by burial in a genizah. In some circles the answer to the question "How are you?" is בָּרוּךְ הַשֵּׁם (*barukh ha-shem*), "Blessed be the Name," which stands for both "Fine, thank you" and "Could be better." On another note, a conversation about Daniel Jonah Goldhagen's book, *Hitler's Willing Executioners*, might end with the emotionally charged יִמַּח שְׁמָם (*yimmah shemam*), May their name be blotted out.

The miracle-working founder of the eighteenth-century Hasidic movement was called the בַּעַל שֵׁם טוֹב (*ba'al shem tov*), the Master of the Good Name. A good name is so valued that the Rabbis of Pirkei Avot, playing on the sound of the words, asserted טוֹב שֵׁם מִשֶּׁמֶן טוֹב (*tov shem mi-shemen tov*), "A good reputation is worth more than precious oils." To damage someone's reputation, מוֹצִיא שֵׁם רָע (*motsi shem ra*), is considered a serious religious transgression.

The word has dozens of idiomatic uses. Jews are exhorted to study Torah לִשְׁמָה (li-shmah), for its own sake. Many righteous acts are done לְשֵׁם שָׁמַיִם (le-shem shamayim), for the sake of heaven. At a circumcision, one blesses the infant by saying כְּשֵׁם שֶׁנִּכְנָס לַבְּרִית (ke-shem she-nikhnas la-berit), "Just as he has entered the Covenant," so may he enter under the wedding canopy. In the Diaspora it is common to give a child both a שֵׁם לוֹעֲזִי (shem lo'azi), secular name, and a שֵׁם עִבְרִי (shem ivri), Hebrew name. Jews believe that one's name and one's nature are related. In the book of Samuel, Nabal's wife soothes David's anger at her husband with כִּשְׁמוֹ כֶּן הוּא (ki-shemo ken hu), "[Nabal] is [a low-life], as his name implies." Of a good person one says שְׁמוֹ הוֹלֵךְ לְפָנָיו (shemo holekh lefanav), his good name precedes him.

Hebrew-language maven Yitzhak Avineri comments at length on the custom among Zionist pioneers of Hebraizing their שֵׁם מִשְׁפָּחָה (shem mishpahah), family name, "Green" for example becoming "Goren." He prefers the Hebraizing of the שֵׁם פְּרָטִי (shem perati), given name, Anatoly for example becoming נָתָן (natan), as in Sharansky. We mention this because the Rabbis taught that by quoting something בְּשֵׁם אוֹמְרוֹ (be-shem omero), giving credit to the source, one brings redemption to the world.

There. It's done. בָּרוּךְ הַשֵּׁם (barukh ha-shem).

tav bet lamed ת-ב-ל

ADD LIFE TO YOUR SPICE

Lovers of Hebrew will want to savor the story of the ways the Hebrew root for spice, ת-ב-ל (*tav, bet, lamed*), has added relish to the language. The first thing we notice is that the commonly accepted word for "spice," found both in the pages of the Talmud and on the shelves of your local Israeli Supersol, is the result of a mistake. It appears that when some readers of the Aramaic plural תְּבָלִין (*tevalin*), spices, saw that word they read it as a singular, תַּבְלִין (*tavlin*), spice, with a plural form תַּבְלִינִים (*tavlinim*), spices. The rest is linguistic history.

Then there is the fact that three seemingly distinct words use the three letters of our root. Thus we have תֶּבֶל (*tevel*, accent on the first syllable), a masculine noun meaning "spice," and תֵּבֵל (*tevel*, accent on the second syllable), a feminine noun meaning "the world." In addition, there is תֶּבֶל (*tevel*, accent on the first syllable), a masculine noun meaning "abomination." How are we going to reconcile these three? Curiously, the first and the third meanings probably derive from the same primary root, ב-ל-ל (*bet, lamed, lamed*), to mix. When you add spices to food you are creating a savory mixture. But when you mix things together you also destroy their purity, somehow creating something unsavory, like, for example, בִּלְבּוּל (*bilbul*), confusion, and הִתְבּוֹלְלוּת (*hitbolelut*), assimilation. As to the second use of the word תֵּבֵל (*tevel*), world, it comes from the root י-ב-ל (*yod, bet, lamed*), to be fruitful, that also gives us the noun יְבוּל (*yevul*), produce.

These linguistic facts did not stop the Rabbis from making some ingenious pluralistic plays-on-words using our root. They

197

said, for example, תֵּבֵל הִיא אֶרֶץ יִשְׂרָאֵל שֶׁהִיא מְתֻבֶּלֶת בַּכֹּל (*tevel hi erets yisrael, she-hi metubelet ba-kol*), "The world, that is the Land of Israel, because it contains all flavors." They also proposed with some zest that the world's first metal-worker, Tubal-Cain, got his name from the fact that he was a תּוּבָל קַיִן (*tubbal-kayin*), a "well-seasoned Cain." For the Rabbis, however, there was only one spice that counted. The Talmud records the following: תַּבְלִין אֶחָד יֵשׁ לָנוּ, וְשַׁבָּת שְׁמוֹ (*tavlin ehad yesh lanu, ve-shabbat shemo*), "We have one spice, and Shabbat is its name."

This playfulness has filtered down to twentieth-century writers. Shalom Aleichem, a Yiddish writer who captured the piquancy of Jewish life in Eastern Europe, has been called by one critic הַתַּבְלָן הַגָּדוֹל (*ha-tablan ha-gadol*), "The great spice man." S.Y. Agnon writes that the conversation of one of his characters is מְתֻבֶּלֶת בְּמִקְרָא וּבְמִשְׁנָה (*metubelet be-mikra u-ve-mishnah*), "spiced with quotations from the Bible and Mishnah." And Chaim Nachman Bialik reports not too gleefully on that מִין תַּבְלִין חָרִיף (*min tavlin harif*), "type of sharp spice" known in some circles as a slap in the face.

Because Jewish culture is not a means for escape from the truths of this world, most Jews will recognize the wisdom in its approach to the spices of life. Just consider the proverb that says אֵין תַּבְלִין כְּרָעָבוֹן (*ein tavlin ki-re'avon*). "There is no better spice than hunger."

Let's eat.

tav kaf nun ת-כ-נ

FORM AND CONTENT

An age-old question asks: What is more important, form or content? The way Judaism answers questions of this sort is to harmonize the two. Thus, תֹּכֶן (*tokhen*), content, is more important than צוּרָה (*tsurah*), form, because form, as any architect will tell you, is a part of content.

The early meanings of the root itself, ת-כ-נ (*tav, kaf, nun*), contain several near synonyms—to examine, estimate, measure—and a meaning that is not so near—to plan—leading to a wide variety of derived words. In other words, multiplicity of meaning is one of the תְּכוּנוֹת (*tekhunot*), characteristics, of our root.

Any book published in modern times has a תֹּכֶן הָעִנְיָנִים (*token ha-inyanim*), table of contents. And yet, in the biblical narrative of the Jewish people's sojourn in Egypt, we are told that although the Israelite slaves were not given straw, they nevertheless had to produce a תֹּכֶן לְבֵנִים (*tokhen levenim*), a quota of bricks. A modern bureaucrat will be asked to work according to a pre-established תָּכְנִית (*tokhnit*), agenda or plan, while a college student will be assigned a תָּכְנִית לְמוּדִים (*tokhnit limudim*), course of study. If a friend calls you in the morning "to do" lunch that noon, and you are already "booked," you answer, in near-Hebrew argot, that you are כְּבַר מְתוּכְנֶנֶת (*kevar metukhnenet*), you already have something on your תָּכְנִית (*tokhnit*), schedule, even if it means you are just going to watch a תָּכְנִית (*tokhnit*), program, on television.

When you go the Jerusalem Theater, an usher will offer you a תָּכְנִיָּה (*tokhniyyah*), program, so that you can identify the actors in the play. Is it possible, הֲיִתָּכֵן? (*ha-yittakhen*), that the star is being replaced by an understudy once again? And speaking of stars, one whose profession it is to gaze into the contents of the heavens is a תּוֹכֵן (tokhen, accent on the second syllable), astronomer. And since Israel has become one of the high-tech leaders in the world, they created new words, like תִּכְנוּת (tikhnut), for computer programming, and תָּכְנָה (tokhnah), for software.

Toward the end of one's high school career, students take a מִבְחַן מַתְכֹּנֶת (mivhan matkonet), a sample test on the model of the all-important Bagrut exam. On certain "half holidays" in Israel, work is carried on בְּמַתְכֹּנֶת שַׁבָּת (be-matkonet shabbat), on a reduced schedule.

You'll find our root as well in a drug store, your kitchen, and even a design studio. If you're not feeling well, your old-fashioned doctor will write you a מַתְכֹּן (matkon), prescription to take to the pharmacist. And if you feel like eating a good home-cooked meal, you just call up your friend, the chef, and ask for a different kind of מַתְכּוֹן (matkon), a recipe. If you have a מַתְכּוֹן לְהַצְלָחָה (matkon le-hatslahah), formula for success, please send it along. Your friendly תַּכָּן (takan), designer, will be only too happy to make you a תֶּכֶן (tekhen), design, for anything from an evening dress to a sofa.

As is Hebrew's way, sometimes one root will lead to the creation of another root. That is how we got the four-letter root ת-כ-נ-נ (tav, kaf, nun, nun), to plan. If you've visited some of the exquisitely livable small towns in Israel, you will not fail to recognize that their charm is due to intelligent תִּכְנוּן עָרִים (tikhnun arim), town planning.

And where, you might ask, is the Jewish content in all this? Some would say that both the צוּרָה (tsurah), form, and the תּוֹכֵן (tokhen), content, of the Hebrew language itself reflect more than adequately the content and provide a מַתְכֹּנֶת (matkonet), framework, for Jewish life. Who are we to argue?

HANGING OUT WITH HEBREW

You can tell a good deal about a religion by the way it addresses ultimate questions about God and man. As Rosh ha-Shanah approaches, for example, most people are judged to be neither basically good nor fundamentally evil. Rather, they are considered to be, during the days preceding Yom Kippur, תְּלוּיִם וְעוֹמְדִים (teluyim ve-omdim), in a state of suspended judgment.

The Hebrew root ת-ל-ה (tav, lamed, heh) in Scripture often refers to the punishment of hanging, as in Megillat Esther, וַיִּתְלוּ אֶת הָמָן עַל הָעֵץ (va-yitlu et haman al ha-ets), "They hanged Haman on the tree." A more philosophical direction is taken in Job's acknowledgment of God's power, recognizing that God תֹּלֶה אֶרֶץ עַל בְּלִימָה (toleh erets al belimah), "suspends the Earth on the Void."

The Rabbis were quick to recognize the connection between suspension and dependency, notably in the case of מִצְוֹות הַתְּלוּיוֹת בָּאָרֶץ (mitsvot ha-teluyot ba-arets), mitzvot that make sense only in Israel. A colorful rabbinic expression using our root, תָּלָה עַצְמוֹ בְּאִילָן גָּדוֹל (talah atsmo be-ilan gadol), does not mean "He hanged himself on a tall tree," but rather, "He pegged his ideas on a great authority."

Today, you might hang your coat on a מִתְלֶה (mitleh), coat rack. Curiously, the word תְּלִי (teli), hanger, is also used for the quiver of arrows hanging from a hunter's shoulder.

We all know that Israel has a certain תְּלוּת כַּלְכָּלִית (telut kalkalit), economic dependency, on the United States. That's why some American communities have recently made it easier to buy locally from Israeli merchants things like that beautiful made-in-Israel תִּלְיוֹן (*tilyon*), pendant, hanging from your neck.

Don't confuse תִּלְיוֹן (*tilyon*) with the word for hangman. That word is found most famously in Chaim Nachman Bialik's passionate poem on the Kishinev pogrom, "On the Slaughter," where the poet angrily offers his own neck to the תַּלְיָן (*talyan*) executioner.

In less stressful times one may concur with the popular Jewish proverb הַכֹּל תָּלוּי בְּמַזָּל (*ha-kol talui be-mazal*), "Everything depends on luck." Or perhaps one would rather agree with the Hebrew slogan of a ballpoint pen company. When it marketed its cartridge pen in Israel, it advertised, הַכֹּל תָּלוּי בְּטִיב הַמִּלּוּי (*ha-kol talui be-tiv ha-milui*), "It all depends on the quality of what's inside." It should surprise no one to learn that this slogan has made it into the vocabulary of Hebrew-speakers who recognize the necessity, sometimes, of suspending judgment. After all, it always depends.

SUGGESTIONS FOR FURTHER BROWSING

Ruth Almagor-Ramon. *A Moment of Hebrew* (*Rega shel Ivrit*). **Tzivonim Publishing. Jerusalem, 2001.**

Everyone who listens to the radio in Israel recognizes the dulcet tones of Menahem Peri, the fellow who comes on for one minute a day to tell us about words newly sanctioned by the Hebrew Language Academy, older words whose meanings may be lost on us, and words and expressions that have tickled the fancy of Ruth Almagor-Ramon, the editor of *Kol Yisrael's* program, *Rega shel Ivrit*. If you've ever longed for a copy of the script of these pieces, then you're in luck. Slightly edited for the printed page, this book contains the text of 300 of these programs. The selections are brief enough to be read when you have only a moment to spare. They are meaty enough to stay with you the whole day. By the way, as Almagor-Ramon reminds us, one minute a day is, as they say, "not exactly." At times it means "the blink of an eye"; at others it means "as long as it takes to say the word *rega*." On the radio it means "as long as it takes to perform a segment of *Rega shel Ivrit*. And then there's Sallah Shabbati, the fictional character who made famous the expression for "Hold it a second," *Rega, hoshvim*.

Edna Lauden and Liora Weinbach, with English translations by Miriam Shani. *Multi Dictionary: Bilingual Learners Dictionary* (*Rav-Milon*). **AD Publishing. Tel-Aviv, 1998.**

This is an excellent dictionary for students at the intermediate and advanced levels who are interested specifically in modern spoken Hebrew. Each entry is given first with its "full" spelling, that is, without vowels (*nekuddot*) but with all the letters needed to permit word recognition, the way it is usually found in books and newspapers. This is followed, to facilitate correct pronunciation, by the spelling with the vowels. Each definition of a Hebrew word is given in English as well as in simple Hebrew. To enable the learner to understand the nuance of a word and to show how a word is used in an authentic setting, a simple Hebrew sentence is given as well. Among the more useful sections of the dictionary are the tables of verbs and prepositions and the many word lists by topic, such as shopping, the restaurant, the family, and more. Particularly helpful are charts of phrases useful in conversation—arranged by topic. There are some fifteen of these, including: how to begin and end a conversation; how to ask for something and invite someone; how to complain (without pulling any punches) or make a suggestion; how to agree, disagree, and apologize; how to thank and compliment, and many more. There are also two very useful lists of medical terms and of expressions that have to do with Jewish religious tradition.

Mordekhay Rosen. *A Moment about Word Etymology (Millah be-Rega).* Holon, 1999.

This book contains the stories of some 2,000 words that have made their way into Hebrew from eighty other languages. Many of the entries were first presented to the Israeli public on the author's radio spot, *Millah be-Rega*. The book is based on the concept that words are the building blocks of culture. Whether you're looking for a word from Aramaic or Akkadian, Greek or Latin, Persian or Arabic, English or French, Russian or German, you'll find it listed in one of the indexes at the back of the book. A word of warning: This book is not made for people with weak arms or weak eyes. It requires some heavy lifting and, because it is so dense, some readers may find the font a bit too small to handle. For those who enjoy digging—and squinting—for treasures, this is an etymological dictionary for you.

Ruvik Rosenthal. *The Language Arena (Ha-Zirah ha-Leshonit).* Am Oved Publishers. Tel-Aviv, 2001.

This book is based on columnist Ruvik Rosenthal's belief that the language spoken by Israelis is not Hebrew at all. Rather, he says, "It is us." For Rosenthal, then, Hebrew paints a portrait of modern-day Israelis. It is for this reason that he divides his book, based on his column of the same name in *Ma'ariv*, into four sections: the multi-cultural arena, the lexical arena, the political arena, and the literary–mass communication arena. These four arenas are further divided into some fifty chapters, dealing with a wide array of fascinating and unexpected language topics, for example: army slang; Yiddish in Hebrew; code words that come from Arabic; the omnipresent expression, "*zeh ma yesh*" (that's all there is); the language of Ehud Barak, Benjamin Netanyahu and Arik Sharon; and translating from American English. As if this selection were not spicy enough, Rosenthal seasons his book further with some eighty alphabetical entries of the "real meaning" of words he considers crucial to understanding Israeli culture today.

Abraham Solomonick, with David Morrison (English Editor). *Maskilon I, II,* and *III*. Gefen Publishing House. Jerusalem, 2001.

This three-volume set puts together Hebrew-learning aids that will be a boon to the intermediate student. *Maskilon I* (787 pages) is a Hebrew-English Dictionary of Verb-Roots that includes 1,640 verb roots and their derivations, a 78-page table of verb conjugations, and an 82-page table that lists all the roots in *Maskilon I*. This table tells you on what page the roots can be found in *Maskilon III*, the set's Hebrew-English Learner's Dictionary. *Maskilon III* (843 pages) also cross-references its entries with those in *Maskilon I*. The advantage of this system is best demonstrated by an example. Look up צלם on page 465 of *Maskilon III*; it will give you the two meanings of the root and then tell you to go to page 284 of *Maskilon I*, where you will find the derivations of each of the meanings of the root. (It's really less complicated than it sounds here.) Two additional features of *Maskilon III* are a list of Hebrew abbreviations and a highly useful collection of Hebrew idioms and their translations. *Maskilon II* is a concise 257-page Hebrew grammar book designed specifically for English speakers. While this volume is not explicitly intended for classroom use, it does include an abundance of useful exercises. The amazing thing about this set is its compactness; each volume is squeezed into a format that measures less than 5x7 inches. Sometimes this means dealing with pages that do not always lie flat. But that's a small price to pay for such a rich reference tool.

ABOUT THE AUTHOR

Joseph Lowin is executive director of the National Center for the Hebrew Language. Previously, Lowin was director of Cultural Services at the National Foundation for Jewish Culture, director of the Midrasha Institute of Jewish Studies, and director of Jewish education at Hadassah. Lowin has a Ph.D. in French language and literature from Yale University. He has held faculty appointments at Yale, the University of Miami, and Touro College and has also taught at Yeshiva University and the State University of New York. He has been a Fulbright Fellow at the Sorbonne and a Jerusalem Fellow at Hebrew University.

The 101 chapters of *HebrewTalk* are based mainly on Lowin's columns about Hebrew written for *Hadassah Magazine* during the past ten years. In addition to *HebrewTalk,* Lowin has published two other books, *HebrewSpeak,* based on the first ten years' columns in *Hadassah Magazine,* and a book of literary criticism on Cynthia Ozick.

Lowin's articles of literary criticism, dealing mainly with Jewish and Israeli fiction, have appeared in the *Jewish Book Annual, Midstream,* the *Revue des Etudes Juives, Jewish Quarterly, Religious Studies Review,* the *Journal of Psychology and Judaism,* the *Yearbook of American Jewish Culture,* and *Hadassah Magazine.*

Joseph Lowin and his wife Judith reside in Rockland County, New York. They have three children, Shari, David and Benjamin.

EKS Publishing is the premier publisher of Hebrew educational materials. In addition to the books listed below, EKS offers audio CDs and cassettes, flashcards, charts, posters, and magnets for students of Hebrew. For a complete catalog call 877-7-HEBREW or visit our website: www.ekspublishing.com.

For Adults

Teach Yourself to Read Hebrew
The First Hebrew Primer
The First Hebrew Reader
Prayerbook Hebrew the Easy Way
The Beginner's Dictionary of Prayerbook Hebrew

For Children

Siddur Shabbat b'Yachad
In the Beginning
The Tower of Babel
Noah's Ark
Lech Lecha
Rebecca
Og the Terrible Series: Comic Book Adventures
    in Prayerbook Hebrew

Chesed Series

Give Me Your Hand
K'vod Hamet: A Guide for the Bereaved
Chesed shel Emet: Guidelines for Taharah